TABLE OF CONTENTS

M000103989

UNIVERSITY CASEBOOK SERIES®

2022 SUPPLEMENT TO
CONSTITUTIONAL LAW
CASES AND MATERIALS
SIXTEENTH EDITION

JONATHAN D. VARAT
Professor of Law Emeritus and Former Dean
University of California, Los Angeles School of Law

VIKRAM D. AMAR
Dean and Iwan Foundation Professor of Law
University of Illinois College of Law

EVAN H. CAMINKER
Branch Rickey Collegiate Professor of Law and Former Dean
University of Michigan Law School

FOUNDATION
PRESS

University Casebook Series is a trademark registered in the U.S. Patent and Trademark Office.

© 2021 LEG, Inc. d/b/a West Academic
© 2022 LEG, Inc. d/b/a West Academic
    444 Cedar Street, Suite 700
    St. Paul, MN 55101
    1-877-888-1330

Printed in the United States of America

ISBN: 978-1-63659-902-1

PREFACE

Page vii. Add to end of Notes on style:

In addition, we have sometimes omitted internal citations and quotation marks from quoted material without specifically indicating that fact.

TABLE OF CASES

The principal cases are in bold type.

UNIVERSITY CASEBOOK SERIES®

2022 SUPPLEMENT TO

CONSTITUTIONAL LAW

CASES AND MATERIALS

SIXTEENTH EDITION

PART 1

THE CONSTITUTION AND THE COURTS: THE JUDICIAL FUNCTION IN CONSTITUTIONAL CASES

CHAPTER 3

THE JURISDICTION OF FEDERAL COURTS IN CONSTITUTIONAL CASES

2. CONSTITUTIONAL LITIGATION INITIATED IN THE FEDERAL COURTS

Page 63. Replace FNa with the following footnote:

Beginning the decade following *Bivens'* recognition of a damages action against federal officials for Fourth Amendment violations, the Court declined 11 times to imply a similar cause of action for other alleged constitutional violations. In Egbert v. Boule, 597 U.S. ___, 142 S.Ct. 1793 (2022), the Court essentially limited *Bivens* and its immediate progeny (a Fifth Amendment sex-discrimination claim and an Eighth Amendment inadequate-care claim) to their facts. "[R]ecognizing a cause of action under *Bivens* is 'a disfavored judicial activity,' " and "in all but the most unusual circumstances, prescribing a cause of action is a job for Congress, not the courts."

Given the Court's limitations on and criticisms of *Bivens*-based causes of action, might there be an argument for the creation of a statutory right of action against federal officials who violate the Constitution? And might even states enact such statutes, creating "converse-1983" claims? See Akhil Amar, *Using State Law to Protect Federal Constitutional Rights: Some Questions and Answers About Converse-1983*, 64 Colo.L.Rev. 159 (1993); Vikram Amar, *Converse § 1983 Suits in Which States Police Federal Agents: An Idea Whose Time Has Arrived*, 69 Brook.L.Rev. 1369 (2004).

3. CASES AND CONTROVERSIES AND JUSTICIABILITY

B. STANDING

1. "CONVENTIONAL" STANDING

Page 74. Add after Village of Arlington Heights v. Metropolitan Housing Development Corp.:

California v. Texas

593 U.S. ___, 141 S.Ct. 2104 (2021).

In 2010, Congress enacted the Patient Protection and Affordable Care Act, 124 Stat. 119, which comprehensively regulated the health insurance industry and included an "individual mandate" that required most Americans to obtain "minimum essential" health insurance coverage. 26 U.S.C. § 5000A(a). The Act also imposed a monetary penalty, scaled according to income, upon individuals who failed to do so. A group of States and other plaintiffs sued to enjoin the Act's operation, arguing that Congress lacked the power to impose the individual mandate and that the mandate was not severable from the rest of the statute's many regulations, and so the entire Act must fall. In 2012, the Supreme Court held (in a 5–4 decision) that the individual mandate exceeded Congress's Commerce Clause power but was a valid exercise of Congress's taxing power. See National Federation of Independent Business v. Sebelius, 567 U.S.

519 (2012).ᵃ In 2017, Congress effectively nullified the penalty for non-purchase, amending the Act to set the penalty amount to $0. Tax Cuts and Jobs Act of 2017, 131 Stat. 2092, 26 U.S.C. § 5000A(c). Post-amendment IRS rules made clear that the statute no longer requires taxpayers to report whether they maintain the insurance coverage prescribed in § 5000A(a). In 2018 Texas and 17 other States, later joined by two individuals, sued various federal officials claiming that the mandate can no longer be defended as a tax in the absence of financial consequences. Arguing that (according to *Sebelius*) Congress has no other power to impose it and repeating that the mandate is not severable from the rest of the Act, they sought an injunction against the Act's enforcement in its entirety.

The Court, in an opinion authored by Justice Breyer and joined by six others, held that the plaintiffs lacked standing to challenge the individual mandate, as "[n]either the individual nor the state plaintiffs have shown that the injury they will suffer or have suffered is 'fairly traceable' to the 'allegedly unlawful conduct' of which they complain."

The Court assumed the individual plaintiffs suffered a financial injury in fact through their purchase of the minimum essential insurance coverage prescribed by § 5000A(a). But the Court held that this injury was not traceable to the mandate: the required Article III injury must be caused by actions of government officials rather than by unenforceable laws on the books. "Their problem lies in the fact that the statutory provision, while it tells them to obtain that coverage, has no means of enforcement. With the penalty zeroed out, the IRS can no longer seek a penalty from those who fail to comply. . . . Because of this, there is no possible Government action that is causally connected to the plaintiffs' injury—the costs of purchasing health insurance. Or to put the matter conversely, that injury is not 'fairly traceable' to any 'allegedly unlawful conduct' of which the plaintiffs complain. Allen v. Wright, 468 U.S. 737, 751 (1984). They have not pointed to any way in which the defendants, the Commissioner of Internal Revenue and the Secretary of Health and Human Services, will act to enforce § 5000A(a). They have not shown how any other federal employees could do so either. In a word, they have not shown that any kind of Government action or conduct has caused or will cause the injury they attribute to § 5000A(a)." The Court continued: "[O]ur cases have consistently spoken of the need to assert an injury that is the result of a statute's actual or threatened *enforcement*, whether today or in the future."

The Article III requirement of redressability also "makes clear that the statutory language alone is not sufficient. To determine whether an injury is redressable, a court will consider the relationship between 'the judicial relief requested' and the 'injury' suffered. *Allen*, 468 U.S., at 753, n. 19. The plaintiffs here sought injunctive relief and a declaratory judgment. The injunctive relief, however, concerned the Act's other provisions that they say are inseverable from the minimum essential coverage requirement. The relief they sought in respect to the only provision they attack as unconstitutional—the minimum essential coverage provision—is declaratory relief, namely, a judicial statement that the provision they attacked is unconstitutional. . . . Remedies, however, ordinarily 'operate with respect to specific parties.' . . . In the absence of any specific party, they do not simply operate 'on legal rules in the abstract.' "

The Court observed that "[t]he matter is not simply technical. To find standing here to attack an unenforceable statutory provision would allow a federal court to issue what would amount to 'an advisory opinion without the possibility of any judicial relief.' . . . It would threaten to grant unelected judges a general authority to conduct oversight of decisions of the elected branches of Government. . . ."

ᵃ   For fuller treatment of those two holdings, see 16th edition text at pp. 183 and 202.

With respect to the state plaintiffs, the Court held that they "have similarly failed to show that they have alleged an 'injury fairly traceable to the defendant's allegedly *unlawful* conduct.'" The States claimed "two kinds of pocketbook injuries." First, they claimed that the individual mandate has led state residents to enroll in various state-operated or state-sponsored insurance programs, for which the states must pay a share of the new enrollees' costs. But "the States also have failed to show how this injury is directly traceable to any actual or possible unlawful Government conduct in enforcing § 5000A(a). . . . That alone is enough to show that they, like the individual plaintiffs, lack Article III standing."

The Court observed another "fatal weakness" of causation: the state plaintiffs failed to show that the individual mandate, without any prospect of penalty, will lead more individuals to enroll in the cost-sharing state programs. "We have said that, where a causal relation between injury and challenged action depends upon the decision of an independent third party (here an individual's decision to enroll in, say, Medicaid), 'standing is not precluded, but it is ordinarily "substantially more difficult" to establish' . . . . To satisfy that burden, the plaintiff must show at the least 'that third parties will likely react in predictable ways.' . . ." But here, "the programs to which the state plaintiffs point offer their recipients many benefits that have nothing to do with the minimum essential coverage provision of § 5000A(a). . . . Given these benefits, neither logic nor intuition suggests that the presence of the [mandate] would lead an individual to enroll in one of those programs that its absence would lead them to ignore. A penalty might have led some inertia-bound individuals to enroll. But without a penalty, what incentive could the provision provide?" The Court concluded: "Unsurprisingly, the States have not demonstrated that an unenforceable mandate will cause their residents to enroll in valuable benefits programs that they would otherwise forgo. It would require far stronger evidence than the States have offered here to support their counterintuitive theory of standing, which rests on a 'highly attenuated chain of possibilities.'"

Second, the state plaintiffs also claimed to suffer additional pocketbook injuries: costs of providing information to beneficiaries of state health plans about their health insurance coverage and costs of providing related information to the IRS. "The problem with these claims, however, is that other provisions of [the] Act, not the minimum essential coverage provision, impose these other requirements. Nothing in the text of these form provisions suggests that they would not operate without § 5000A(a). . . . To show that the minimum essential coverage requirement is unconstitutional would not show that enforcement of any of these other provisions violates the Constitution. The state plaintiffs do not claim the contrary. The Government's conduct in question is therefore not 'fairly traceable' to enforcement of the 'allegedly unlawful' provision of which the plaintiffs complain—§ 5000A(a). *Allen*, 468 U.S., at 751." For the same reason, the Court dismissed other asserted pocketbook injuries linked to other expenditure-inducing provisions of the Act.

Justice Alito, joined by Justice Gorsuch, dissented. He argued that "[t]he States have clearly shown that they suffer concrete and particularized financial injuries that are traceable to the conduct of the Federal Government." The dissent did not claim these injuries were directly traceable to the challenged individual mandate *per se*. Rather, the dissent's theory of traceability "proceeds in two steps." The States argued first that the mandate is unconstitutional; and second that the cost-imposing provisions of the Act cannot be severed from the mandate. If both steps were accepted as alleged, then "it follows that the Government cannot lawfully enforce those obligations against the States." In other words, the dissent accepted a "standing-through-inseverability" theory: the assumption of inseverability creates the required Article III connection between the assertedly illegal conduct (the individual mandate) and the asserted injury (costs imposed by the Act's other provisions).[b]

The Court did not address the dissent's "novel alternative theory of standing," declining to consider it because it was not presented in either the lower courts or the petition for certiorari.[c]

Page 76. Add after Gill v. Whitford:

Carney v. Adams, 593 U.S. ___, 141 S.Ct. 493 (2021). The Delaware Constitution's political-balance requirements for several major courts dictate that no more than a bare majority of judges "shall be of the same political party" and the other judges "shall be of the other major political party," so only Democrats or Republicans may serve as judges on these courts. Adams, a registered independent, claimed these requirements violated his First Amendment right of freedom of association. The Court held that Adams lacked standing because, based on the record at summary judgment, he was not "able and ready" to apply for a judicial vacancy and therefore lacked a concrete, particularized, and imminent injury. The Court refused to credit Adams' claim that he wanted to apply to become a judge on one of these courts: his statement of intent "stand[s] alone without any actual past injury, without reference to an anticipated timeframe, without prior judgeship applications, without prior relevant conversations, without efforts to determine likely openings, without other preparations or investigations, and without any other supporting evidence." The Court noted that Adams, within a matter of weeks, had read a law review article arguing the exclusion of independent-party judges is unconstitutional; switched his party affiliation from Democrat to independent; and then filed suit. These circumstances all "suggest[ ] an abstract, generalized grievance, not an actual desire to become a judge."

Uzuegbunam v. Preczewski, 593 U.S. ___, 141 S.Ct. 792 (2021). A college's free speech zone policy prohibited speech that "disturbs the peace and/or comfort of person(s)." After being stopped from speaking based on listeners' complaints, a student sued various college officials charged with enforcing the speech policy for violating his First Amendment rights. The college discontinued the policy, rendering the student's claim for injunctive relief moot. The Court held that the student still had standing to seek nominal damages, however, because they would serve to redress his completed First Amendment violation. The Court based this characterization of nominal damages on history: the prevailing rule at common law permitted a party whose rights were invaded to recover nominal damages without furnishing evidence of actual damage. Rather than purely symbolic, nominal damages were considered the default remedy unless and until the plaintiff showed she was entitled to some other form of damages. So while "a single dollar often cannot provide full redress," even a partial remedy constituted redress under the common law and thus nominal damages satisfy the redressability element of modern standing requirements. Chief Justice Roberts' lone dissent, complaining that "federal courts will be required to give advisory opinions

---

[b]   Reaching the merits, the dissent would have declared the individual mandate unconstitutional, found the mandate inseverable from the provisions imposing costs on the state plaintiffs, and enjoined enforcement of each of these challenged injury-causing provisions.

[c]   Justice Thomas concurred in the Court's opinion, writing separately that this alternative theory "offers a connection between harm and unlawful conduct" and "might well support standing in some circumstances, as it has some support in history and our case law." But he agreed with the Court that this standing-through-inseverability argument was not properly addressed here.

For a deeper dive into the standing-through-inseverability theory, see Vikram Amar, Caminker, & Mazzone, *"Standing" In Unfamiliar Territory: Part Two in a Series on the California v. Texas Affordable Care Act Case,* justia.com, https://verdict.justia.com/2020/10/13/standing-in-unfamiliar-territory-part-two-in-a-series-on-the-california-v-texas-affordable-care-act-case (2020).

whenever a plaintiff tacks on a request for a dollar," argued in response that at least the defendant should be able to fully moot the claim for nominal damages by "fork[ing] over a buck" so that this claim would not itself require a court to reach the merits.

2.   TAXPAYER AND CITIZEN STANDING

Citizen Standing

Page 84. Add after Spokeo, Inc. v. Robins:

TransUnion LLC v. Ramirez
593 U.S. ___, 141 S.Ct. 2190, 210 L.Ed.2d 568 (2021).

■ JUSTICE KAVANAUGH delivered the opinion of the Court.

To have Article III standing to sue in federal court, plaintiffs must demonstrate, among other things, that they suffered a concrete harm. No concrete harm, no standing. Central to assessing concreteness is whether the asserted harm has a "close relationship" to a harm traditionally recognized as providing a basis for a lawsuit in American courts—such as physical harm, monetary harm, or various intangible harms including (as relevant here) reputational harm. Spokeo, Inc. v. Robins, 578 U.S. 330, 340–341 (2016).

In this case, a class of 8,185 individuals sued TransUnion, a credit reporting agency, in federal court under the Fair Credit Reporting Act. The plaintiffs claimed that TransUnion failed to use reasonable procedures to ensure the accuracy of their credit files, as maintained internally by TransUnion. For 1,853 of the class members, TransUnion provided misleading credit reports to third-party businesses. We conclude that those 1,853 class members have demonstrated concrete reputational harm and thus have Article III standing to sue on the reasonable-procedures claim. The internal credit files of the other 6,332 class members were *not* provided to third-party businesses during the relevant time period. We conclude that those 6,332 class members have not demonstrated concrete harm and thus lack Article III standing to sue on the reasonable-procedures claim.

In two other claims, all 8,185 class members complained about formatting defects in certain mailings sent to them by TransUnion. But the class members other than the named plaintiff Sergio Ramirez have not demonstrated that the alleged formatting errors caused them any concrete harm. Therefore, except for Ramirez, the class members do not have standing as to those two claims.

Over Judge McKeown's dissent, the U.S. Court of Appeals for the Ninth Circuit ruled that all 8,185 class members have standing as to all three claims. The Court of Appeals approved a class damages award of about $40 million. In light of our conclusion that (i) only 1,853 class members have standing for the reasonable-procedures claim and (ii) only Ramirez himself has standing for the two formatting claims relating to the mailings, we reverse the judgment of the Ninth Circuit and remand the case for further proceedings consistent with this opinion.

I

[In 1970, Congress passed the Fair Credit Reporting Act. 84 Stat. 1127, as amended, 15 U.S.C. § 1681 *et seq.* In order to promote "fair and accurate credit reporting" and to protect consumer privacy, the Act regulates the consumer reporting agencies that compile and disseminate personal information about consumers. Three requirements are relevant here. First, consumer reporting agencies must "follow reasonable procedures to assure maximum possible accuracy" in consumer reports. § 1681e(b). Second, the agencies must, upon request, disclose to the consumer "[a]ll information in the consumer's file at the time of the request." § 1681g(a)(1). Third, the agencies must "provide to a consumer, with each written disclosure by the agency to the consumer," a "summary of rights" prepared by the Consumer Financial Protection Bureau (CFPB). § 1681g(c)(2). The Act creates a cause of action for injured consumers: "Any person who willfully fails to comply with any requirement imposed under this subchapter with respect to any consumer is liable to that consumer" for actual damages or for statutory damages not less than $100 and not more than $1,000, as well as for punitive damages and attorney's fees. § 1681n(a).

[TransUnion, one of the "Big Three" credit reporting agencies, compiles personal and financial information about individual consumers to create consumer reports, which it then sells to entities such as banks, landlords, and car dealerships that request information about consumers' creditworthiness. Beginning in 2002, TransUnion introduced an add-on product called OFAC Name Screen Alert. OFAC, the U.S. Treasury Department's Office of Foreign Assets Control, maintains a list of "specially designated nationals" who threaten America's national security (such as terrorists, drug traffickers, or other serious criminals), with whom it is generally unlawful to transact business. When a business requested OFAC in addition to other consumer information, TransUnion used third-party software to compare the consumer's name against the OFAC list. If the consumer's first and last name matched the first and last name of an individual on OFAC's list, then TransUnion would place an alert on the credit report indicating that the consumer's name was a "potential match." TransUnion did not compare any data other than first and last names (for example, middle names, initials, or birth dates). Unsurprisingly, TransUnion's process generated many false positives, as thousands of law-abiding Americans share a first and last name with one of the terrorists, drug traffickers, or serious criminals on OFAC's list.

[In 2011, Sergio Ramirez tried to purchase a car but was refused when the dealer obtained his credit report through TransUnion and learned that Ramirez matched a name on the OFAC database. Ramirez called TransUnion to request a copy of his credit file; he received a mailing that included his file and the statutorily required summary of rights prepared by the CFPB but did not mention the OFAC alert. TransUnion then mailed Ramirez a second letter alerting him that his name was considered a potential match to names on the OFAC list, but this second mailing did not include an additional copy of the summary of rights. TransUnion eventually removed the OFAC alert from Ramirez's file.

[In February 2012, Ramirez sued TransUnion and alleged three violations of the Fair Credit Reporting Act: TransUnion (1) failed to follow reasonable procedures to ensure the accuracy of information in his credit file; (2) failed to provide him with all of the information in his credit file upon his request; and (3) failed to provide him with a summary of his rights "with each written disclosure," because TransUnion's second mailing did not contain a summary of his rights. The district court certified a class of all people in the United States to whom TransUnion sent a mailing similar in form to Ramirez's second mailing during the period from January 1, 2011, to July 26, 2011. The parties stipulated that the class contained 8,185 members, of which only 1,853 members (including Ramirez) had their credit reports disseminated by TransUnion to potential creditors during the same time period. The district court ruled that all 8,185 class members had Article III standing to assert all three claims, and after trial the jury awarded the plaintiffs more than $60 million in statutory and punitive damages. The

U.S. Court of Appeals for the Ninth Circuit affirmed in relevant part (though reducing the punitive damages award), over a dissent arguing that only the 1,853 class members whose reports were actually disseminated had standing to pursue the reasonable-procedures claim and only Ramirez had standing to pursue the two claims related to deficient mailings.]

. . .

II

The question in this case is whether the 8,185 class members have Article III standing as to their three claims. In Part II, we summarize the requirements of Article III standing—in particular, the requirement that plaintiffs demonstrate a "concrete harm." In Part III, we then apply the concrete-harm requirement to the plaintiffs' lawsuit against TransUnion.

A

. . . Article III confines the federal judicial power to the resolution of "Cases" and "Controversies." For there to be a case or controversy under Article III, the plaintiff must have a " 'personal stake' " in the case—in other words, standing. . . . To demonstrate their personal stake, plaintiffs must be able to sufficiently answer the question: " 'What's it to you?' " Scalia, The Doctrine of Standing as an Essential Element of the Separation of Powers, 17 Suffolk U. L. Rev. 881, 882 (1983).

To answer that question in a way sufficient to establish standing, a plaintiff must show (i) that he suffered an injury in fact that is concrete, particularized, and actual or imminent; (ii) that the injury was likely caused by the defendant; and (iii) that the injury would likely be redressed by judicial relief. Lujan v. Defenders of Wildlife, 504 U.S. 555, 560–561 (1992). If "the plaintiff does not claim to have suffered an injury that the defendant caused and the court can remedy, there is no case or controversy for the federal court to resolve." . . .

Requiring a plaintiff to demonstrate a concrete and particularized injury caused by the defendant and redressable by the court ensures that federal courts decide only "the rights of individuals," Marbury v. Madison, 1 Cranch 137, 170 (1803), and that federal courts exercise "their proper function in a limited and separated government," Roberts, Article III Limits on Statutory Standing, 42 Duke L. J. 1219, 1224 (1993). Under Article III, federal courts do not adjudicate hypothetical or abstract disputes. . . .

B

The question in this case focuses on the Article III requirement that the plaintiff's injury in fact be "concrete"—that is, "real, and not abstract." Spokeo, Inc. v. Robins, 578 U.S. 330, 340 (2016) . . . . What makes a harm concrete for purposes of Article III? As a general matter, the Court has explained that "history and tradition offer a meaningful guide to the types of cases that Article III empowers federal courts to consider." . . . And with respect to the concrete-harm requirement in particular, this Court's opinion in Spokeo v. Robins indicated that courts should assess whether the alleged injury to the plaintiff has a "close relationship" to a harm "traditionally" recognized as providing a basis for a lawsuit in American courts. 578 U.S., at 341. That inquiry asks whether plaintiffs have identified a close historical or common-law analogue for their asserted injury. Spokeo does not require an exact duplicate in American history and tradition. But Spokeo is not an open-ended invitation for federal courts to loosen Article III based on contemporary, evolving beliefs about what kinds of suits should be heard in federal courts.

As *Spokeo* explained, certain harms readily qualify as concrete injuries under Article III. The most obvious are traditional tangible harms, such as physical harms and monetary harms. If a defendant has caused physical or monetary injury to the plaintiff, the plaintiff has suffered a concrete injury in fact under Article III.

Various intangible harms can also be concrete. Chief among them are injuries with a close relationship to harms traditionally recognized as providing a basis for lawsuits in American courts. *Id.*, at 340–341. Those include, for example, reputational harms, disclosure of private information, and intrusion upon seclusion. . . . And those traditional harms may also include harms specified by the Constitution itself. See, *e.g.*, *Spokeo*, 578 U.S., at 340 . . . (abridgment of free speech), and Church of Lukumi Babalu Aye, Inc. v. Hialeah, 508 U.S. 520 (1993) (infringement of free exercise)).

In determining whether a harm is sufficiently concrete to qualify as an injury in fact, the Court in *Spokeo* said that Congress's views may be "instructive." 578 U.S., at 341. Courts must afford due respect to Congress's decision to impose a statutory prohibition or obligation on a defendant, and to grant a plaintiff a cause of action to sue over the defendant's violation of that statutory prohibition or obligation. See *id.*, at 340–341. In that way, Congress may "elevate to the status of legally cognizable injuries concrete, *de facto* injuries that were previously inadequate in law." *Id.*, at 341 . . . . But even though "Congress may 'elevate' harms that 'exist' in the real world before Congress recognized them to actionable legal status, it may not simply enact an injury into existence, using its lawmaking power to transform something that is not remotely harmful into something that is." . . . .

Importantly, this Court has rejected the proposition that "a plaintiff automatically satisfies the injury-in-fact requirement whenever a statute grants a person a statutory right and purports to authorize that person to sue to vindicate that right." *Spokeo*, 578 U.S., at 341. As the Court emphasized in *Spokeo*, "Article III standing requires a concrete injury even in the context of a statutory violation." *Ibid.*

. . .

For standing purposes, therefore, an important difference exists between (i) a plaintiff's statutory cause of action to sue a defendant over the defendant's violation of federal law, and (ii) a plaintiff's suffering concrete harm because of the defendant's violation of federal law. Congress may enact legal prohibitions and obligations. And Congress may create causes of action for plaintiffs to sue defendants who violate those legal prohibitions or obligations. But under Article III, an injury in law is not an injury in fact. Only those plaintiffs who have been *concretely harmed* by a defendant's statutory violation may sue that private defendant over that violation in federal court. . . .[1]

---

[1] The lead dissent [authored by Justice Thomas] notes that the terminology of injury in fact became prevalent only in the latter half of the 20th century. That is unsurprising because until the 20th century, Congress did not often afford federal "citizen suit"-style causes of action to private plaintiffs who did not suffer concrete harms. For example, until the 20th century, Congress generally did not create "citizen suit" causes of action for private plaintiffs to sue the Government. . . . Moreover, until Abbott Laboratories v. Gardner, 387 U.S. 136 (1967), a plaintiff often could not bring a pre-enforcement suit against a Government agency or official under the Administrative Procedure Act arguing that an agency rule was unlawful; instead, a party could raise such an argument only in an enforcement action. Likewise, until the 20th century, Congress rarely created "citizen suit"-style causes of action for suits against private parties by private plaintiffs who had not suffered a concrete harm. All told, until the 20th century, this Court had little reason to emphasize the injury-in-fact requirement because, until the 20th century, there were relatively few instances where litigants without concrete injuries had a cause of action to sue in federal court. The situation has changed markedly, especially over the last 50 years or so. During that time, Congress has created many novel and expansive causes of action that in turn have required greater judicial focus on the requirements of Article III. See, *e.g.*, Spokeo, Inc. v. Robins, 578 U.S. 330 (2016); . . . . Lujan v. Defenders of Wildlife, 504 U.S. 555 (1992).

. . .

A regime where Congress could freely authorize *unharmed* plaintiffs to sue defendants who violate federal law not only would violate Article III but also would infringe on the Executive Branch's Article II authority. We accept the "displacement of the democratically elected branches when necessary to decide an actual case." Roberts, 42 Duke L. J., at 1230. But otherwise, the choice of how to prioritize and how aggressively to pursue legal actions against defendants who violate the law falls within the discretion of the Executive Branch, not within the purview of private plaintiffs (and their attorneys). Private plaintiffs are not accountable to the people and are not charged with pursuing the public interest in enforcing a defendant's general compliance with regulatory law. See *Lujan*, 504 U.S., at 577.

In sum, the concrete-harm requirement is essential to the Constitution's separation of powers. To be sure, the concrete-harm requirement can be difficult to apply in some cases. Some advocate that the concrete-harm requirement be ditched altogether, on the theory that it would be more efficient or convenient to simply say that a statutory violation and a cause of action suffice to afford a plaintiff standing. But as the Court has often stated, "the fact that a given law or procedure is efficient, convenient, and useful in facilitating functions of government, standing alone, will not save it if it is contrary to the Constitution." . . . So it is here.[3]

III

We now apply those fundamental standing principles to this lawsuit. . . .

. . .

A

We first address the plaintiffs' claim that TransUnion failed to "follow reasonable procedures to assure maximum possible accuracy" of the plaintiffs' credit files maintained by TransUnion. . . . In particular, the plaintiffs argue that TransUnion did not do enough to ensure that OFAC alerts labeling them as potential terrorists were not included in their credit files.

Assuming that the plaintiffs are correct that TransUnion violated its obligations under the Fair Credit Reporting Act to use reasonable procedures in internally maintaining the credit files, we must determine whether the 8,185 class members suffered concrete harm from TransUnion's failure to employ reasonable procedures.

1

Start with the 1,853 class members (including the named plaintiff Ramirez) whose reports were disseminated to third-party businesses. The plaintiffs argue that the

---

[3] [Justice Thomas's] lead dissent would reject the core standing principle that a plaintiff must always have suffered a concrete harm, and would cast aside decades of precedent articulating that requirement, such as *Spokeo* [and] *Lujan*. . . . As we see it, the dissent's theory would largely outsource Article III to Congress. As we understand the dissent's theory, a suit seeking to enforce "general compliance with regulatory law" would not suffice for Article III standing because such a suit seeks to vindicate a duty owed to the whole community. . . . But under the dissent's theory, so long as Congress frames a defendant's obligation to comply with regulatory law as an obligation owed to *individuals*, any suit to vindicate that obligation suddenly suffices for Article III. Suppose, for example, that Congress passes a law purporting to give all American citizens an individual right to clean air and clean water, as well as a cause of action to sue and recover $100 in damages from any business that violates any pollution law anywhere in the United States. The dissent apparently would find standing in such a case. We respectfully disagree. In our view, unharmed plaintiffs who seek to sue under such a law are still doing no more than enforcing general compliance with regulatory law. And under Article III and this Court's precedents, Congress may not authorize plaintiffs who have not suffered concrete harms to sue in federal court simply to enforce general compliance with regulatory law.

publication to a third party of a credit report bearing a misleading OFAC alert injures the subject of the report. The plaintiffs contend that this injury bears a "close relationship" to a harm traditionally recognized as providing a basis for a lawsuit in American courts—namely, the reputational harm associated with the tort of defamation. Spokeo, Inc. v. Robins, 578 U.S. 330, 341 (2016).

We agree with the plaintiffs. Under longstanding American law, a person is injured when a defamatory statement "that would subject him to hatred, contempt, or ridicule" is published to a third party. . . . TransUnion provided third parties with credit reports containing OFAC alerts that labeled the class members as potential terrorists, drug traffickers, or serious criminals. The 1,853 class members therefore suffered a harm with a "close relationship" to the harm associated with the tort of defamation. We have no trouble concluding that the 1,853 class members suffered a concrete harm that qualifies as an injury in fact.

. . .

2

The remaining 6,332 class members are a different story [because] TransUnion did not provide those plaintiffs' credit information to any potential creditors during the class period from January 2011 to July 2011. Given the absence of dissemination, we must determine whether the 6,332 class members suffered some other concrete harm for purposes of Article III.

. . .

[The answer is no, as] there is "no historical or common-law analog where the mere existence of inaccurate information, absent dissemination, amounts to concrete injury." . . . "Since the basis of the action for words was the loss of credit or fame, and not the insult, it was always necessary to show a publication of the words."

. . . The mere presence of an inaccuracy in an internal credit file, if it is not disclosed to a third party, causes no concrete harm. In cases such as these where allegedly inaccurate or misleading information sits in a company database, the plaintiffs' harm is roughly the same, legally speaking, as if someone wrote a defamatory letter and then stored it in her desk drawer. A letter that is not sent does not harm anyone, no matter how insulting the letter is. So too here.

Because the plaintiffs cannot demonstrate that the misleading information in the internal credit files itself constitutes a concrete harm, the plaintiffs advance a separate argument based on an asserted *risk of future harm*. They say that the 6,332 class members suffered a concrete injury for Article III purposes because the existence of misleading OFAC alerts in their internal credit files exposed them to a material risk that the information would be disseminated in the future to third parties and thereby cause them harm. The plaintiffs rely on language from *Spokeo* where the Court said that "the risk of real harm" (or as the Court otherwise stated, a "material risk of harm") can sometimes "satisfy the requirement of concreteness." 578 U.S., at 341–342 (citing Clapper v. Amnesty Int'l USA, 568 U.S. 398 (2013)).

. . . But importantly, *Clapper* involved a suit for *injunctive relief* . . . [and] a plaintiff's standing to seek injunctive relief does not necessarily mean that the plaintiff has standing to seek retrospective damages.

TransUnion advances a persuasive argument that in a suit for damages, the mere risk of future harm, standing alone, cannot qualify as a concrete harm—at least unless the exposure to the risk of future harm itself causes a *separate* concrete harm. . . .[7] TransUnion contends that if an individual is exposed to a risk of future harm, time will eventually reveal whether the risk materializes in the form of actual harm. If the risk of future harm materializes and the individual suffers a concrete harm, then the harm itself, and not the pre-existing risk, will constitute a basis for the person's injury and for damages. If the risk of future harm does *not* materialize, then the individual cannot establish a concrete harm sufficient for standing, according to TransUnion.

. . .

Here, the 6,332 plaintiffs did not demonstrate that the risk of future harm materialized—that is, that the inaccurate OFAC alerts in their internal TransUnion credit files were ever provided to third parties or caused a denial of credit. Nor did those plaintiffs present evidence that the class members were independently harmed by their exposure to the risk itself—that is, that they suffered some other injury (such as an emotional injury) from the mere risk that their credit reports would be provided to third-party businesses. Therefore, the 6,332 plaintiffs' argument for standing for their damages claims based on an asserted risk of future harm is unavailing.

Even apart from that fundamental problem with their argument based on the risk of future harm . . . the risk of dissemination to third parties . . . was too speculative to support Article III standing. . . . The plaintiffs claimed that TransUnion could have divulged their misleading credit information to a third party at any moment. But the plaintiffs did not demonstrate a sufficient likelihood that their individual credit information would be requested by third-party businesses and provided by TransUnion during the relevant time period. Nor did the plaintiffs demonstrate that there was a sufficient likelihood that TransUnion would otherwise intentionally or accidentally release their information to third parties. "Because no evidence in the record establishes a serious likelihood of disclosure, we cannot simply presume a material risk of concrete harm." . . .

Moreover, the plaintiffs did not present any evidence that the 6,332 class members even *knew* that there were OFAC alerts in their internal TransUnion credit files. If those plaintiffs prevailed in this case, many of them would first learn that they were "injured" when they received a check compensating them for their supposed "injury." It is difficult to see how a risk of future harm could supply the basis for a plaintiff's standing when the plaintiff did not even know that there was a risk of future harm.

. . .

                                        B

We next address the plaintiffs' standing to recover damages for two other claims in the complaint: the disclosure claim and the summary-of-rights claim. Those two claims are intertwined.

In the disclosure claim, the plaintiffs alleged that TransUnion breached its obligation to provide them with their complete credit files upon request. According to the plaintiffs, TransUnion sent the plaintiffs copies of their credit files that omitted the

---

[7] For example, a plaintiff's knowledge that he or she is exposed to a risk of future physical, monetary, or reputational harm could cause its own current emotional or psychological harm. We take no position on whether or how such an emotional or psychological harm could suffice for Article III purposes—for example, by analogy to the tort of intentional infliction of emotional distress. . . . The plaintiffs here have not relied on such a theory of Article III harm. They have not claimed an emotional distress injury from the risk that a misleading credit report might be sent to a third-party business. Nor could they do so, given that the 6,332 plaintiffs have not established that they were even aware of the misleading information in the internal credit files maintained at TransUnion.

OFAC information, and then in a second mailing sent the OFAC information. . . . In the summary-of-rights claim, the plaintiffs further asserted that TransUnion should have included another summary of rights in that second mailing—the mailing that included the OFAC information. . . . As the plaintiffs note, the disclosure and summary-of-rights requirements are designed to protect consumers' interests in learning of any inaccuracies in their credit files so that they can promptly correct the files before they are disseminated to third parties.

In support of standing, the plaintiffs thus contend that the TransUnion mailings were formatted incorrectly and deprived them of their right to receive information in the format required by statute. But the plaintiffs have not demonstrated that the format of TransUnion's mailings caused them a harm with a close relationship to a harm traditionally recognized as providing a basis for a lawsuit in American courts. See *Spokeo*, 578 U.S., at 341. In fact, they do not demonstrate that they suffered any harm *at all* from the formatting violations. The plaintiffs presented no evidence that, other than Ramirez, "a single other class member so much as *opened* the dual mailings," "nor that they were confused, distressed, or relied on the information in any way." . . . The plaintiffs put forth no evidence, moreover, that the plaintiffs would have tried to correct their credit files—and thereby prevented dissemination of a misleading report—had they been sent the information in the proper format. . . . Without any evidence of harm caused by the format of the mailings, these are "bare procedural violation[s], divorced from any concrete harm." *Spokeo*, 578 U.S., at 341. That does not suffice for Article III standing.

. . .

For its part, the United States as *amicus curiae*, but not the plaintiffs, separately asserts that the plaintiffs suffered a concrete "informational injury" under several of this Court's precedents. See Federal Election Comm'n v. Akins, 524 U.S. 11 (1998) . . . . We disagree. The plaintiffs did not allege that they failed to receive any required information. They argued only that they received it *in the wrong format*. Therefore, *Akins* [does] not control here. In addition, those cases involved denial of information subject to public-disclosure or sunshine laws that entitle all members of the public to certain information. This case does not involve such a public-disclosure law. . . . Moreover, the plaintiffs have identified no "downstream consequences" from failing to receive the required information. . . . They did not demonstrate, for example, that the alleged information deficit hindered their ability to correct erroneous information before it was later sent to third parties. An "asserted informational injury that causes no adverse effects cannot satisfy Article III." . . .

* * *

No concrete harm, no standing. The 1,853 class members whose credit reports were provided to third-party businesses suffered a concrete harm and thus have standing as to the reasonable-procedures claim. The 6,332 class members whose credit reports were not provided to third-party businesses did not suffer a concrete harm and thus do not have standing as to the reasonable-procedures claim. As for the claims pertaining to the format of TransUnion's mailings, none of the 8,185 class members other than the named plaintiff Ramirez suffered a concrete harm.

We reverse the judgment of the U.S. Court of Appeals for the Ninth Circuit and remand the case for further proceedings consistent with this opinion. . . .

It is so ordered.

■ JUSTICE THOMAS, with whom JUSTICE BREYER, JUSTICE SOTOMAYOR, AND JUSTICE KAGAN join, dissenting.

TransUnion generated credit reports that erroneously flagged many law-abiding people as potential terrorists and drug traffickers. In doing so, TransUnion violated several provisions of the Fair Credit Reporting Act (FCRA) that entitle consumers to accuracy in credit-reporting procedures; to receive information in their credit files; and to receive a summary of their rights. Yet despite Congress' judgment that such misdeeds deserve redress, the majority decides that TransUnion's actions are so insignificant that the Constitution prohibits consumers from vindicating their rights in federal court. The Constitution does no such thing.

. . .

II

A

. . .

. . . Article III "does not extend the judicial power to every violation of the constitution" or federal law "which may possibly take place." . . . Rather, the power extends only "to 'a case in law or equity,' in which a *right*, under such law, is asserted." . . .

Key to the scope of the judicial power, then, is whether an individual asserts his or her own rights. At the time of the founding, whether a court possessed judicial power over an action with no showing of actual damages depended on whether the plaintiff sought to enforce a right held privately by an individual or a duty owed broadly to the community. See Spokeo, Inc. v. Robins, 578 U.S. 330, 344–346 (2016) (Thomas, J., concurring) . . . . Where an individual sought to sue someone for a violation of his private rights, such as trespass on his land, the plaintiff needed only to allege the violation. . . . Courts typically did not require any showing of actual damage. See Uzuegbunam v. Preczewski, 592 U.S.___, ___ (2021). But where an individual sued based on the violation of a duty owed broadly to the whole community, such as the overgrazing of public lands, courts required "not only *injuria* [legal injury] but also *damnum* [damage]." *Spokeo*, 578 U.S., at 346 (Thomas, J., concurring) . . . .

This distinction mattered not only for traditional common-law rights, but also for newly created statutory ones. The First Congress enacted a law defining copyrights and gave copyright holders the right to sue infringing persons in order to recover statutory damages, even if the holder "could not show monetary loss." . . . In the patent context, a defendant challenged an infringement suit brought under a similar law. Along the lines of what TransUnion argues here, the infringer contended that "the making of a machine cannot be an offence, because no action lies, except for actual damage, and there can be no actual damages, or even a rule for damages, for an infringement by making a machine." . . . Riding circuit, Justice Story rejected that theory, noting that the plaintiff could sue in federal court merely by alleging a violation of a private right: "[W]here the law gives an action for a particular act, the doing of that act imports of itself a damage to the party" because "[e]very violation of a right imports some damage." . . .[2]

---

[2] The "public rights" terminology has been used to refer to two different concepts. . . . Here, in contrast, the term "public rights" refers to duties owed collectively to the community. For example, Congress owes a duty to all Americans to legislate within its constitutional confines. But not every single American can sue over Congress' failure to do so. Only individuals who, at a minimum, establish harm beyond the mere violation of that constitutional duty can sue. . . .

The principle that the violation of an individual right gives rise to an actionable harm was widespread at the founding, in early American history, and in many modern cases. See *Uzuegbunam*, 592 U.S., at ___ (collecting cases); Havens Realty Corp. v. Coleman, 455 U.S. 363, 373 (1982) ("[T]he actual or threatened injury required by Art. III may exist solely by virtue of statutes creating legal rights, the invasion of which creates standing" . . . .) And this understanding accords proper respect for the power of Congress and other legislatures to define legal rights. No one could seriously dispute, for example, that a violation of property rights is actionable, but as a general matter, "[p]roperty rights are created by the State." Palazzolo v. Rhode Island, 533 U.S. 606, 626 (2001). In light of this history, tradition, and common practice, our test should be clear: So long as a "statute fixes a minimum of recovery . . ., there would seem to be no doubt of the right of one who establishes a technical ground of action to recover this minimum sum without any specific showing of loss." T. Cooley, Law of Torts *271. While the Court today discusses the supposed failure to show "injury in fact," courts for centuries held that injury in law to a private right was enough to create a case or controversy.

B

Here, each class member established a violation of his or her private rights. The jury found that TransUnion violated three separate duties created by statute. . . . All three of those duties are owed to individuals, not to the community writ large. . . .

Were there any doubt that consumer reporting agencies owe these duties to specific individuals—and not to the larger community—Congress created a cause of action providing that "[a]ny person who willfully fails to comply" with an FCRA requirement "with respect to any *consumer* is liable to *that consumer*." § 1681n(a) (emphasis added). If a consumer reporting agency breaches any FCRA duty owed to a specific consumer, then that individual (not all consumers) may sue the agency. No one disputes that each class member possesses this cause of action. And no one disputes that the jury found that TransUnion violated each class member's individual rights. The plaintiffs thus have a sufficient injury to sue in federal court.

C

The Court chooses a different approach. Rejecting this history, the majority holds that the mere violation of a personal legal right is *not*—and never can be—an injury sufficient to establish standing. What matters for the Court is only that the "injury in fact be 'concrete.'" "No concrete harm, no standing."

That may be a pithy catchphrase, but it is worth pausing to ask why "concrete" injury in fact should be the sole inquiry. After all, it was not until 1970—"180 years after the ratification of Article III"—that this Court even introduced the "injury in fact" (as opposed to injury in law) concept of standing. . . . And the concept then was not even about constitutional standing; it concerned a *statutory* cause of action under the Administrative Procedure Act. . . .

The Court later took this statutory requirement and began to graft it onto its constitutional standing analysis. See, *e.g.,* Warth v. Seldin, 422 U.S. 490 (1975). But even then, injury in fact served as an *additional* way to get into federal court. Article III injury still could "exist solely by virtue of 'statutes creating legal rights, the invasion of which creates standing.'" *Id.*, at 500 . . . . So the introduction of an injury-in-fact requirement, in effect, "represented a substantial broadening of access to the federal courts." Simon v. Eastern Ky. Welfare Rights Organization, 426 U.S. 26, 39 (1976). A plaintiff could now invoke a federal court's judicial power by establishing injury by virtue of a violated legal right *or* by alleging some *other* type of "personal interest." *Ibid.*

In the context of public rights, the Court continued to require more than just a legal violation. In Lujan v. Defenders of Wildlife, 504 U.S. 555 (1992), for example, the Court concluded that several environmental organizations lacked standing to challenge a regulation about interagency communications, even though the organizations invoked a citizen-suit provision allowing " 'any person [to] commence a civil suit . . . to enjoin any person . . . who is alleged to be in violation of' " the law. . . . Echoing the historical distinction between duties owed to individuals and those owed to the community, the Court explained that a plaintiff must do more than raise "a generally available grievance about government—claiming only harm to his and every citizen's interest in proper application of the Constitution and laws." 504 U.S., at 573. "Vindicating the *public* interest (including the public interest in Government observance of the Constitution and laws) is the function of Congress and the Chief Executive." *Id.,* at 576. " 'The province of the court,' " in contrast, " 'is, solely, to decide on the rights of individuals.' " *Ibid.* (quoting Marbury v. Madison, 1 Cranch 137, 170 (1803)).

. . .

In *Spokeo*, the Court built on this approach. Based on a few sentences from *Lujan* . . . the Court concluded that a plaintiff does not automatically "satisf[y] the injury-in-fact requirement whenever a statute grants a person a statutory right and purports to authorize that person to sue to vindicate that right." *Spokeo*, 578 U.S., at 341. But the Court made clear that "Congress is well positioned to identify intangible harms that meet minimum Article III requirements" and explained that "the violation of a procedural right granted by statute *can be* sufficient in some circumstances to constitute injury in fact." *Id.,* at 341, 342 (emphasis added).

Reconciling these statements has proved to be a challenge. . . . But "[t]he historical restrictions on standing" offer considerable guidance. . . . A statute that creates a public right plus a citizen-suit cause of action is insufficient by itself to establish standing. See *Lujan*, 504 U.S., at 576.[4] A statute that creates a private right and a cause of action, however, *does* gives plaintiffs an adequate interest in vindicating their private rights in federal court. . . .

The majority today, however, takes the road less traveled: "[U]nder Article III, an injury in law is not an injury in fact." . . . No matter if the right is personal or if the legislature deems the right worthy of legal protection, legislatures are constitutionally unable to offer the protection of the federal courts for anything other than money, bodily integrity, and anything else that this Court thinks looks close enough to rights existing at common law. The 1970s injury-in-fact theory has now displaced the traditional gateway into federal courts.

This approach is remarkable in both its novelty and effects. Never before has this Court declared that legal injury is *inherently* insufficient to support standing.[5] And

---

[4] But see Caminker, Comment, The Constitutionality of *Qui Tam* Actions, 99 Yale L. J. 341, 342, n. 3 (1989) ("Six statutes [enacted by the First Congress] imposed penalties and/or forfeitures for conduct injurious to the general public and expressly authorized suits by private informers, with the recovery being shared between the informer and the United States"); McCulloch v. Maryland, 4 Wheat. 316, 317, 321–322 (1819) (reviewing "an action of debt brought by the defendant in error . . . who sued as well for himself as for the State of Maryland . . . to recover certain penalties").

[5] See, *e.g.,* Lujan v. Defenders of Wildlife, 504 U.S. 555, 578 (1992) ("Nothing in this contradicts the principle that the injury required by Art. III may exist solely by virtue of 'statutes creating legal rights, the invasion of which creates standing' . . ."); Warth v. Seldin, 422 U.S. 490, 514 (1975) ("Congress may create a statutory right or entitlement the alleged deprivation of which can confer standing to sue even where the plaintiff would have suffered no judicially cognizable injury in the absence of statute"); Linda R. S. v. Richard D., 410 U.S. 614, 617, n. 3 (1973) ("Congress may enact statutes creating legal rights, the invasion of which creates standing, even though no injury would exist without the statute").

never before has this Court declared that legislatures are constitutionally precluded from creating legal rights enforceable in federal court if those rights deviate too far from their common-law roots. According to the majority, courts alone have the power to sift and weigh harms to decide whether they merit the Federal Judiciary's attention. In the name of protecting the separation of powers, this Court has relieved the legislature of its power to create and define rights.

III

Even assuming that this Court should be in the business of second-guessing private rights, this is a rather odd case to say that Congress went too far. TransUnion's misconduct here is exactly the sort of thing that has long merited legal redress.

As an initial matter, this Court has recognized that the unlawful withholding of requested information causes "a sufficiently distinct injury to provide standing to sue." Public Citizen v. Department of Justice, 491 U.S. 440, 449 (1989); see also *Havens Realty Corp.*, 455 U.S., at 374. Here, TransUnion unlawfully withheld from each class member the OFAC version of his or her credit report that the class member requested. And TransUnion unlawfully failed to send a summary of rights. The majority's response is to contend that the plaintiffs actually did not allege that they failed to receive any required information; they alleged only that they received it in the *"wrong format."*

That reframing finds little support in the complaint . . . [and] also finds no footing in the record. . . .

Were there any doubt about the facts below, we have the helpful benefit of a jury verdict. . . .

. . .

And then there is the standalone harm caused by the rather extreme errors in the credit reports. The majority (rightly) decides that having one's identity falsely and publically associated with terrorism and drug trafficking is itself a concrete harm. For good reason. This case is a particularly grave example of the harm this Court identified as central to the FCRA: "curb[ing] the dissemination of false information." *Spokeo*, 578 U.S., at 342. And it aligns closely with a "harm that has traditionally been regarded as providing a basis for a lawsuit." *Id.*, at 341. . . .

The question this Court has identified as key, then, is whether a plaintiff established "a degree of risk" that is "sufficient to meet the concreteness requirement." *Spokeo,* 578 U.S., at 343. Here, in a 7-month period, it is undisputed that nearly 25 percent of the class had false OFAC-flags sent to potential creditors. . . . If 25 percent is insufficient, then, pray tell, what percentage is?

The majority deflects this line of analysis by all but eliminating the risk-of-harm analysis. According to the majority, an elevated risk of harm simply shows that a concrete harm is *imminent* and thus may support only a claim for injunctive relief. But this reworking of *Spokeo* fails for two reasons. First, it ignores what *Spokeo* said: "[Our opinion] does not mean . . . that the risk of real harm cannot satisfy the requirement of concreteness." *Spokeo*, 578 U.S., at 341. Second, it ignores what *Spokeo* did. The Court in *Spokeo* remanded the respondent's claims for statutory damages to the Ninth Circuit to consider "whether the . . . violations alleged in this case entail a degree of risk sufficient to meet the concreteness requirement." *Id.*, at 342–343. The theory that risk of harm matters only for injunctive relief is thus squarely foreclosed by *Spokeo* itself.

. . .

But even setting aside everything already mentioned—the Constitution's text, history, precedent, financial harm, libel, the risk of publication, and actual disclosure to a third party—one need only tap into common sense to know that receiving a letter identifying you as a potential drug trafficker or terrorist is harmful. All the more so when the information comes in the context of a credit report, the entire purpose of which is to demonstrate that a person can be trusted.

And if this sort of confusing and frustrating communication is insufficient to establish a real injury, one wonders what could rise to that level. If, instead of falsely identifying Ramirez as a potential drug trafficker or terrorist, TransUnion had flagged him as a "potential" child molester, would that alone still be insufficient to open the courthouse doors? What about falsely labeling a person a racist? Including a slur on the report? Or what about openly reducing a person's credit score by several points because of his race? If none of these constitutes an injury in fact, how can that possibly square with our past cases indicating that the inability to "observe an animal species, even for purely esthetic purposes, . . . undeniably" is? *Lujan*, 504 U.S., at 562 . . . .

And if some of these examples do cause sufficiently "concrete" and "real"—though "intangible"—harms, how do *we* go about picking and choosing which ones do and which do not? I see no way to engage in this "inescapably value-laden" inquiry without it "devolv[ing] into [pure] policy judgment." . . . Weighing the harms caused by specific facts and choosing remedies seems to me like a much better fit for legislatures and juries than for this Court.

. . .

I respectfully dissent.

■ JUSTICE KAGAN, with whom JUSTICE BREYER and JUSTICE SOTOMAYOR join, dissenting.

. . .

. . . The Court here transforms standing law from a doctrine of judicial modesty into a tool of judicial aggrandizement. It holds, for the first time, that a specific class of plaintiffs whom Congress allowed to bring a lawsuit cannot do so under Article III. I join Justice Thomas's dissent, which explains why the majority's decision is so mistaken. As he recounts, our Article III precedents teach that Congress has broad "power to create and define rights." . . . And Congress may protect those rights by authorizing suits not only for past harms but also for the material risk of future ones. See *Spokeo*, 578 U.S., at 341–343 . . . . Under those precedents, this case should be easy. In the Fair Credit Reporting Act, Congress determined to protect consumers' reputations from inaccurate credit reporting. TransUnion willfully violated that statute's provisions by preparing credit files that falsely called the plaintiffs potential terrorists, and by obscuring that fact when the plaintiffs requested copies of their files. To say, as the majority does, that the resulting injuries did not " 'exist' in the real world" is to inhabit a world I don't know. And to make that claim in the face of Congress's contrary judgment is to exceed the judiciary's "proper—and properly limited—role." *Warth*, 422 U.S., at 498 . . . .

. . .

I differ with Justice Thomas on just one matter, unlikely to make much difference in practice. In his view, any "violation of an individual right" created by Congress gives rise to Article III standing. But in *Spokeo*, this Court held that "Article III requires a concrete injury even in the context of a statutory violation." 578 U.S., at 341. I continue to adhere to that view, but think it should lead to the same result as Justice Thomas's approach in all but highly unusual cases. As *Spokeo* recognized, "Congress is well positioned to identify [both tangible and] intangible harms" meeting Article III standards. *Ibid.* Article III requires for concreteness only a "real harm" (that is, a harm that "actually exist[s]") or a "risk of real harm." *Ibid.* And as today's decision definitively proves, Congress is better suited than courts to determine when something causes a harm or risk of harm in the real world. For that reason, courts should give deference to those congressional judgments. Overriding an authorization to sue is appropriate when but only when Congress could not reasonably have thought that a suit will contribute to compensating or preventing the harm at issue. Subject to that qualification, I join Justice Thomas's dissent in full.

5.   LEGISLATIVE STANDING

Page 93. Add after Virginia House of Delegates v. Bethune-Hill, before § C on Mootness:

Berger v. North Carolina State Conference of NAACP
497 U.S. ___, 142 S.Ct. 2191 (2022).

The North Carolina NAACP sued the members of the State Board of Elections in federal court, seeking to enjoin the Board from enforcing a state statute requiring voters to present photo IDs (with limited exceptions). Per state law, the state Attorney General (an independently elected state official) represented the defendant Board members. As also expressly authorized by state law, the speaker of the State House of Representatives and the president pro tempore of the State Senate moved to intervene to defend the constitutionality of the voter ID statute, arguing that neither the Board members nor the Attorney General would adequately represent their legislative interests. The Fourth Circuit Court of Appeals ultimately ruled en banc that the legislative leaders were not entitled to intervene as defendants under Federal Rule of Civil Procedure 24(a)(2) because their interests were adequately represented by the defendant Board members.

The Supreme Court reversed (8–1). Writing for the Court, Justice Gorsuch started with the unquestioned premises that "States possess a legitimate interest in the continued enforce[ment] of [their] own statutes"; that "States may organize themselves in a variety of ways"; and that "when a State chooses to allocate authority among different officials who do not answer to one another, different interests and perspectives, all important to the administration of state government, may emerge." And "appropriate respect for these realities suggests that federal courts should rarely question that a State's interests will be practically impaired or impeded if its duly authorized representatives are excluded from federal litigation challenging state law." Citing Virginia House of Delegates v. Bethune-Hill, 139 S.Ct. 1945 (2019) [see Casebook 16th ed. p. 92], the Court held that "a State must be able to designate agents to represent it in federal court and may authorize its legislature to litigate on the State's behalf." (cleaned up) And citing Hollingsworth v. Perry, 570 U.S. 693 (2013) [see Casebook 16th ed. p. 88], the Court "stressed that state law may provide for other officials, besides an attorney general, to speak for the State in federal court as some states have done for their presiding legislative officers." As a result, "where a State chooses to divide its sovereign authority among different officials and authorize their participation in a suit challenging state law, a full consideration of the State's practical interests may require the involvement of different voices with different perspectives. To hold otherwise would risk allowing a private plaintiff to pick its preferred defendants and potentially silence those whom the State deems essential to a fair understanding of its interests."

PART 2

ALLOCATION OF GOVERNMENTAL POWERS: THE NATION AND THE STATES; THE PRESIDENT, THE CONGRESS, AND THE COURTS

CHAPTER 4

THE SCOPE OF NATIONAL POWER

2. SOURCES OF NATIONAL POWER: EARLY DEVELOPMENTS

A. THE MARSHALL COURT'S VIEW

Page 131. In the Note on *McCulloch and Limits on State Power to Tax and Regulate Federal Entities* add after the sentence ending "federal entities or federal property.":

A good recent example is United States v. Washington, 597 U.S. ___, 142 S.Ct. 1976 (2022), where a unanimous Court struck down a Washington state law that, by its terms, applied only to federal workers at one federal facility in the state, and made it easier for those workers to obtain workers' compensation, thus raising workers' compensation costs for the Federal Government. As the Court remarked, it has come to understand the so-called intergovernmental immunities doctrine "as prohibiting state laws that *either* regulat[e] the United States directly *or* discriminat[e] against the Federal Government or those with whom it deals (*e.g.*, contractors). . . . We have said that a state law discriminates against the Federal Government or its contractors if it single[s] them out for less favorable treatment."

3. THE SCOPE OF NATIONAL POWER TODAY

F. OTHER FEDERAL POWERS

1. FISCAL POWERS

Page 229. In the report of the Norman v. Baltimore & Ohio Railroad Co. case add as footnote "c" the following after the sentence "The Congress may pass bankruptcy acts.":

   c   As the Court reminded in Siegel v. Fitzgerald, 597 U.S. ___, 142 S.Ct. 1770 (2022), Congress's powers in the bankruptcy realm are limited by the language in Article I providing that Congress is authorized to establish "uniform Laws on the subject of Bankruptcies throughout the United States." The *Siegel* Court struck down a congressional enactment of a significant fee increase that was non-uniform in that it exempted debtors in six judicial districts in two States (North Carolina and Alabama), by permitting those districts to opt out of the so-called United States Trustee Program, a mechanism to transfer administrative functions previously handled by bankruptcy judges to U.S. Trustees within the Department of Justice.

CHAPTER 5

STATE SOVEREIGNTY AND FEDERAL REGULATION

2. ENFORCEMENT OF FEDERAL RIGHTS IN SUITS AGAINST STATE OFFICERS: THE ELEVENTH AMENDMENT

Page 266. In the Note discussing *Application of the Eleventh Amendment in Suits for "Retroactive Relief"* add directly before the last paragraph:

Two other limitations on the Ex Parte Young device have emerged (or at least been made more salient) in recent years. One is the requirement that there be an enforcement connection between the state official sued and the challenged provision. Since 2010 the federal courts of appeals have begun to engage more thoroughly and much more frequently the question of precisely which state officers have a sufficient connection to enforcement of the challenged law or regulation so as to be subject such officers to federal injunctions under the Ex Parte Young doctrine.

And in late 2021, the Supreme Court itself decided an important case in this area involving a newfangled abortion regulation from Texas. Texas Senate Bill 8 (SB 8)—known colloquially as the Texas Heartbeat Act—was enacted in 2021 and prohibits physicians from performing or inducing an abortion if the physician has detected a fetal heartbeat. SB 8 does not permit state officials to bring criminal prosecutions or civil actions to enforce the law, but instead authorizes and contemplates "private civil actions" in which private plaintiffs can obtain injunctions and statutory damages awards against those who perform or assist with prohibited abortions. Abortion providers filed suit in federal court seeking pre-enforcement review of SB 8 (which they alleged ran afoul of Supreme Court precedent recognizing constitutional protections for reproductive choices), naming a variety of defendants, including a state-court judge, a state-court clerk, the state Attorney General, various other state administrators and a single private defendant (whom plaintiffs believed was inclined to invoke SB 8 against them).

After the district court denied various motions to dismiss and the Fifth Circuit Court of Appeals stayed proceedings in the district court pending its review of defendant's appeals on the merits, the Supreme Court in Whole Woman's Health v. Jackson, ___ U.S. ___, 142 S.Ct. 522 (2021) granted certiorari before judgment and, in a 5–4 ruling authored by Justice Gorsuch and joined by Justices Thomas, Alito, Kavanaugh and Barrett, affirmed the district court in part, reversed in part, and remanded. The Court held that the Ex Parte Young device did not permit the inclusion of the state-court judges or state-court clerks as defendants. The plaintiffs had asserted an intent ultimately to certify a federal class and request an order enjoining *all* state court clerks from docketing SB 8 cases, and *all* state-court judges from hearing them. But the Court reminded that the Ex Parte Young device is grounded in traditional equity practice, and this traditional exception does not normally permit federal courts to issue injunctions against state-court judges or clerks preventing them from processing cases in the first place. The traditional remedy against such officials has instead been some form of appeal. As stated in Ex parte Young itself, "an injunction against a state court" or its "machinery" "would be a violation of the whole scheme of our Government."

The Court also ruled that the Texas Attorney General should be dismissed since plaintiffs had not identified any enforcement authority the Attorney General possesses in connection with SB 8 that a federal court might enjoin him from exercising, and the private defendant should be dismissed because the plaintiffs had not contested his sworn declaration that he had no intent of invoking SB 8 against them. The Court (with eight Justices in agreement) did permit the suit to go forward against various other state administrators who may or must take (somewhat minor) enforcement actions against the petitioners, but whose involvement wouldn't prevent private plaintiffs from suing or state courts from entering judgments. The 5-justice majority did note that pre-enforcement cases in federal court are not the only way that state laws that arguably violate the federal Constitution can be challenged. State courts can entertain pre-enforcement challenges, and any individual sued under any state law (including SB 8) may raise state and federal constitutional arguments in his or her defense.

Page 267. In the Note discussing *Congressional Power to Abrogate Eleventh Amendment Immunity and Subject States to Suit in Federal Court* add footnote "1" at the end of the description of Central Virginia Community College v. Katz:

[1]   Building on *Katz*'s reasoning of state waiver with regard to certain federal functions at the founding, the Court in Torres v. Texas Dept. of Public Safety, 597 U.S. ___, 242 S.Ct. 2455 (2022), found that, in joining together to form a Union, the States agreed to sacrifice their sovereign immunity for the good of the common defense. Accordingly, the Court upheld the availability of private damage actions in state courts against non-consenting states under the Uniformed Services Employment and Reemployment Rights Act of 1994 (USERRA), which gives returning servicemembers the right to reclaim their prior jobs with state employers and authorizes suit if those employers refuse to accommodate veterans' service-related disabilities.

CHAPTER 7

SEPARATION OF POWERS

2. ALLOCATION OF LAWMAKING AUTHORITY BETWEEN THE LEGISLATIVE AND EXECUTIVE BRANCHES

Page 394. Add after Clinton v. City of New York, before § 3 on Presidential Control:

Biden v. Missouri
___ U.S. ___, 142 S.Ct. 647 (2022).

National Federation of Independent Business v. Department of Labor
___ U.S. ___, 142 S.Ct. 661 (2022).

On January 13, 2022, the Supreme Court was asked to issue a stay or lift a stay of lower court proceedings that were considering challenges to two administrative regulations seeking to require or encourage certain populations to vaccinate themselves against COVID-19 during the coronavirus pandemic. In Biden v. Missouri, ___ U.S. ___, 142 S.Ct. 647 (2022), lower courts had preliminarily enjoined a requirement issued by the Secretary of Health and Human Services that, in order to receive Medicare and Medicaid funding, participating medical facilities must ensure that their staff—unless exempt for medical or religious reasons—are vaccinated. The primary question was whether the regulation was authorized by the governing congressional statute, which gave the Secretary power to promulgate "requirements as [he] finds necessary in the interest of the health and safety of individuals who are furnished services in the institution." 42 U.S.C. § 1395x(e)(9) [this provision referred to hospitals; other provisions authorized the same for outpatient rehabilitation facilities, skilled nursing facilities, and ambulatory surgical centers]. Through a per curiam opinion, the Court agreed to stay the preliminary injunctions (thus permitting the regulation to take effect) after concluding among other things that the petitioners were likely to win on the merits that the regulation was authorized by statute. Because the vaccine mandate would "substantially reduce the likelihood that healthcare workers will contract the virus and transmit it to their patients," the rule "fits neatly within the language of the statute." The Court observed that many other regulations similarly dictate "a host of conditions that address the safe and effective provision of healthcare" including some that "relate to the qualifications and duties of healthcare workers themselves." Notably, the Court conceded "[o]f course the vaccine mandate goes further than what the Secretary has done in the past to implement infection control. But he has never had to address an infection problem of this scale and scope before. In any event, there can be no doubt that addressing infection problems in Medicare and Medicaid facilities is what he does."

Justice Thomas, joined by Justices Alito, Gorsuch, and Barrett, dissented because in their view the government "has not made a strong showing that this hodgepodge of [statutory] provisions authorizes a national vaccine mandate. We presume that Congress does not hide 'fundamental details of a regulatory scheme in vague or ancillary provisions.' Yet here, the Government proposes to find virtually unlimited vaccination power, over millions of healthcare workers, in definitional provisions, a saving clause, and a provision regarding long-term care facilities' sanitation procedures." The dissent also proclaimed " '[w]e expect Congress to speak clearly when authorizing an agency to exercise powers of vast economic and political significance.' And we expect Congress to use 'exceedingly clear language if it wishes to significantly alter the balance between state and federal power.' "

In National Federation of Independent Business v. Department of Labor, ___ U.S. ___, 142 S.Ct. 661 (2022), the Court issued a stay against a vaccine-mandate regulation issued by the Secretary of Labor through the Occupational Safety and Health Administration. Again to address the coronavirus pandemic, OSHA issued an emergency rule requiring all employers with at least 100 employees to require their employees (with few exceptions) either to get vaccination or to wear masks and regularly test themselves for COVID-19. Noncompliant employees must be "removed from the workplace." After receiving applications from lower court proceedings to stay the regulation pending their consideration of the merits, the Court (again through a per curiam opinion) granted the stay after concluding among other things that the petitioners were likely to win on the merits that the regulation was not authorized by statute. Tracking Justice Thomas's dissent in the companion *Biden* case, the Court again observed that " '[w]e expect Congress to speak clearly when authorizing an agency to exercise powers of vast economic and political significance.' " The Court's primary concern was that the "Act empowers the Secretary to set *workplace* safety standard, not broad public health measures." The Act's "provisions typically speak to hazards that employees face at work. And no provision of the Act addresses public health more generally, which falls outside of OSHA's sphere of expertise." While recognizing that unvaccinated (or unmasked) employees are more likely than others to contract COVID-19 at work, the Court responded that such a risk "is not an *occupational* hazard in most [workplaces]. . . . Permitting OSHA to regulate the hazards of daily life—simply because most Americans have jobs and face those same risks while on the clock—would significantly expand OSHA's regulatory authority without clear congressional authorization."

Justice Gorsuch, joined by Justices Thomas and Alito, concurred, focusing on the separation of powers issues raised by congressional delegations of authority to administrative agencies. Justice Gorsuch invoked a "major questions doctrine" in concluding that Congress had not given OSHA sufficiently broad authority to issue the vaccination mandate. "Why does the major questions doctrine matter? It ensures that the national government's power to make the laws that govern us remain where Article I of the Constitution says it belongs—with the people's elected representatives. If administrative agencies seek to regulate the daily lives and liberties of millions of Americans, the doctrine says, they must at least be able to trace that power to a clear grant of authority from Congress. In this respect, the major questions doctrine is closely related to what is sometimes called the nondelegation doctrine. . . . Both are designed to protect the separation of powers and ensure that any new laws governing the lives of Americans are subject to the robust democratic processes the Constitution demands."

Justice Breyer, joined by Justices Sotomayor and Kagan, dissented. They claimed that "OSHA's rule perfectly fits the language of the applicable statutory provision." That provision "commands . . . OSHA to issue an emergency temporary standard whenever it determines '(A) that employees are exposed to grave danger from exposure to substances or agents determined to be toxic or physically harmful or from new hazards, and (B) that such emergency standard is necessary to protect employees from such danger.' 29 U.S.C. § 655(c)(1). They explained why vaccination does in fact "protect employees from workplace hazards" and the statute is "indifferent to whether a hazard in the workplace is also found elsewhere." And if "OSHA's Standard is far-reaching—applying to many millions of American workers—it no more than reflects the scope of the crisis. . . . It is perverse, given these circumstances, to read the Act's grant of emergency powers in the way the majority does—as constraining OSHA from addressing one of the gravest workplace hazards in the agency's history." The Standard "is part of what the agency was built for." The dissent then addressed the "underlying" question of "[w] decides how much protection, and of what kind, American workers need from COVID-19? An agency with expertise in workplace health and safety, acting as Congress and the President authorized? Or a court, lacking any knowledge of how to safeguard workplaces, and insulated from responsibility for any damage it causes?"

West Virginia v. Environmental Protection Agency

597 U.S. ___, 142 S.Ct. 2587, ___ L.Ed.2d ___ (2022).

■ CHIEF JUSTICE ROBERTS delivered the opinion of the Court.

[In 2015, the Environmental Protection Agency (EPA) promulgated the Clean Power Plan rule, which addressed carbon dioxide (CO_2) emissions from existing coal- and natural-gas-fired power plants as a means of reducing the country's contribution to climate warming. For authority, the Agency cited Section 111(d) of the Clean Air Act, which authorizes regulation of certain pollutants from both new and existing sources. 42 U.S. C. § 7411(d). This statutory section "operates as a gap-filler," empowering EPA to regulate harmful emissions not already controlled under the agency's two primary pollution control regimes. Prior to the Clean Power Plan, EPA had used § 111(d) only a handful of times since its enactment in 1970.

[Under the Clean Air Act, although the States set the actual enforceable rules governing power plants and other sources), EPA determines the amount of pollution reduction that the States must achieve. The Agency derives that amount by determining the "best system of emission reduction . . . that has been adequately demonstrated," or the BSER, for the type of source at issue. States then submit plans identifying the emissions restrictions they intend to implement in order to comply with the EPA-decreed pollution ceilings.

[EPA's Clean Power Plan was premised on the Agency's earlier finding that CO_2 is an "air pollutant" that "may reasonably be anticipated to endanger public health or welfare" by causing climate change. 80 Fed. Reg. 64530. CO_2 was not already regulated by other pollution control programs. Applying § 111(d), EPA determined that with respect to CO_2, the "best system or emission reduction" for existing coal and natural gas plants included three types of measures. The first was "heat rate improvements" at coal-fired plants, technologies the plants could use to burn coal more cleanly. The second and third measures involved a very different approach: "generation shifting" in electricity production from higher-emitting to lower emitting producers. The second measure required shifting electricity generation from coal-fired power plants to cleaner natural-gas-fired plants. The third measure required additional shifting to renewable energy sources, mostly solar and wind. EPA explained that, to implement the needed shift to cleaner sources, an operator could reduce its coal or natural gas plant's own production of electricity, build or invest in a new or existing natural gas plant, wind farm, or solar installation, or purchase emission credits as part of a cap-and-trade regime (the latter program permits producers who reduce their emissions to sell a credit for that amount to other producers who can then count that credited savings toward meeting their own emission caps). After considering a wide range of potential stringencies for the BSER and modeling how much more electricity both natural gas and renewable sources could supply without causing undue cost increases or reducing the overall power supply, EPA decided to mandate what it considered to be a "reasonable" amount of generation shifting. The Agency projected, for instance, that coal could feasibly be reduced to only 27% of national electricity generation by 2030, down from 38% in 2014, though this reduction would cost billions of dollars in compliance costs (due to higher electricity prices), require the retirement of dozens of coal plants, and eliminate tens of thousands of jobs.

[The day EPA promulgated the Clean Power Plan, many states and private parties challenged it by petitioning for review in the D.C. Circuit Court of Appeals. The Supreme Court stayed the Plan, preventing it from taking effect. The new Trump Administration ultimately repealed the Plan in 2019, replacing it with an alternative Affordable Clean Energy (ACE) rule that focused solely on requiring existing coal plants to burn more cleanly (which concededly would produce only small reductions in CO_2 emissions). Many states and private parties then petitioned for review in the D.C. Circuit to challenge the Trump Administration's repeal and replacement of the Clean Power Plan, and other states and private parties intervened to defend both actions. The Court of Appeals vacated EPA's repeal-and-replacement of the Plan and remanded to the Agency for further consideration. The Supreme Court granted various petitions for certiorari.[a]]

. . .

III

A

. . . The issue here is whether restructuring the Nation's overall mix of electricity generation, to transition from 38% coal to 27% coal by 2030, can be the "best system of emission reduction" within the meaning of Section 111.

"It is a fundamental canon of statutory construction that the words of a statute must be read in their context and with a view to their place in the overall statutory scheme." *Davis v. Michigan Dept. of Treasury*, 489 U.S. 803, 809 (1989). Where the statute at issue is one that confers authority upon an administrative agency, that inquiry must be "shaped, at least in some measure, by the nature of the question presented"—whether Congress in fact meant to confer the power the agency has asserted. *FDA v. Brown & Williamson Tobacco Corp.*, 529 U.S. 120, 159 (2000). In the ordinary case, that context has no great effect on the appropriate analysis. Nonetheless, our precedent teaches that there are "extraordinary cases" that call for a different approach—cases in which the "history and the breadth of the authority that [the agency] has asserted," and the "economic and political significance" of that assertion, provide a "reason to hesitate before concluding that Congress" meant to confer such authority.

Such cases have arisen from all corners of the administrative state. [The Court briefly described cases denying the Food and Drug Administration's authority to regulate and ban tobacco products, the Centers for Disease Control and Prevention's authority to mandate a nationwide eviction moratorium in response to the COVID-19 pandemic, the Occupational Safety and Health Administration's mandate that employers of large companies either obtain a COVID-19 vaccination or undergo weekly testing, among others.]

---

[a]   After the appellate court's ruling issued on January 19, 2021, the new Biden Administration indicated it wanted time to consider yet a different rule rather than to reinstate the Clean Power Plan, raising a question as to whether the Court lacked Article III jurisdiction to hear this challenge because the controversy over the Plan had become moot. The Court unanimously rejected this jurisdictional concern based on the voluntary cessation doctrine, though the dissent questioned whether why, under the circumstances, the majority felt it necessary to grant discretionary review over this case in the first place.

In *Brown & Williamson*, for instance, the Food and Drug Administration claimed that its authority over "drugs" and "devices" included the power to regulate, and even ban, tobacco products. *Id.*, at 126–127. We rejected that "expansive construction of the statute," concluding that "Congress could not have intended to delegate" such a sweeping and consequential authority "in so cryptic a fashion." *Id.*, at 160. [Discussion of other cases omitted.] . . .

All of these regulatory assertions had a colorable textual basis. And yet, in each case, given the various circumstances, "common sense as to the manner in which Congress [would have been] likely to delegate" such power to the agency at issue, *Brown & Williamson*, 529 U.S., at 133, made it very unlikely that Congress had actually done so. Extraordinary grants of regulatory authority are rarely accomplished through "modest words," "vague terms," or "subtle device[s]." Nor does Congress typically use oblique or elliptical language to empower an agency to make a "radical or fundamental change" to a statutory scheme. Agencies have only those powers given to them by Congress, and "enabling legislation" is generally not an "open book to which the agency [may] add pages and change the plot line." We presume that "Congress intends to make major policy decisions itself, not leave those decisions to agencies." *United States Telecom Assn. v. FCC*, 855 F. 3d 381, 419 (CADC 2017) (Kavanaugh, J., dissenting from denial of rehearing en banc).

Thus, in certain extraordinary cases, both separation of powers principles and a practical understanding of legislative intent make us "reluctant to read into ambiguous statutory text" the delegation claimed to be lurking there. To convince us otherwise, something more than a merely plausible textual basis for the agency action is necessary. The agency instead must point to "clear congressional authorization" for the power it claims.

The dissent criticizes us for "announc[ing] the arrival" of this major questions doctrine, and argues that each of the decisions just cited simply followed our "ordinary method" of "normal statutory interpretation." But in what the dissent calls the "key case" in this area, *Brown & Williamson*, the Court could not have been clearer: "In extraordinary cases . . . there may be reason to hesitate" before accepting a reading of a statute that would, under more "ordinary" circumstances, be upheld. 529 U.S., at 159. Or, as we put it more recently, we "typically greet" assertions of "extravagant statutory power over the national economy" with "skepticism." The dissent attempts to fit the analysis in these cases within routine statutory interpretation, but the bottom line—a requirement of "clear congressional authorization"—confirms that the approach under the major questions doctrine is distinct.

As for the major questions doctrine "label[ ], it took hold because it refers to an identifiable body of law that has developed over a series of significant cases all addressing a particular and recurring problem: agencies asserting highly consequential power beyond what Congress could reasonably be understood to have granted. . . .

B

Under our precedents, this is a major questions case. In arguing that Section 111(d) empowers it to substantially restructure the American energy market, EPA "claim[ed] to discover in a long-extant statute an unheralded power" representing a "transformative expansion in [its] regulatory authority." It located that newfound power in the vague language of an "ancillary provision[ ]" of the Act, one that was designed to function as a gap filler and had rarely been used in the preceding decades. And the Agency's discovery allowed it to adopt a regulatory program that Congress had conspicuously and repeatedly declined to enact itself. Given these circumstances, there is every reason to "hesitate before concluding that Congress" meant to confer on EPA the authority it claims under Section 111(d).

Prior to 2015, EPA had always set emissions limits under Section 111 based on the application of measures that would reduce pollution by causing the regulated source to operate more cleanly. It had never devised a cap by looking to a "system" that would reduce pollution simply by "shifting" polluting activity "from dirtier to cleaner sources." . . .

[EPA itself described the sort of "systems of emissions reduction" it had previously mandated as "more traditional air pollution control measures."] But, the Agency explained, in order to "control[ ] CO2 from affected [plants] at levels . . . necessary to mitigate the dangers presented by climate change," it could not base the emissions limit on "measures that improve efficiency at the power plants" [because the] quantity of emissions reductions resulting from the application of these measures" would have been "too small." . . .

This view of EPA's authority was not only unprecedented; it also effected a "fundamental revision of the statute, changing it from [one sort of] scheme of . . . regulation" into an entirely different kind. Under the Agency's prior view of Section 111, its role was limited to ensuring the efficient pollution performance of each individual regulated source. Under that paradigm, if a source was already operating at that level, there was nothing more for EPA to do. Under its newly "discover[ed]" authority, however, EPA can demand much greater reductions in emissions based on a very different kind of policy judgment: that it would be "best" if coal made up a much smaller share of national electricity generation. And on this view of EPA's authority, it could go further, perhaps forcing coal plants to "shift" away virtually all of their generation—*i.e.*, to cease making power altogether. . . .

We also find it "highly unlikely that Congress would leave" to "agency discretion" the decision of how much coal-based generation there should be over the coming decades. *Brown & Williamson*, 529 U.S., at 160 ("We are confident that Congress could not have intended to delegate a decision of such economic and political significance to an agency in so cryptic a fashion."). The basic and consequential tradeoffs involved in such a choice are ones that Congress would likely have intended for itself. Congress certainly has not conferred a like authority upon EPA anywhere else in the Clean Air Act. The last place one would expect to find it is in the previously little-used backwater of Section 111(d). . . .

Finally, we cannot ignore that [EPA enacted] a program that, long after the dangers posed by greenhouse gas emissions "had become well known, Congress considered and rejected" multiple times [offering several examples]. . . .

C

Given these circumstances, our precedent counsels skepticism toward EPA's claim that Section 111 empowers it to devise carbon emissions caps based on a generation shifting approach. To overcome that skepticism, the Government must—under the major questions doctrine—point to "clear congressional authorization" to regulate in that manner.

All the Government can offer, however, is the Agency's authority to establish emissions caps at a level reflecting "the application of the best system of emission reduction . . . adequately demonstrated." 42 U.S.C. § 7411(a)(1). As a matter of "definitional possibilities," generation shifting can be described as a "system"—"an aggregation or assemblage of objects united by some form of regular interaction,"— capable of reducing emissions. But of course almost anything could constitute such a "system"; shorn of all context, the word is an empty vessel. Such a vague statutory grant is not close to the sort of clear authorization required by our precedents.

The Government, echoed by the other respondents, looks to other provisions of the Clean Air Act for support. It points out that the Act elsewhere uses the word "system" . . . to describe cap-and-trade schemes or other sector-wide mechanisms for reducing pollution [discussion of examples omitted]. . . .

These arguments, however, concern an interpretive question that is not at issue. We have no occasion to decide whether the statutory phrase "system of emission reduction" refers *exclusively* to measures that improve the pollution performance of individual sources, such that all other actions are ineligible to qualify as the BSER. To be sure, it is pertinent to our analysis that EPA has acted consistent with such a limitation for the first four decades of the statute's existence. But the only interpretive question before us, and the only one we answer, is more narrow: whether the "best system of emission reduction" identified by EPA in the Clean Power Plan was within the authority granted to the Agency in Section 111(d) of the Clean Air Act. For the reasons given, the answer is no.

* * *

Capping carbon dioxide emissions at a level that will force a nationwide transition away from the use of coal to generate electricity may be a sensible "solution to the crisis of the day." But it is not plausible that Congress gave EPA the authority to adopt on its own such a regulatory scheme in Section 111(d). A decision of such magnitude and consequence rests with Congress itself, or an agency acting pursuant to a clear delegation from that representative body. The judgment of the Court of Appeals for the District of Columbia Circuit is reversed, and the cases are remanded for further proceedings consistent with this opinion.

It is so ordered.

■ JUSTICE GORSUCH, with whom JUSTICE ALITO joins, concurring.

. . . I join the Court's opinion and write to offer some additional observations about the doctrine on which it rests.

I

A

One of the Judiciary's most solemn duties is to ensure that acts of Congress are applied in accordance with the Constitution in the cases that come before us. To help fulfill that duty, courts have developed certain "clear-statement" rules. These rules assume that, absent a clear statement otherwise, Congress means for its laws to operate in congruence with the Constitution rather than test its bounds. In this way, these clear-statement rules help courts "act as faithful agents of the Constitution." A. Barrett, Substantive Canons and Faithful Agency, 90 B. U. L. Rev. 109, 169 (2010).

Consider some examples. The Constitution prohibits Congress from passing laws imposing various types of retroactive liability. Consistent with this rule, Chief Justice Marshall long ago advised that "a court . . . ought to struggle hard against a [statutory] construction which will, by a retrospective operation, affect the rights of parties." *United States v. Schooner Peggy*, 1 Cranch 103, 110 (1801). . . .

The Constitution also incorporates the doctrine of sovereign immunity. To enforce that doctrine, courts have consistently held that "nothing but express words, or an insurmountable implication" would justify the conclusion that lawmakers intended to abrogate the States' sovereign immunity. . . .

The major questions doctrine works in much the same way to protect the Constitution's separation of powers. In Article I, "the People" vested "[a]ll" federal "legislative powers . . . in Congress." As Chief Justice Marshall put it, this means that "important subjects . . . must be entirely regulated by the legislature itself," even if Congress may leave the Executive "to act under such general provisions to fill up the details." *Wayman v. Southard*, 10 Wheat. 1, 42–43 (1825). Doubtless, what qualifies as an important subject and what constitutes a detail may be debated. But no less than its rules against retroactive legislation or protecting sovereign immunity, the Constitution's rule vesting federal legislative power in Congress is "vital to the integrity and maintenance of the system of government ordained by the Constitution."

It is vital because the framers believed that a republic—a thing of the people— would be more likely to enact just laws than a regime administered by a ruling class of largely unaccountable "ministers." The Federalist No. 11 (A. Hamilton). From time to time, some have questioned that assessment. But by vesting the lawmaking power in the people's elected representatives, the Constitution sought to ensure "not only that all power [w]ould be derived from the people," but also "that those [e]ntrusted with it should be kept in dependence on the people." *Id.*, No. 37 (J. Madison). The Constitution, too, placed its trust not in the hands of "a few, but [in] a number of hands," *ibid.*, so that those who make our laws would better reflect the diversity of the people they represent and have an "immediate dependence on, and an intimate sympathy with, the people." *Id.*, No. 52 (J. Madison). . . .

Admittedly, lawmaking under our Constitution can be difficult. But that is nothing particular to our time nor any accident. The framers believed that the power to make new laws regulating private conduct was a grave one that could, if not properly checked, pose a serious threat to individual liberty. See The Federalist No. 48 (J. Madison); see also *id.*, No. 73 (A. Hamilton). As a result, the framers deliberately sought to make lawmaking difficult by insisting that two houses of Congress must agree to any new law and the President must concur or a legislative supermajority must override his veto.

The difficulty of the design sought to serve other ends too. By effectively requiring a broad consensus to pass legislation, the Constitution sought to ensure that any new laws would enjoy wide social acceptance, profit from input by an array of different perspectives during their consideration, and thanks to all this prove stable over time. See *id.*, No. 10, at 82–84 (J. Madison). The need for compromise inherent in this design also sought to protect minorities by ensuring that their votes would often decide the fate of proposed legislation—allowing them to wield real power alongside the majority. See *id.*, No. 51 (J. Madison). The difficulty of legislating at the federal level aimed as well to preserve room for lawmaking "by governments more local and more accountable than a distant federal" authority, and in this way allow States to serve as "laborator[ies]" for "novel social and economic experiments."

Permitting Congress to divest its legislative power to the Executive Branch would "dash [this] whole scheme." Legislation would risk becoming nothing more than the will of the current President, or, worse yet, the will of unelected officials barely responsive to him. In a world like that, agencies could churn out new laws more or less at whim. Intrusions on liberty would not be difficult and rare, but easy and profuse. See The Federalist No. 47 (J. Madison); No. 62 (J. Madison). Stability would be lost, with vast numbers of laws changing with every new presidential administration. . . . [L]aws would more often bear the support only of the party currently in power. Powerful special interests, which are sometimes "uniquely" able to influence the agendas of administrative agencies, would flourish while others would be left to ever-shifting winds.

Finally, little would remain to stop agencies from moving into areas where state authority has traditionally predominated. . . .

B

Much as constitutional rules about retroactive legislation and sovereign immunity have their corollary clear-statement rules, Article I's Vesting Clause has its own: the major questions doctrine. Some version of this clear-statement rule can be traced to at least 1897, when this Court confronted a case involving the Interstate Commerce Commission, the federal government's "first modern regulatory agency." . . . In fact, this Court applied the major questions doctrine in "all corners of the administrative state," whether the issue at hand involved an agency's asserted power to regulate tobacco products, ban drugs used in physician-assisted suicide, extend Clean Air Act regulations to private homes, impose an eviction moratorium, or enforce a vaccine mandate.

. . .

II

A

Turning from the doctrine's function to its application, it seems to me that our cases supply a good deal of guidance about when an agency action involves a major question for which clear congressional authority is required.

First, this Court has indicated that the doctrine applies when an agency claims the power to resolve a matter of great "political significance," or end an "earnest and profound debate across the country." . . . Relatedly, this Court has found it telling when Congress has "considered and rejected" bills authorizing something akin to the agency's proposed course of action. That too may be a sign that an agency is attempting to "work [a]round" the legislative process to resolve for itself a question of great political significance.

Second, this Court has said that an agency must point to clear congressional authorization when it seeks to regulate a "significant portion of the American economy," or require "billions of dollars in spending" by private persons or entities. The Court has held that regulating tobacco products, eliminating rate regulation in the telecommunications industry, subjecting private homes to Clean Air Act restrictions, and suspending local housing laws and regulations can sometimes check this box.

Third, this Court has said that the major questions doctrine may apply when an agency seeks to "intrud[e] into an area that is the particular domain of state law." . . .

While this list of triggers may not be exclusive, each of the signs the Court has found significant in the past is present here, making this a relatively easy case for the doctrine's application. . . .

. . . None of this is to say the policy the agency seeks to pursue is unwise or should not be pursued. It is only to say that the agency seeks to resolve for itself the sort of question normally reserved for Congress. As a result, we look for clear evidence that the people's representatives in Congress have actually afforded the agency the power it claims.

B

At this point, the question becomes what qualifies as a clear congressional statement authorizing an agency's action. Courts have long experience applying clear-statement rules throughout the law, and our cases have identified several telling clues in this context too.

First, courts must look to the legislative provisions on which the agency seeks to rely "with a view to their place in the overall statutory scheme." "[O]blique or elliptical language" will not supply a clear statement. Nor may agencies seek to hide "elephants in mouseholes," or rely on "gap filler" provisions. . . .

Second, courts may examine the age and focus of the statute the agency invokes in relation to the problem the agency seeks to address. As the Court puts it today, it is unlikely that Congress will make an "[e]xtraordinary gran[t] of regulatory authority" through "vague language" in "a long-extant statute." . . . [A]n agency's attempt to deploy an old statute focused on one problem to solve a new and different problem may also be a warning sign that it is acting without clear congressional authority. . . .

Third, courts may examine the agency's past interpretations of the relevant statute. A "contemporaneous" and long-held Executive Branch interpretation of a statute is entitled to some weight as evidence of the statute's original charge to an agency. Conversely, in *NFIB v. OSHA*, [142 S.Ct. 661 (2022)], the Court found it "telling that OSHA, in its half century of existence, ha[d] never before adopted a broad public health regulation" under the statute that the agency sought to invoke as authority for a nationwide vaccine mandate. . . .

Fourth, skepticism may be merited when there is a mismatch between an agency's challenged action and its congressionally assigned mission and expertise. As the Court explains, "[w]hen an agency has no comparative expertise in making certain policy judgments, . . . Congress presumably would not task it with doing so." . . .

Asking these questions again yields a clear answer in our case. As the Court details, the agency before us cites no specific statutory authority allowing it to transform the Nation's electrical power supply. Instead, the agency relies on a rarely invoked statutory provision that was passed with little debate and has been characterized as an "obscure, never-used section of the law." Nor has the agency previously interpreted the relevant provision to confer on it such vast authority; there is no original, longstanding, and consistent interpretation meriting judicial respect. Finally, there is a "mismatch" between the EPA's expertise over environmental matters and the agency's claim that "Congress implicitly tasked it, and it alone, with balancing the many vital considerations of national policy implicated in deciding how Americans will get their energy." Such a claimed power "requires technical and policy expertise *not* traditionally needed in [the] EPA's regulatory development." . . .

III

. . . When Congress seems slow to solve problems, it may be only natural that those in the Executive Branch might seek to take matters into their own hands. But the Constitution does not authorize agencies to use pen-and-phone regulations as substitutes for laws passed by the people's representatives. In our Republic, "[i]t is the peculiar province of the legislature to prescribe general rules for the government of society." *Fletcher v. Peck*, 6 Cranch 87, 136 (1810). Because today's decision helps safeguard that foundational constitutional promise, I am pleased to concur.

■ JUSTICE KAGAN, with whom JUSTICE BREYER and JUSTICE SOTOMAYOR join, dissenting.

Today, the Court strips the Environmental Protection Agency (EPA) of the power Congress gave it to respond to "the most pressing environmental challenge of our time." *Massachusetts v. EPA*, 549 U.S. 497, 505 (2007).

Climate change's causes and dangers are no longer subject to serious doubt. Modern science is "unequivocal that human influence"—in particular, the emission of green-house gases like carbon dioxide—"has warmed the atmosphere, ocean and land."

Intergovernmental Panel on Climate Change, Sixth Assessment Report, The Physical Science Basis: Headline Statements 1 (2021). The Earth is now warmer than at any time "in the history of modern civilization," with the six warmest years on record all occurring in the last decade. U.S. Global Change Research Program, Fourth National Climate Assessment, Vol. I, p.10 (2017); Brief for Climate Scientists as *Amici Curiae* 8. The rise in temperatures brings with it "increases in heat-related deaths," "coastal inundation and erosion," "more frequent and intense hurricanes, floods, and other extreme weather events," "drought," "destruction of ecosystems," and "potentially significant disruptions of food production." *American Elec. Power Co. v. Connecticut*, 564 U.S. 410, 417 (2011). If the current rate of emissions continues, children born this year could live to see parts of the Eastern seaboard swallowed by the ocean. See Brief for Climate Scientists as *Amici Curiae* 6. Rising waters, scorching heat, and other severe weather conditions could force "mass migration events[,] political crises, civil unrest," and "even state failure." Dept. of Defense, Climate Risk Analysis 8 (2021). And by the end of this century, climate change could be the cause of "4.6 million excess yearly deaths." See R. Bressler, The Mortality Cost of Carbon, 12 Nature Communications 4467, p. 5 (2021).

Congress charged EPA with addressing those potentially catastrophic harms, including through regulation of fossil-fuel-fired power plants. Section 111 of the Clean Air Act directs EPA to regulate stationary sources of any substance that "causes, or contributes significantly to, air pollution" and that "may reasonably be anticipated to endanger public health or welfare." Carbon dioxide and other greenhouse gases fit that description. See *Massachusetts*, 549 U.S., at 528–532. EPA thus serves as the Nation's "primary regulator of greenhouse gas emissions." And among the most significant of the entities it regulates are fossil-fuel-fired (mainly coal- and natural-gas-fired) power plants. Today, those electricity-producing plants are responsible for about one quarter of the Nation's greenhouse gas emissions. Curbing that output is a necessary part of any effective approach for addressing climate change.

. . . This Court has obstructed EPA's effort from the beginning. Right after the Obama administration issued the Clean Power Plan, the Court stayed its implementation. That action was unprecedented: Never before had the Court stayed a regulation then under review in the lower courts. . . .

The limits the majority now puts on EPA's authority fly in the face of the statute Congress wrote. . . . The majority today overrides that legislative choice. In so doing, it deprives EPA of the power needed—and the power granted—to curb the emission of greenhouse gases.

I

. . . As the Senate Report explained, Section 111(d) guarantees that "there should be no gaps in control activities pertaining to stationary source emissions that pose any significant danger to public health or welfare." Reflecting that language, the majority calls Section 111(d) a "gap-filler." It might also be thought of as a backstop or catch-all provision, protecting against pollutants that the [two primary pollution control] programs let go by. But the section is *not*, as the majority further claims, an "ancillary provision" or a statutory "backwater." That characterization is a non-sequitur. That something is a backstop does not make it a backwater. Even if they are needed only infrequently, backstops can perform a critical function—and this one surely does. Again, Section 111(d) tells EPA that when a pollutant—like carbon dioxide—is not regulated through other programs, EPA must undertake a further regulatory effort to control that substance's emission from existing stationary sources. In that way, Section 111(d) operates to ensure that the Act achieves comprehensive pollution control.

Section 111 describes the prescribed regulatory effort in expansive terms. . . . [T]he provision instructs EPA to decide upon the "best system of emission reduction which . . . has been adequately demonstrated." The provision tells EPA, in making that determination, to take account of both costs and varied "nonair" impacts (on health, the environment, and the supply of energy). And the provision finally directs EPA to set the particular emissions limit achievable through use of the demonstrated "best system." Taken as a whole, the section provides regulatory flexibility and discretion. It imposes, to be sure, meaningful constraints: Take into account costs and nonair impacts, and make sure the best system has a proven track record. But the core command—go find the best system of emission reduction—gives broad authority to EPA.

If that flexibility is not apparent on the provision's face, consider some dictionary definitions—supposedly a staple of this Court's supposedly textualist method of reading statutes. A "system" is "a complex unity formed of many often diverse parts subject to a common plan or serving a common purpose." Webster's Third New International Dictionary 2322 (1971). Or again: a "system" is "[a]n organized and coordinated method; a procedure." American Heritage Dictionary 1768 (5th ed. 2018). . . . Congress used an obviously broad word (though surrounding it with constraints) to give EPA lots of latitude in deciding how to set emissions limits. And contra the majority, a broad term is not the same thing as a "vague" one. A broad term is comprehensive, extensive, wide-ranging; a "vague" term is unclear, ambiguous, hazy. (Once again, dictionaries would tell the tale.) So EPA was quite right in stating in the Clean Power Plan that the "[p]lain meaning" of the term "system" in Section 111 refers to "a set of measures that work together to reduce emissions." 80 Fed. Reg. 64762. Another of this Court's opinions, involving a matter other than the bogeyman of environmental regulation, might have stopped there.

For generation shifting fits comfortably within the conventional meaning of a "system of emission reduction." Consider one of the most common mechanisms of generation shifting: the use of a cap-and-trade scheme. Here is how the majority describes cap and trade: "Under such a scheme, sources that receive a reduction in their emissions can sell a credit representing the value of that reduction to others, who are able to count it toward their own applicable emissions caps." Does that sound like a "system" to you? It does to me too. And it also has to this Court. In the past, we have explained that "[t]his type of 'cap-and-trade' *system* cuts costs while still reducing pollution to target levels.". . . .

Other statutory provisions confirm the point [discussing other parts of the Clean Air Act]. . . .

There is also a flipside point . . . [Q]uite a number of statutory sections confine EPA's emissions-reduction efforts to technological controls—essentially, equipment or processes that can be put into place at a particular facility [giving examples]. . . . None of those provisions would allow EPA to set emissions limits based on generation shifting, as the Agency acknowledges. But nothing like the language of those provisions is included in Section 111. That matters under normal rules of statutory interpretation. As Justice Scalia once wrote for the Court: "We do not lightly assume that Congress has omitted from its adopted text requirements that it nonetheless intends to apply, and our reluctance is even greater when Congress has shown elsewhere in the same statute that it knows how to make such a requirement manifest."

. . . Section 111 does not impose *any* constraints—technological or otherwise—on EPA's authority to regulate stationary sources (except for those stated, like cost). In somehow (and to some extent) saying otherwise, the majority flouts the statutory text.

"Congress," this Court has said, "knows to speak in plain terms when it wishes to circumscribe, and in capacious terms when it wishes to enlarge, agency discretion." In Section 111, Congress spoke in capacious terms. It knew that "without regulatory flexibility, changing circumstances and scientific developments would soon render the Clean Air Act obsolete." *Massachusetts*, 549 U.S., at 532. So the provision enables EPA to base emissions limits for existing stationary sources on the "best system." That system may be technological in nature; it may be whatever else the majority has in mind; or, most important here, it may be generation shifting. The statute does not care. And when Congress uses "expansive language" to authorize agency action, courts generally may not "impos[e] limits on [the] agency's discretion." . . .

II

. . .

A

"[T]he words of a statute," as the majority states, "must be read in their context and with a view to their place in the overall statutory scheme." . . . So too, a court "must be guided to a degree by common sense as to the manner in which Congress is likely to delegate." . . .

. . . The majority today goes beyond those sensible principles. It announces the arrival of the "major questions doctrine," which replaces normal text-in-context statutory interpretation with some tougher-to-satisfy set of rules. Apparently, there is now a two-step inquiry. First, a court must decide, by looking at some panoply of factors, whether agency action presents an "extraordinary case[]." If it does, the agency "must point to clear congressional authorization for the power it claims," someplace over and above the normal statutory basis we require. The result is statutory interpretation of an unusual kind. It is not until page 28 of a 31-page opinion that the majority begins to seriously discuss the meaning of Section 111. And even then, it does not address straight-up what should be the question: Does the text of that provision, when read in context and with a common-sense awareness of how Congress delegates, authorize the agency action here?

The majority claims it is just following precedent, but that is not so. The Court has never even used the term "major questions doctrine" before. And in the relevant cases, the Court has done statutory construction of a familiar sort. It has looked to the text of a delegation. It has addressed how an agency's view of that text works—or fails to do so—in the context of a broader statutory scheme. And it has asked, in a common-sensical (or call it purposive) vein, about what Congress would have made of the agency's view—otherwise said, whether Congress would naturally have delegated authority over some important question to the agency, given its expertise and experience. In short, in assessing the scope of a delegation, the Court has considered—without multiple steps, triggers, or special presumptions—the fit between the power claimed, the agency claiming it, and the broader statutory design. [Discussion of several cases omitted]

. . . The eyebrow-raise is indeed a consistent presence in these cases, responding to something the Court found anomalous—looked at from Congress's point of view—in a particular agency's exercise of authority. In each case, the Court thought, the agency had strayed out of its lane, to an area where it had neither expertise nor experience. The Attorney General making healthcare policy, the regulator of pharmaceutical concerns deciding the fate of the tobacco industry, and so on. And in each case, the proof that the agency had roamed too far afield lay in the statutory scheme itself. The agency action collided with other statutory provisions; if the former were allowed, the latter could not mean what they said or could not work as intended. FDA having to declare tobacco "safe" to avoid shutting down an industry; or EPA having literally to change hard numbers contained in the Clean Air Act. There, according to the Court, the statutory framework was "not designed to grant" the authority claimed. The agency's "singular" assertion of power "would render the statute unrecognizable to the Congress" that wrote it.

B

The Court today faces no such singular assertion of agency power. As I have already explained, nothing in the Clean Air Act (or, for that matter, any other statute) conflicts with EPA's reading of Section 111. Notably, the majority does not dispute that point. Of course, it views Section 111 (if for unexplained reasons) as less clear than I do. But nowhere does the majority provide evidence from within the statute itself that the Clean Power Plan conflicts with or undermines Congress's design. That fact alone makes this case different from all the cases described above. As to the other critical matter in those cases—is the agency operating outside its sphere of expertise?—the majority at least tries to say something. It claims EPA has no "comparative expertise" in "balancing the many vital considerations of national policy" implicated in regulating electricity sources. But that is wrong. [Extensive discussion of EPA's relevant expertise omitted.]

. . . Why, then, be "skeptic[al]" of EPA's exercise of authority? When there is no misfit, of the kind apparent in our precedents, between the regulation, the agency, and the statutory design? Although the majority offers a flurry of complaints, they come down in the end to this: The Clean Power Plan is a big new thing, issued under a minor statutory provision. See [majority opinion] (labeling the Plan "transformative" and "unprecedented" and calling Section 111(d) an "ancillary" "backwater"). I have already addressed the back half of that argument: In fact, there is nothing insignificant about Section 111(d), which was intended to ensure that EPA would limit existing stationary sources' emissions of otherwise unregulated pollutants (however few or many there were). And the front half of the argument doesn't work either. The Clean Power Plan was not so big [because the energy industry exceeded the Plan's projected reductions even though it never went into effect]. It was not so new [because EPA had already employed cap-and-trade schemes to reduce mercury emissions].

. . . In any event, newness might be perfectly legitimate—even required—from Congress's point of view. I do not dispute that an agency's longstanding practice may inform a court's interpretation of a statute delegating the agency power. But it is equally true, as *Brown & Williamson* recognized, that agency practices are "not carved in stone." 529 U.S., at 156–157. Congress makes broad delegations in part so that agencies can "adapt their rules and policies to the demands of changing circumstances." *Id.*, at 157. To keep faith with that congressional choice, courts must give agencies "ample latitude" to revisit, rethink, and revise their regulatory approaches. *Ibid.* So it is here. Section 111(d) was written, as I've shown, to give EPA plenty of leeway. . . .

And contra the majority, it is that [enacting] Congress's choice which counts, not any later one's. The majority says it "cannot ignore" that Congress in recent years has "considered and rejected" cap-and-trade schemes. But under normal principles of statutory construction, the majority *should* ignore that fact (just as I should ignore that Congress failed to enact bills barring EPA from implementing the Clean Power Plan). As we have explained time and again, failed legislation "offers a particularly dangerous basis on which to rest an interpretation of an existing law a different and earlier Congress" adopted. *Bostock v. Clayton County*, 590 U.S. ___ (2020); see *Sullivan v. Finkelstein*, 496 U.S. 617, 632 (1990) (Scalia, J., concurring in part) ("Arguments based on subsequent legislative history" should "not be taken seriously, not even in a footnote"). . . . That leaves the Court in much the same place it was when deciding *Massachusetts v. EPA*. Said the Court then: "That subsequent Congresses have eschewed enacting binding emissions limitations to combat global warming tells us nothing about what Congress meant" when it enacted the Clean Air Act. 549 U.S., at 529–530. And so the Court recognized EPA's authority to regulate carbon dioxide. But that Court was not this Court; and this Court deprives EPA of the authority Congress gave it in Section 111(d) to respond to the same environmental danger.

III

Some years ago, I remarked that "[w]e're all textualists now." It seems I was wrong. The current Court is textualist only when being so suits it. When that method would frustrate broader goals, special canons like the "major questions doctrine" magically appear as get-out-of-text-free cards. Today, one of those broader goals makes itself clear: Prevent agencies from doing important work, even though that is what Congress directed. That anti-administrative-state stance shows up in the majority opinion, and it suffuses the concurrence.

The kind of agency delegations at issue here go all the way back to this Nation's founding. "[T]he founding era," scholars have shown, "wasn't concerned about delegation." E. Posner & A. Vermeule, Interring the Nondelegation Doctrine, 69 U. Chi. L. Rev. 1721, 1734 (2002). The records of the Constitutional Convention, the ratification debates, the Federalist—none of them suggests any significant limit on Congress's capacity to delegate policymaking authority to the Executive Branch. And neither does any early practice. The very first Congress gave sweeping authority to the Executive Branch to resolve some of the day's most pressing problems, including questions of "territorial administration," "Indian affairs," "foreign and domestic debt," "military service," and "the federal courts." J. Mortenson & N. Bagley, Delegation at the Founding, 121 Colum. L. Rev. 277, 349 (2021). That Congress, to use a few examples, gave the Executive power to devise a licensing scheme for trading with Indians; to craft appropriate laws for the Territories; and to decide how to pay down the (potentially ruinous) national debt. See *id*. Barely anyone objected on delegation grounds. See *id*. at 281–282, 332, 339.

It is not surprising that Congress has always delegated, and continues to do so—including on important policy issues. As this Court has recognized, it is often "unreasonable and impracticable" for Congress to do anything else. In all times, but ever more in "our increasingly complex society," the Legislature "simply cannot do its job absent an ability to delegate power under broad general directives." Consider just two reasons why.

First, Members of Congress often don't know enough—and know they don't know enough—to regulate sensibly on an issue. Of course, Members can and do provide overall direction. But then they rely, as all of us rely in our daily lives, on people with greater expertise and experience. Those people are found in agencies. Congress looks to them to make specific judgments about how to achieve its more general objectives. And it does so especially, though by no means exclusively, when an issue has a scientific or technical dimension. . . .

Second and relatedly, Members of Congress often can't know enough—and again, know they can't—to keep regulatory schemes working across time. Congress usually can't predict the future—can't anticipate changing circumstances and the way they will affect varied regulatory techniques. Nor can Congress (realistically) keep track of and respond to fast-flowing developments as they occur. Once again, that is most obviously true when it comes to scientific and technical matters. The "best system of emission reduction" is not today what it was yesterday, and will surely be something different tomorrow. So for this reason too, a rational Congress delegates. It enables an agency to adapt old regulatory approaches to new times, to ensure that a statutory program remains effective.

Over time, the administrative delegations Congress has made have helped to build a modern Nation. Congress wanted fewer workers killed in industrial accidents. It wanted to prevent plane crashes, and reduce the deadliness of car wrecks. It wanted to ensure that consumer products didn't catch fire. It wanted to stop the routine adulteration of food and improve the safety and efficacy of medications. And it wanted cleaner air and water. If an American could go back in time, she might be astonished by how much progress has occurred in all those areas. It didn't happen through legislation alone. It happened because Congress gave broad-ranging powers to administrative agencies, and those agencies then filled in—rule by rule by rule—Congress's policy outlines. . . . In short, when it comes to delegations, there are good reasons for Congress (within extremely broad limits) to get to call the shots. Congress knows about how government works in ways courts don't. More specifically, Congress knows what mix of legislative and administrative action conduces to good policy. Courts should be modest.

. . . The subject matter of the regulation here makes the Court's intervention all the more troubling. Whatever else this Court may know about, it does not have a clue about how to address climate change. And let's say the obvious: The stakes here are high. Yet the Court today prevents congressionally authorized agency action to curb power plants' carbon dioxide emissions. The Court appoints itself—instead of Congress or the expert agency—the decisionmaker on climate policy. I cannot think of many things more frightening. Respectfully, I dissent.

3. PRESIDENTIAL CONTROL OVER THE EXECUTIVE BRANCH

Page 413. Add after Seila Law, LLC v. Consumer Financial Protection Bureau:

Collins v. Yellin

593 U.S. ___, 141 S.Ct. 1761, 210 L.Ed.2d 432 (2021).

■ JUSTICE ALITO delivered the opinion of the Court. . . .

Fannie Mae and Freddie Mac are two of the Nation's leading sources of mortgage financing. When the housing crisis hit in 2008, the companies suffered significant losses, and many feared that their troubling financial condition would imperil the national economy. To address that concern, Congress enacted the Housing and Economic Recovery Act of 2008 (Recovery Act), 122 Stat. 2654, 12 U.S.C. § 4501 *et seq.* Among other things, that law created the Federal Housing Finance Agency (FHFA), "an independent agency" tasked with regulating the companies and, if necessary, stepping in as their conservator or receiver. At its head, Congress installed a single Director, whom the President could remove only "for cause." . . .

Shortly after the FHFA came into existence, it placed Fannie Mae and Freddie Mac into conservatorship and negotiated agreements for the companies with the Department of Treasury. Under those agreements, Treasury committed to providing each company with up to $100 billion in capital, and in exchange received, among other things, senior preferred shares and quarterly fixed-rate dividends. Four years later, the FHFA and Treasury amended the agreements and replaced the fixed-rate dividend formula with a variable one that required the companies to make quarterly payments consisting of their entire net worth minus a small specified capital reserve. This deal, which the parties refer to as the "third amendment" . . . caused the companies to transfer enormous amounts of wealth to Treasury. It also resulted in a slew of lawsuits, including the one before us today.

A group of Fannie Mae's and Freddie Mac's shareholders challenged the third amendment on statutory and constitutional grounds. With respect to their statutory claim, the shareholders contended that the Agency exceeded its authority as a conservator under the Recovery Act when it agreed to a variable dividend formula that would transfer nearly all of the companies' net worth to the Federal Government. And with respect to their constitutional claim, the shareholders argued that the FHFA's structure violates the separation of powers because the Agency is led by a single Director who may be removed by the President only "for cause." . . . They sought declaratory and injunctive relief, including an order requiring Treasury either to return the variable dividend payments or to re-characterize those payments as a pay down on Treasury's investment.

We hold that the shareholders' statutory claim is barred by the Recovery Act, which prohibits courts from taking "any action to restrain or affect the exercise of [the] powers or functions of the Agency as a conservator." § 4617(f). But we conclude that the FHFA's structure violates the separation of powers, and we remand for further proceedings to determine what remedy, if any, the shareholders are entitled to receive on their constitutional claim.

I

A

. . .

The FHFA is led by a single Director who is appointed by the President with the advice and consent of the Senate. §§ 4512(a), (b)(1). The Director serves a 5-year term but may be removed by the President "for cause." § 4512(b)(2). The Director is permitted to choose three deputies to assist in running the Agency's various divisions, and the Director sits as Chairman of the Federal Housing Finance Oversight Board, which advises the Agency about matters of strategy and policy. . . . Since its inception, the FHFA has had three Senate-confirmed Directors, and in times of their absence, various Acting Directors have been selected to lead the Agency on an interim basis. . . .

. . .

II

[The Court rejected the shareholders' statutory claim. The FHFA did not exceed its authority as a conservator under the Act, and so the claim was barred by the Recovery Act's anti-injunction clause.]

. . .

III

We now consider the shareholders' claim that the statutory restriction on the President's power to remove the FHFA Director . . . is unconstitutional.

A

Before turning to the merits of this question, however, we must address threshold issues raised in the lower court or by the federal parties and appointed *amicus*.

. . .

[The Court held that the shareholders had standing to sue; a post-oral argument fourth amendment did not moot the claim for retrospective relief; a statutory "succession clause" effecting a limited transfer of stockholders' rights did not bar the suit; and the fact that the third amendment was adopted when FHFA was led by a removable-at-will Acting Director did not avoid a potential constitutional defect because the amendment's harm continued under a succession of removal-protected confirmed Directors.]

[W]e now proceed to the merits of the shareholders' constitutional argument.

B

The Recovery Act's for-cause restriction on the President's removal authority violates the separation of powers. Indeed, our decision last Term in *Seila Law* [v. CFPB] is all but dispositive. There, we held that Congress could not limit the President's power to remove the Director of the Consumer Financial Protection Bureau (CFPB) to instances of "inefficiency, neglect, or malfeasance." . . . We did "not revisit our prior decisions allowing certain limitations on the President's removal power," but we found "compelling reasons not to extend those precedents to the novel context of an independent agency led by a single Director." . . . "Such an agency," we observed, "lacks a foundation in historical practice and clashes with constitutional structure by concentrating power in a unilateral actor insulated from Presidential control." . . .

A straightforward application of our reasoning in *Seila Law* dictates the result here. The FHFA (like the CFPB) is an agency led by a single Director, and the Recovery Act (like the Dodd-Frank Act) restricts the President's removal power. Fulfilling his obligation to defend the constitutionality of the Recovery Act's removal restriction, *amicus*[a] attempts to distinguish the FHFA from the CFPB. We do not find any of these distinctions sufficient to justify a different result.

1

Amicus first argues that Congress should have greater leeway to restrict the President's power to remove the FHFA Director because the FHFA's authority is more limited than that of the CFPB. *Amicus* points out that the CFPB administers 19 statutes while the FHFA administers only 1; the CFPB regulates millions of individuals and businesses whereas the FHFA regulates a small number of Government-sponsored enterprises; the CFPB has broad rule-making and enforcement authority and the FHFA has little; and the CFPB receives a large budget from the Federal Reserve while the FHFA collects roughly half the amount from regulated entities.

We have noted differences between these two agencies. See *Seila Law*, 591 U.S., at ___ (noting that the FHFA "regulates primarily Government-sponsored enterprises, not purely private actors"). But the nature and breadth of an agency's authority is not dispositive in determining whether Congress may limit the President's power to remove its head. The President's removal power serves vital purposes even when the officer subject to removal is not the head of one of the largest and most powerful agencies. The removal power helps the President maintain a degree of control over the subordinates he needs to carry out his duties as the head of the Executive Branch, and it works to ensure that these subordinates serve the people effectively and in accordance with the policies that the people presumably elected the President to promote. . . . In addition, because the President, unlike agency officials, is elected, this control is essential to subject Executive Branch actions to a degree of electoral accountability. . . . At-will removal ensures that "the lowest officers, the middle grade, and the highest, will depend, as they ought, on the President, and the President on the community." . . . These purposes are implicated whenever an agency does important work, and nothing about

---

[a] Because the federal parties did not defend the statute's constitutionality, the Court appointed an *amicus* to do so.

the size or role of the FHFA convinces us that its Director should be treated differently from the Director of the CFPB. The test that *amicus* proposes would also lead to severe practical problems. *Amicus* does not propose any clear standard to distinguish agencies whose leaders must be removable at will from those whose leaders may be protected from at-will removal. This case is illustrative. As *amicus* points out, the CFPB might be thought to wield more power than the FHFA in some respects. But the FHFA might in other respects be considered more powerful than the CFPB.

. . .

Courts are not well-suited to weigh the relative importance of the regulatory and enforcement authority of disparate agencies, and we do not think that the constitutionality of removal restrictions hinges on such an inquiry.

. . .

[The Court rejected two other purported distinctions: "when [FHFA] steps into the shoes of a regulated entity as its conservator or receiver, it takes on the status of a private party and thus does not wield executive power," and FHFA regulates Government-sponsored enterprises rather than private actors.]

4

Finally, *amicus* contends that there is no constitutional problem in this case because the Recovery Act offers only "modest [tenure] protection." That is so, *amicus* claims, because the for-cause standard would be satisfied whenever a Director "disobey[ed] a lawful [Presidential] order," including one about the Agency's policy discretion.

We acknowledge that the Recovery Act's "for cause" restriction appears to give the President more removal authority than other removal provisions reviewed by this Court. See, *e.g., Seila Law,* 591 U.S., at ___ ("for 'inefficiency, neglect of duty, or malfeasance in office' "); *Morrison* [v. Olson], 487 U.S., at 663 (" 'for good cause, physical disability, mental incapacity, or any other condition that substantially impairs the performance of [his or her] duties' "); *Bowsher* [v. Synar], *supra*, at 728 ("by joint resolution of Congress" due to " 'permanent disability,' " " 'inefficiency,' " " 'neglect of duty,' " " 'malfeasance,' " " 'a felony[,] or conduct involving moral turpitude' "); *Humphrey's Executor* v. *United States*, 295 U.S. 602, 619 (1935) (" ' "for inefficiency, neglect of duty, or malfeasance in office" ' "); *Myers* [v. United States], 272 U.S., at 107 (" 'by and with the advice and consent of the Senate' "). And it is certainly true that disobeying an order is generally regarded as "cause" for removal. See NLRB v. Electrical Workers, 346 U.S. 464, 475 (1953) ("The legal principle that insubordination, disobedience or disloyalty is adequate cause for discharge is plain enough").

But as we explained last Term, the Constitution prohibits even "modest restrictions" on the President's power to remove the head of an agency with a single top officer. *Seila Law.* . . . The President must be able to remove not just officers who disobey his commands but also those he finds "negligent and inefficient," *Myers,* 272 U.S., at 135, those who exercise their discretion in a way that is not "intelligen[t] or wis[e]," *ibid.,* those who have "different views of policy," *id.,* at 131, those who come "from a competing political party who is dead set against [the President's] agenda," *Seila Law,* . . . and those in whom he has simply lost confidence, *Myers, supra,* at 124. *Amicus* recognizes that " 'for cause' . . . does not mean the same thing as 'at will,' " . . . and therefore the removal restriction in the Recovery Act violates the separation of powers.

C

Having found that the removal restriction violates the Constitution, we turn to the shareholders' request for [prospective] relief. . . .

. . .

[The Court rejected the shareholders' argument that the third amendment must be completely undone because it was adopted and implemented by officers who lacked constitutional authority.] "All the officers who headed the FHFA during the time in question were properly *appointed*. Although the statute unconstitutionally limited the President's authority to *remove* the confirmed Directors, there was no constitutional defect in the statutorily prescribed method of appointment to that office. As a result, there is no reason to regard any of the actions taken by the FHFA in relation to the third amendment as void."

. . .

[With respect to the shareholders' claim that absent the unconstitutional removal restriction the President might have replaced a Director who supervised the third amendment's implementation or a Director might have behaved differently, the] "parties' arguments should be resolved in the first instance by the lower courts."

* * *

The judgment of the Court of Appeals is affirmed in part, reversed in part, and vacated in part, and the case is remanded for further proceedings consistent with this opinion.

It is so ordered.

■ JUSTICE THOMAS, concurring.

I join the Court's opinion in full. I agree that the Directors were properly appointed and could lawfully exercise executive power. And I agree that, to the extent a Government action violates the Constitution, the remedy should fit the injury. But I write separately because I worry that the Court and the parties have glossed over a fundamental problem with removal-restriction cases such as these: The Government does not necessarily act unlawfully even if a removal restriction is unlawful in the abstract.

[Justice Thomas noted the parties assumed that if the Director's removal protection is unconstitutional then the shareholders were injured by unlawful agency action. "Our recent precedents have not clearly questioned this premise, and on this premise, the Court correctly resolves the remaining legal issues. But in the future, parties and courts should ensure not only that a provision is unlawful but also that unlawful *action* was taken." Here, Justice Thomas challenged each of the shareholders' four arguments as to why the removal problem meant the agency's actions were themselves illegal; he concluded that, "absent an unlawful act, the shareholders are not entitled to a remedy." That said, Justice Thomas did "not understand the parties to have sought review of these issues in this Court," and so he invited the Fifth Circuit to "consider this issue on remand."]

. . .

■ JUSTICE KAGAN, with whom JUSTICE BREYER and JUSTICE SOTOMAYOR join as to Part II, concurring in part and concurring in the judgment in part.

Faced with a global financial crisis, Congress created the Federal Housing Finance Agency (FHFA) and gave it broad powers to rescue the Nation's mortgage market. I join the Court in deciding that the FHFA wielded its authority within statutory limits. On the main constitutional question, though, I concur only in the judgment. *Stare decisis* compels the conclusion that the FHFA's for-cause removal provision violates the Constitution. But the majority's opinion rests on faulty theoretical premises and goes further than it needs to. I also write to address the remedial question. The majority's analysis, which I join, well explains why backwards-looking relief is not always necessary to redress a removal violation. . . .

I

I agree with the majority that *Seila Law* . . . governs the constitutional question here. In *Seila Law*, the Court held that an "agency led by a single [d]irector and vested with significant executive power" comports with the Constitution only if the President can fire the director at will. 591 U.S., at ___. I dissented from that decision—vehemently. See *id.*, at ___ (Kagan, J., dissenting) ("The text of the Constitution, the history of the country, the precedents of this Court, and the need for sound and adaptable governance—all stand against the majority's opinion"). But the "doctrine of *stare decisis* requires us, absent special circumstances, to treat like cases alike"—even when that means adhering to a wrong decision. . . . So the issue now is not whether *Seila Law* was correct. The question is whether that case is distinguishable from this one. And it is not. As I observed in *Seila Law*, the FHFA "plays a crucial role in overseeing the mortgage market, on which millions of Americans annually rely." . . . It thus wields "significant executive power," much as the agency in *Seila Law* did. And I agree with the majority that there is no other legally relevant distinction between the two.

For two reasons, however, I do not join the majority's discussion of the constitutional issue. First is the majority's political theory. Throughout the relevant part of its opinion, the majority offers a contestable—and, in my opinion, deeply flawed—account of how our government should work. At-will removal authority, the majority intones, "is essential to subject Executive Branch actions to a degree of electoral accountability"—and so courts should grant the President that power in cases like this one. I see the matter differently (as, I might add, did the Framers). *Seila Law*, 591 U.S., at ___ (Kagan, J., dissenting). The right way to ensure that government operates with "electoral accountability" is to lodge decisions about its structure with, well, "the branches accountable to the people." *Id.*, at ___; see *id.*, at ___ (the Constitution "instructs Congress, not this Court, to decide on agency design"). I will subscribe to decisions contrary to my view where precedent, fairly read, controls (and there is no special justification for reversal). But I will not join the majority's mistaken musings about how to create "a workable government." *Id.*, at ___ (quoting Youngstown Sheet & Tube Co. v. Sawyer, 343 U.S. 579, 635 (1952) (Jackson, J., concurring)).

My second objection is to the majority's extension of *Seila Law*'s holding. Again and again, *Seila Law* emphasized that its rule was limited to single-director agencies "wield[ing] significant executive power." 591 U.S., at ___ (plurality opinion) . . . . To take *Seila Law* at its word is to acknowledge where it left off: If an agency did not exercise "significant executive power," the constitutionality of a removal restriction would remain an open question. . . . But today's majority careens right past that boundary line. Without even mentioning *Seila Law*'s "significant executive power" framing, the majority announces that, actually, "the constitutionality of removal restrictions" does not "hinge[ ]" on "the nature and breadth of an agency's authority." Any "agency led by a single Director," no matter how much executive power it wields, now becomes subject to the requirement of at-will removal. And the majority's broadening is gratuitous— unnecessary to resolve the dispute here. As the opinion later explains, the FHFA exercises plenty of executive authority: Indeed, it might "be considered more powerful than the CFPB." So the majority could easily have stayed within, rather than reached out beyond, the rule *Seila Law* created.

In thus departing from *Seila Law*, the majority strays from its own obligation to respect precedent. To ensure that our decisions reflect the "evenhanded" and "consistent development of legal principles," not just shifts in the Court's personnel, s*tare decisis* demands something of Justices previously on the losing side. . . . They (meaning here, I) must fairly apply decisions with which they disagree. But fidelity to precedent also places demands on the winners. They must apply the Court's precedents—limits and all—wherever they can, rather than widen them unnecessarily at the first opportunity. Because today's majority does not conform to that command, I concur in the judgment only.

II

I join in full the majority's discussion of the proper remedy for the constitutional violation it finds. . . .

■ JUSTICE GORSUCH, concurring in part.

I agree with the Court on the merits and am pleased to join nearly all of its opinion. I part ways only when it comes to the question of remedy addressed in Part III-C.

[Justice Gorsuch argued that the traditional remedy for the wrongful exercise of executive authority would be to "set aside the Director's ultra vires actions as 'contrary to constitutional right,'" and this is true even where "the Director was unconstitutionally insulated from removal rather than unconstitutionally appointed." He chastised the Court for "guessing what legislative scheme Congress would have adopted in some hypothetical but-for world" and "task[ing] lower courts and the parties with reconstructing how executive agents would have reacted to it."]

. . .

. . . I would take a simpler and more familiar path. Whether unconstitutionally installed or improperly unsupervised, officials cannot wield executive power except as Article II provides. . . . [W]here individuals are burdened by unconstitutional executive action, they are "entitled to relief." . . .

■ JUSTICE SOTOMAYOR, with whom JUSTICE BREYER joins, concurring in part and dissenting in part.

Prior to 2010, this Court had gone the greater part of a century since it last prevented Congress from protecting an Executive Branch officer from unfettered Presidential removal. Yet today, for the third time in just over a decade, the Court strikes down the tenure protections Congress provided an independent agency's leadership.

Last Term, the Court held in *Seila Law* . . . that for-cause removal protection for the Director of the Consumer Financial Protection Bureau (CFPB) violated the separation of powers. As an "independent agency led by a single Director and vested with significant executive power," the Court reasoned, the CFPB had "no basis in history and no place in our constitutional structure." . . . *Seila Law* expressly distinguished the Federal Housing Finance Agency (FHFA), another independent Agency headed by a single Director, on the ground that the FHFA does not possess "regulatory or enforcement authority remotely comparable to that exercised by the CFPB." . . . Moreover, the Court found it significant that, unlike the CFPB, the FHFA "regulates primarily Government-sponsored enterprises, not purely private actors." . . .

Nevertheless, the Court today holds that the FHFA and CFPB are comparable after all, and that any differences between the two are irrelevant to the constitutional separation of powers. That reasoning cannot be squared with this Court's precedents, least of all last Term's *Seila Law*. I respectfully dissent in part from the Court's opinion and from the corresponding portions of the judgment.[1]

. . .

II

Where Congress is silent on the question, the general rule is that the President may remove Executive Branch officers at will. See Myers v. United States, 272 U.S. 52, 126 (1926). Throughout our Nation's history, however, Congress has identified particular officers who, because of the nature of their office, require a degree of independence from Presidential control. Those officers may be removed from their posts only for cause. Often, Congress has granted financial regulators such independence in order to bolster public confidence that financial policy is guided by long-term thinking, not short-term political expediency. . . . Other times, Congress has provided tenure protection to officers who investigate other Government actors and thus might face conflicts of interest if directly controlled by the President. . . .

In a line of decisions spanning more than half a century, this Court consistently approved of independent agencies and independent counsels within the Executive Branch. See Humphrey's Executor v. United States, 295 U.S. 602 (1935); Wiener v. United States, 357 U.S. 349 (1958); Morrison v. Olson, 487 U.S. 654 (1988). In recent years, however, the Court has taken an unprecedentedly active role in policing Congress' decisions about which officers should enjoy independence. See *Seila Law*, . . .; Free Enterprise Fund v. Public Company Accounting Oversight Bd., 561 U.S. 477 (2010). These decisions have focused almost exclusively on perceived threats to the separation of powers posed by limiting the President's removal power, while largely ignoring the Court's own encroachment on Congress' constitutional authority to structure the Executive Branch as it deems necessary.

Never before, however, has the Court forbidden simple for-cause tenure protection for an Executive Branch officer who neither exercises significant executive power nor regulates the affairs of private parties. Because the FHFA Director fits that description, this Court's precedent, separation-of-powers principles, and proper respect for Congress all support leaving in place Congress' limits on the grounds upon which the President may remove the Director.

A

In *Seila Law*, the Court held that the CFPB Director, an individual with "the authority to bring the coercive power of the state to bear on millions of private citizens and businesses," . . . must be removable by the President at will. In so holding, the Court declined to overrule *Humphrey's Executor* and *Morrison*, which respectively upheld the independence of the Federal Trade Commission's (FTC) five-member board and an independent counsel tasked with investigating Government malfeasance. See 591 U.S., at ___ ("[W]e do not revisit *Humphrey's Executor* or any other precedent today"). Instead,

---

[1]   . . . I join also Part II of Justice Kagan's concurrence concerning the proper remedial analysis for the Fifth Circuit to conduct on remand. Finally, I note that Justice Thomas' arguments that an improper removal restriction does not necessarily render agency action unlawful warrant further consideration in an appropriate case.

Seila Law opted not to "extend those precedents" to the CFPB, "an independent agency led by a single Director and vested with significant executive power." 591 U.S., at ___.[2]

The Court today concludes that the reasoning of *Seila Law* "dictates" that the FHFA is unconstitutionally structured because it, too, is led by a single Director. But *Seila Law* did not hold that an independent agency may never be run by a single individual with tenure protection. Rather, that decision stated, repeatedly, that its holding was limited to a single-director agency with "significant executive power." . . . The question, therefore, is not whether the FHFA is headed by a single Director, but whether the FHFA wields "significant" executive power. It does not.

. . .

. . . As the Court recognized in *Seila Law*, the FHFA does "not involve regulatory or enforcement authority remotely comparable to that exercised by the CFPB." . . . . It is in "an entirely different league" from the CFPB. 591 U.S., at ___, n. 8.

B

Because the FHFA does not possess significant executive power, the question under *Seila Law* is whether this Court's decisions upholding for-cause removal provisions in *Humphrey's Executor* and *Morrison* should be "extend[ed]" to the FHFA Director. The clear answer is yes.

Not only does the FHFA lack significant executive power, the authority it does possess is exercised over other governmental actors. In that respect, the FHFA Director mimics the independent counsel whose tenure protections were upheld in *Morrison*. . . .

. . .

Historical considerations further confirm the constitutionality of the FHFA Director's independence. Single-director independent agencies with limited executive power, like the FHFA, boast a more storied pedigree than do single-director independent agencies with significant executive power, like the CFPB. . . . [The Comptroller of the Currency, the Office of Special Counsel, and the Social Security Administration] provide historical support for an agency with the FHFA's limited purview.

The FHFA also draws on a long tradition of independence enjoyed by financial regulators, including the Comptroller of the Treasury, the Second Bank of the United States, the Federal Reserve Board, the Securities and Exchange Commission, the Commodity Futures Trading Commission, and the Federal Deposit Insurance Corporation. . . . The public has long accepted (indeed, expected) that financial regulators will best perform their duties if separated from the political exigencies and pressures of the present moment.

. . .

To recap, the FHFA does not wield significant executive power, the executive power it does wield is exercised over Government affiliates, and its independence is supported by historical tradition. All considerations weigh in favor of recognizing Congress' power to make the FHFA Director removable only for cause.

III

The Court disagrees. After *Seila Law*, the Court reasons, all that matters is that "[t]he FHFA (like the CFPB) is an agency led by a single Director." From that, the

---

[2] As Justice Kagan explained in dissent, *Seila Law* rested on implausible recharacterizations of this Court's separation-of-powers jurisprudence. I continue to believe that *Seila Law* was wrongly decided. Whatever the merits of that decision, however, it does not support invalidating the FHFA Director's independence.

unconstitutionality of the FHFA Director's independence follows virtually *a fortiori*. The Court reaches that conclusion by disavowing the very distinctions it relied upon just last Term in *Seila Law* in striking down the CFPB Director's independence.

. . .

The Court's position unduly encroaches on Congress' judgments about which executive officers can and should enjoy a degree of independence from Presidential removal, and it cannot be squared with *Seila Law*, which relied extensively on such agency comparisons. . . .

. . .

. . . That the Court is unwilling to stick to the methodology it articulated just last Term in *Seila Law* is a telltale sign that the Court's separation-of-powers jurisprudence has only continued to lose its way.

IV

. . . Because I would afford Congress the freedom it has long possessed to make officers like the FHFA Director independent from Presidential control, I respectfully dissent.

United States v. Arthrex, Inc.

593 U.S. ___, 141 S.Ct. 1970 (2021).

Building on Edmond v. United States, 520 U.S. 651 (1997), the Court explored the distinction between "principal officers" and "inferior officers." Per the Appointments Clause, principal officers must be nominated by the president and confirmed by the Senate; Congress may vest the appointment of inferior officers "in the President alone, in the Courts of Law, or in the Heads of Departments." Art. II, § 2, cl. 2.

The Patent and Trademark Office (PTO), an executive agency within the Department of Commerce, grants and issues patents in the name of the United States. The PTO has a single Director who is a principal officer, presidentially appointed and Senate confirmed. As agency head, the Director provides "policy direction and management supervision" for PTO officers and employees. Decisions about patents made by primary examiners are reviewed by the Patent Trial and Appeal Board (PTAB), an executive adjudicatory body within the PTO. The PTAB sits in panels of at least three members drawn from the Director, several senior administrators, and more than 200 Administrative Patent Judges (APJs). The APJs are appointed by the Secretary of Commerce.

Inter partes review is a process through which the PTAB can also take a second look at patents previously issued by the PTO, reconsidering whether those patents satisfy the novelty and nonobviousness requirements for inventions. The Director has unreviewable discretion to institute inter partes review. The Director designates at least three members of the PTAB (typically three APJs) to conduct such proceedings, which resemble civil litigation. The PTAB must issue a final written decision on all of the challenged patent claims within 12 to 18 months of institution. Sometimes billions of dollars hang in the balance. Losing parties may seek judicial review in the Court of Appeals for the Federal Circuit, where the Director can intervene to defend or disavow the Board's decision. The Federal Circuit reviews the PTAB's application of patentability standards *de novo* and its underlying factual determinations for substantial evidence.

In 2015, Arthrex, Inc. secured a patent on a surgical device for reattaching soft tissue to bone without tying a knot. Arthrex soon claimed that two companies had infringed the patent, and the dispute went through the PTO's inter partes review process. Three APJs formed the PTAB panel and ultimately concluded that Arthrex's own patent was invalid. On appeal to the Federal Circuit, Arthrex challenged the inter partes process on the ground that the three APJs should be considered principal officers and so their appointment by the Secretary of Commerce (rather than through presidential nomination and Senate confirmation) was unconstitutional. The Federal Circuit agreed. To remedy the violation the panel invalidated the APJs' tenure protections, concluding that making them removable at will by the Secretary of Commerce converted them into inferior officers.

Chief Justice Roberts wrote the opinion of the Court with respect to the merits of the Appointments Clause challenge, joined by Justices Alito, Gorsuch, Kavanaugh, and Barrett. These five Justices concluded that the current APJ regime is unconstitutional. The Court first connected the Appointments Clause with presidential accountability: "The President is 'responsible for the actions of the Executive Branch' and 'cannot delegate [that] ultimate responsibility or the active obligation to supervise that goes with it.' . . . The Framers recognized, of course, that 'no single person could fulfill that responsibility alone, [and] expected that the President would rely on subordinate officers for assistance.' " . . .

"Today, thousands of officers wield executive power on behalf of the President in the name of the United States. That power acquires its legitimacy and accountability to the public through 'a clear and effective chain of command' down from the President, on whom all the people vote. . . .

"Assigning the nomination power to the President guarantees accountability for the appointees' actions because the 'blame of a bad nomination would fall upon the president singly and absolutely.' The Federalist No. 77, p. 517 (J. Cooke ed. 1961) (A. Hamilton). . . ."

The Court observed that APJs are clearly officers, "not 'lesser functionaries' such as employees or contractors—because they 'exercis[e] significant authority pursuant to the laws of the United States.' " The question was whether "the nature of their responsibilities is consistent with their method of appointment" as inferior officers.

"The starting point for . . . analysis is our opinion in *Edmond*. There we explained that '[w]hether one is an "inferior" officer depends on whether he has a superior' other than the President. 520 U.S., at 662. An inferior officer must be 'directed and supervised at some level by others who were appointed by Presidential nomination with the advice and consent of the Senate.' *Id.*, at 663.

"In *Edmond*, we applied this test to adjudicative officials within the Executive Branch—specifically, Coast Guard Court of Criminal Appeals judges appointed by the Secretary of Transportation. See *id.*, at 658. We held that the judges were inferior officers because they were effectively supervised by a combination of Presidentially nominated and Senate confirmed officers in the Executive Branch . . . . 'What is significant,' we concluded, 'is that the judges of the Court of Criminal Appeals have no power to render a final decision on behalf of the United States unless permitted to do so by other Executive officers.' *Id.*, at 665.

"Congress structured the PTAB differently, providing only half of the 'divided' supervision to which judges of the Court of Criminal Appeals were subject. *Id.*, at 664. Like the Judge Advocate General, the PTO Director possesses powers of 'administrative oversight.' *Ibid.* The Director fixes the rate of pay for APJs, controls the decision whether to institute inter partes review, and selects the APJs to reconsider the validity of the patent. . . . The Director also promulgates regulations governing inter partes review, issues prospective guidance on patentability issues, and designates past PTAB decisions as 'precedential' for future panels. . . . He is the boss, except when it comes to the one thing that makes the APJs officers exercising "significant authority" in the first place—their power to issue decisions on patentability. . . . In contrast to the scheme approved by *Edmond*, no principal officer at any level within the Executive Branch 'direct[s] and supervise[s]' the work of APJs in that regard. 520 U.S., at 663.

"*Edmond* goes a long way toward resolving this dispute. What was 'significant' to the outcome there—review by a superior executive officer—is absent here: APJs have the 'power to render a final decision on behalf of the United States' without any such review by their nominal superior or any other principal officer in the Executive Branch. *Id.*, at 665. The only possibility of review is a petition for rehearing, but Congress unambiguously specified that '[o]nly the Patent and Trial Appeal Board may grant rehearings.' . . . Such review simply repeats the arrangement challenged as unconstitutional in this suit.

"This 'diffusion of power carries with it a diffusion of accountability.' . . . The restrictions on review relieve the Director of responsibility for the final decisions rendered by APJs purportedly under his charge. The principal dissent's observation that 'the Director alone has the power to take final action to cancel a patent claim or confirm it,' (opinion of Thomas, J.), simply ignores the undisputed fact that the Director's 'power' in that regard is limited to carrying out the ministerial duty that he 'shall issue and publish a certificate' canceling or confirming patent claims he had previously allowed, as dictated by the APJs' final decision. . . ."

The Court rejected as insufficient other steps the Director might take to influence the PTAB's decisionmaking process, including deciding whether or not to seek inter partes review, choosing APJs to decide a particular case whom she thinks might be predisposed to her views, vacating an unfavorable panel decision before it becomes final, and intervening in the rehearing process by again stacking the panel. But the Court viewed this as extending the problem, describing it as a "roadmap for the Director to evade a statutory prohibition on review without having him take responsibility for the ultimate decision. . . . Even if the Director succeeds in procuring his preferred outcome, such machinations blur the lines of accountability demanded by the Appointments Clause."

"Given the insulation of PTAB decisions from any executive review, the President can neither oversee the PTAB himself nor 'attribute the Board's failings to those whom he *can* oversee.' . . . APJs accordingly exercise power that conflicts with the design of the Appointments Clause 'to preserve political accountability.' *Edmond*, 520 U.S., at 663.

"The principal dissent dutifully undertakes to apply the governing test from *Edmond*, (opinion of Thomas, J.), but its heart is plainly not in it. For example, the dissent rejects any distinction between 'inferior-officer power' and 'principal-officer power,' but *Edmond* calls for exactly that: an appraisal of how much power an officer exercises free from control by a superior. The dissent pigeonholes this consideration as the sole province of the Vesting Clause, but *Edmond* recognized the Appointments Clause as a 'significant structural safeguard[ ]' that 'preserve[s] political accountability' through direction and supervision of subordinates—in other words, through a chain of command. 520 U.S., at 659, 663. The dissent would have the Court focus on the location of an officer in the agency 'organizational chart,' but as we explained in *Edmond*, '[i]t is not enough that other officers may be identified who formally maintain a higher rank, or possess responsibilities of a greater magnitude,' 520 U.S., at 662–663. The dissent stresses that 'at least two levels of authority' separate the President from PTAB decisions, but the unchecked exercise of executive power by an officer buried many layers beneath the President poses more, not less, of a constitutional problem. Conspicuously absent from the dissent is any concern for the President's ability to 'discharge his own constitutional duty of seeing that the laws be faithfully executed.' Myers v. United States, 272 U.S. 52, 135 (1926)."

The Court claimed that "[h]istory reinforces the conclusion that the unreviewable executive power exercised by APJs is incompatible with their status as inferior officers," canvassing some early congressional statutes and mid-19th century Court opinions. The Court posited that "Congress has carried the model of principal officer review into the modern administrative state," citing some examples and distinguishing others, and then tracing the history of the patent system itself.

The Court concluded:

"We hold that the unreviewable authority wielded by APJs during inter partes review is incompatible with their appointment by the Secretary to an inferior office. The principal dissent repeatedly charges that we never say whether APJs are principal officers who were not appointed in the manner required by the Appointments Clause, or instead inferior officers exceeding the permissible scope of their duties under that Clause. . . . But both formulations describe the same constitutional violation: Only an officer properly appointed to a principal office may issue a final decision binding the Executive Branch in the proceeding before us."

"In reaching this conclusion, we do not attempt to 'set forth an exclusive criterion for distinguishing between principal and inferior officers for Appointments Clause purposes." *Edmond*, 520 U.S., at 661. Many decisions by inferior officers do not bind the Executive Branch to exercise executive power in a particular manner, and we do not address supervision outside the context of adjudication. Here, however, Congress has assigned APJs 'significant authority' in adjudicating the public rights of private parties, while also insulating their decisions from review and their offices from removal."

While joining the majority opinion on the merits, Justice Gorsuch added that the Appointments Clause works hand-in-glove with the vesting of executive power in the President alone. While the framers expected the President to rely on others for help, "the framers took pains to ensure those subordinates would always remain responsible to the President and thus, ultimately, to the people. Because it is the President's duty to take care that the laws be faithfully executed, Art. II, § 3, the framers sought to ensure he possessed 'the power of *appointing, overseeing, and controlling* those who execute the laws.' 1 Annals of Cong. 463 (Madison)." In Justice Gorsuch's view, this entails that an inferior officer "must be both '*subordinate* to a[n] officer in the Executive Branch' and 'under the direct control of the President' through a 'chain of command.' *Morrison*, 487 U.S., at 720–21 (Scalia, J., dissenting)."

Justice Thomas wrote the principal dissent on the Appointments Clause merits, joined by Justices Breyer, Sotomayor, and Kagan. This dissent observed that the "Court has been careful not to create a rigid test to divide principal officers . . . from inferior ones. . . . Instead, the Court's opinions have traditionally used a case-by-case analysis. And those analyses invariably result in this Court deferring to Congress' choice of which constitutional appointment process works best." Justice Thomas read *Edmond* to create a "two-part guide": an inferior officer "must be lower in rank to 'a superior,'" and the "inferior officer's work must be 'directed and supervised at some level by others who were'" presidentially nominated and Senate confirmed. Here, the patent ALJs "are lower in rank to at least two different officers"—the PTO's Director and the Secretary of

Commerce. Under *Edmond*, the fact that neither of the superiors have "complete control" does not preclude the ALJ's inferior status. And "[t]he Director here possesses even greater functional power over the Board than that possessed by the Judge Advocate General" declared an inferior officer in *Edmond*; collectively, the Director's avenues of potential control ensure that the ALJs " 'have no power to render a final decision on behalf of the United States unless permitted to do so by other Executive officers.' [*Edmond*, 520 U.S.,] at 665."

Justice Thomas claimed that, under the Court's reading, "most of *Edmond* is superfluous: All that matters is whether the Director has the statutory authority to individually reverse Board decisions." But there is no precedent or historical support for this singular focus, and the "Court in *Edmond* considered all the means of supervision and control exercised by the superior officers."

"Perhaps the better way to understand the Court's opinion today is as creating a new form of intrabranch separation-of-powers law. Traditionally, the Court's task when resolving Appointments Clause challenges has been to discern whether the challenged official qualifies as a specific sort of officer and whether his appointment complies with the Constitution. . . . If the official's appointment is inconsistent with the constitutional appointment process for the position he holds, then the Court provides a remedy. . . .

"Today's majority leaves that tried-and-true approach behind. It never expressly tells us whether administrative patent judges are inferior officers or principal. And the Court never tells us whether the appointment process complies with the Constitution. The closest the Court comes is to say that 'the source of the constitutional violation' is *not* 'the appointment of [administrative patent judges] by the Secretary.' Under our precedent and the Constitution's text, that should resolve the suit. If the appointment process for administrative patent judges—appointment by the Secretary—does not violate the Constitution, then administrative patent judges must be inferior officers. See Art. II, § 2, cl. 2. And if administrative patent judges are inferior officers and have been properly appointed as such, then the Appointments Clause challenge fails. . . .

"The majority's new Appointments Clause doctrine, though, has nothing to do with the validity of an officer's appointment. Instead, it polices the dispersion of executive power among officers. Echoing our doctrine that Congress may not mix duties and powers from different branches into one actor, the Court finds that the constitutional problem here is that Congress has given a specific power—the authority to finally adjudicate inter partes review disputes—to one type of executive officer that the Constitution gives to another. . . . That analysis is doubly flawed.

"For one thing, our separation-of-powers analysis does not fit. The Constitution recognizes executive, legislative, and judicial power, and it vests those powers in specific branches. Nowhere does the Constitution acknowledge any such thing as 'inferior-officer power' or 'principal-officer power.' And it certainly does not distinguish between these sorts of powers in the Appointments Clause.

. . .

"More broadly, interpreting the Appointments Clause to bar any nonprincipal officer from taking 'final' action poses serious line-drawing problems. The majority assures that not every decision by an inferior officer must be reviewable by a superior officer. But this sparks more questions than it answers. Can a line prosecutor offer a plea deal without sign off from a principal officer? If faced with a life-threatening scenario, can an FBI agent use deadly force to subdue a suspect? Or if an inferior officer temporarily fills a vacant office tasked with making final decisions, do those decisions violate the Appointments Clause? And are courts around the country supposed to sort through lists of each officer's (or employee's) duties, categorize each one as principal or inferior, and then excise any that look problematic?

"Beyond those questions, the majority's nebulous approach also leaves open the question of how much 'principal-officer power' someone must wield before he becomes a principal officer. What happens if an officer typically engages in normal inferior-officer work but also has several principal-officer duties? . . ."

Writing further only for himself, Justice Thomas said "at some point it may be worth taking a closer look at whether the functional element of our test in *Edmond*—the part that the Court relies on today—aligns with the text, history, and structure of the Constitution. The founding era history surrounding the Inferior Officer Clause points to at least three different definitions of an inferior officer, none of which requires a case-by-case functional examination of exactly how much supervision and control another officer has. The rationales on which *Edmond* relies to graft a functional element into the inferior-officer inquiry do not withstand close scrutiny." Justice Thomas noted that "[e]arly discussions of inferior officers reflect at least three understandings of who these officers were—and who they were not—under the Appointments Clause. Though I do not purport to decide today which is best, it is worth noting that administrative patent judges would be inferior under each." Some framing discussions "divide[d] all executive officers into three categories: heads of departments, superior officers, and inferior officers." . . . Some "held a second understanding: Inferior officers encompass nearly *all* officers," other than the "Ambassadors, other public Ministers and Consuls" specifically identified in the Constitution. And some "Framers endorsed a third understanding, which distinguished just between inferior and principal officers. . . . This principal-inferior dichotomy also finds roots in the structure of the Constitution, which specifically identifies both principal officers (in the Opinions Clause and the Twenty-fifth Amendment) and inferior officers (in the Appointments Clause)." Under this view, mirrored by contemporary dictionary definitions, a " 'principal' officer is '[a] head' officer; 'a chief; not a second.' 2 Johnson, Dictionary of the English Language. Other executive officers would, by definition, be lower than or subordinate to these head officers." Justice Thomas concluded that, "[r]egardless of which of the three interpretations is correct, all lead to the same result here. Administrative patent judges are inferior officers."

Justice Breyer, joined by Justices Sotomayor and Kagan, filed another dissent on the Appointments Clause merits as well. "*First*, in my view, the Court should interpret the Appointments Clause as granting Congress a degree of leeway to establish and empower federal offices. Neither that Clause nor anything else in the Constitution describes the degree of control that a superior officer must exercise over the decisions of an inferior officer. . . ."

"*Second*, I believe the Court, when deciding cases such as these, should conduct a functional examination of the offices and duties in question rather than a formalist, judicial-rules-based approach. In advocating for a 'functional approach,' I mean an approach that would take account of, and place weight on, why Congress enacted a particular statutory limitation. It would also consider the practical consequences that are likely to follow from Congress' chosen scheme. . . . In this suit, a functional approach, which considers purposes and consequences, undermines the Court's result. . . .

. . .

"More broadly, I see the Court's decision as one part of a larger shift in our separation-of-powers jurisprudence. The Court applied a similarly formal approach in *Free Enterprise Fund* . . . [and] *Seila Law* . . . . My dissent in the first case and Justice

Kagan's dissent in the second explain in greater detail why we believed that this shift toward formalism was a mistake.

"I continue to believe that a more functional approach to constitutional interpretation in this area is superior. As for this particular suit, the consequences of the majority's rule are clear. The nature of the PTAB calls for technically correct adjudicatory decisions. . . . [T]hat fact calls for greater, not less, independence from those potentially influenced by political factors. The Court's decision prevents Congress from establishing a patent scheme consistent with that idea.

"But there are further reasons for a functional approach that extend beyond the bounds of patent adjudication. First, the Executive Branch has many different constituent bodies, many different bureaus, many different agencies, many different tasks, many different kinds of employees. Administration comes in many different shapes and sizes. Appreciating this variety is especially important in the context of administrative adjudication, which typically demands decisionmaking (at least where policy made by others is simply applied) that is free of political influence. . . .

"Second, the Constitution is not a detailed tax code, and for good reason. The Nation's desires and needs change, sometimes over long periods of time. In the 19th century the Judiciary may not have foreseen the changes that produced the New Deal, along with its accompanying changes in the nature of the tasks that Government was expected to perform. We may not now easily foresee just what kinds of tasks present or future technological changes will call for. The Founders wrote a Constitution that they believed was flexible enough to respond to new needs as those needs developed and changed over the course of decades or centuries. At the same time, they designed a Constitution that would protect certain basic principles. A principle that prevents Congress from affording inferior level adjudicators some decisionmaking independence was not among them.

"Finally, the Executive Branch and Congress are more likely than are judges to understand how to implement the tasks that Congress has written into legislation. That understanding encompasses the nature of different mechanisms of bureaucratic control that may apply to the many thousands of administrators who will carry out those tasks. And it includes an awareness of the reasonable limits that can be placed on supervisors to ensure that those working under them enjoy a degree of freedom sufficient to carry out their responsibilities. Considered as a group, unelected judges have little, if any, experience related to this kind of a problem."

* * *

The five-Justice majority that found the PTAB's current structure to violate the Appointments Clause fractured over the appropriate remedy. No Justice agreed with the Federal Circuit's remedial order below, which would have invalidated the for-cause removal restrictions on APGs to make them removable at will by the Secretary of Commerce. Chief Justice Roberts, joined by Justices Alito, Kavanaugh, and Barrett (the "remedial plurality"), argued instead that "[i]n every respect save the insulation of their decisions from review within the Executive Branch, APJs appear to be inferior officers." So they "conclude[d] that a tailored approach is the appropriate one: Section 6(c) cannot constitutionally be enforced to the extent that its requirements prevent the Director from reviewing final decisions rendered by APJs. . . . The Director accordingly may review final PTAB decisions and, upon review, may issue decisions himself on behalf of the Board."

By contrast, Justice Gorsuch argued that, following "traditional remedial principles," the Court ought "not presume a power to 'sever' and excise portions of statutes in response to constitutional violations" but instead should "simply decline[ ] to enforce the statute in the case or controversy at hand." So here he would remedy the Appointment Clause violation merely by " 'setting aside' the PTAB decision in this case."

This fracturing created an unusual impasse, as the Court's overall lineup lacked a majority-backed disposition—four Justices would remedy the constitutional violation in one way, one Justice would remedy the violation in a different way, and four Justices found no constitutional violation and therefore would impose no remedy at all.[a] With this alignment, the Court could not issue a judgment per majority rule.

Justice Breyer (still joined by Justices Sotomayor and Kagan) broke the impasse by supporting the remedial plurality's bottom line: "For the reasons I have set forth above, I do not agree with the Court's basic constitutional determination. For purposes of determining a remedy, however, I recognize that a majority of the Court has reached a contrary conclusion. On this score, I believe that any remedy should be tailored to the constitutional violation. Under the Court's new [merits] test, the current statutory scheme is defective only because the APJ's decisions are not reviewable by the Director alone. The Court's remedy [by which Justice Breyer actually meant the solution advocated by the remedial plurality] addresses that specific problem, and for that reason I agree with its remedial holding." This created a seven-Justice coalition empowering the Director to review and supplant final PTAB decisions, even though only four of the seven sincerely believed such a remedy was necessary.

For historical examples and discussion of the propriety of such intra-case deference for strategic institutional reasons, see Caminker, *Sincere and Strategic Voting Norms on Multimember Courts*, 97 Mich.L.Rev. 2297 (1999).

---

[a]   Justice Thomas did opine that the remedial plurality's proposed solution did not fit its characterization of the constitutional problem.

PART 3

GOVERNMENT AND THE INDIVIDUAL: THE PROTECTION OF LIBERTY AND PROPERTY UNDER THE DUE PROCESS AND EQUAL PROTECTION CLAUSES

CHAPTER 9

THE DUE PROCESS, CONTRACT, AND TAKINGS CLAUSES AND THE REVIEW OF THE REASONABLENESS OF LEGISLATION

1. ECONOMIC REGULATORY LEGISLATION

C. THE TAKINGS CLAUSE OF THE FIFTH AMENDMENT—WHAT DOES IT ADD TO DUE PROCESS?

2. MANDATED ACCESS TO PROPERTY

Page 558. Delete the sentence before Dolan v. City of Tigard and add the following:

What do the following cases add?

Page 570. Add at end of subsection:

Cedar Point Nursery v. Hassid

594 U.S. ___, 141 S.Ct. 2063, 210 L.Ed.2d 369 (2021).

■ CHIEF JUSTICE ROBERTS delivered the opinion of the Court.

A California regulation grants labor organizations a "right to take access" to an agricultural employer's property in order to solicit support for unionization. Cal. Code Regs., tit. 8, § 20900(e)(1)(C) (2020). Agricultural employers must allow union organizers onto their property for up to three hours per day, 120 days per year. The question presented is whether the access regulation constitutes a *per se* physical taking under the Fifth and Fourteenth Amendments.

[The regulation promulgated by the state Agricultural Labor Relations Board required a labor organization to file a written notice with the Board and serve a copy on the employer in order to take access. It set limits on how many organizers could "enter the employer's property for up to one hour before work, one hour during the lunch break, and one hour after work"; prohibited "disruptive conduct" but otherwise allowed organizers to "meet and talk with employees as they wish"; and provided that "[i]nterference with organizers' right of access may constitute an unfair labor practice" which could "result in sanctions against the employer[.]"

[Two growers (one also a shipper), who employ hundreds of workers—none of whom live on the growers' property—sought declaratory and injunctive relief against several Board members, "argu[ing] that the access regulation effected an unconstitutional *per se* physical taking under the Fifth and Fourteenth Amendments by appropriating without compensation an easement for union organizers to enter their property." The district court ruled against the growers, and a divided Ninth Circuit affirmed.]

II

A

. . . The Founders recognized that the protection of private property is indispensable to the promotion of individual freedom. . . . This Court agrees, having noted that protection of property rights is "necessary to preserve freedom" and "empowers persons to shape and to plan their own destiny in a world where governments are always eager to do so for them." Murr v. Wisconsin . . . .

When the government physically acquires private property for a public use, the Takings Clause imposes a clear and categorical obligation to provide the owner with just compensation. . . . The government commits a physical taking when it uses its power of eminent domain to formally condemn property[,] . . . when [it] physically takes possession of property without acquiring title to it[, and] . . . when it occupies property— say, by recurring flooding as a result of building a dam. . . .

When the government, rather than appropriating private property for itself or a third party, instead imposes regulations that restrict an owner's ability to use his own property, a different standard applies. . . . To determine whether a use restriction effects a taking, this Court has generally applied the flexible test developed in *Penn Central*, ...

Our cases have often described use restrictions that go "too far" as "regulatory takings." . . . But that label can mislead. Government action that physically appropriates property is no less a physical taking because it arises from a regulation. . . . The essential question is . . . whether the government has physically taken property for itself or someone else—by whatever means—or has instead restricted a property owner's ability to use his own property. . . . Whenever a regulation results in a physical appropriation of property, a *per se* taking has occurred, and *Penn Central* has no place.

B

The access regulation appropriates a right to invade the growers' property and therefore constitutes a *per se* physical taking. The regulation grants union organizers a right to physically enter and occupy the growers' land for three hours per day, 120 days per year. Rather than restraining the growers' use of their own property, the regulation appropriates for the enjoyment of third parties the owners' right to exclude.

The right to exclude is "one of the most treasured" rights of property ownership. Loretto v. Teleprompter Manhattan CATV Corp., 458 U.S. 419, 435 (1982). . . . [W]e have stated that the right to exclude is "universally held to be a fundamental element of the property right," and is "one of the most essential sticks in the bundle of rights that are commonly characterized as property." Kaiser Aetna v. United States, 444 U.S. 164, 176, 179–180 (1979); see Dolan v. City of Tigard, 512 U.S. 374, 384, 393 (1994); Nollan v. California Coastal Comm'n, 483 U.S. 825, 831 (1987) . . . .

Given the central importance to property ownership of the right to exclude, it comes as little surprise that the Court has long treated government-authorized physical invasions as takings requiring just compensation. The Court has often described the property interest taken as a servitude or an easement.

. . .

In Loretto v. Teleprompter Manhattan CATV Corp., we made clear that a permanent physical occupation constitutes a *per se* taking regardless whether it results in only a trivial economic loss. . . .

We reiterated that the appropriation of an easement constitutes a physical taking in Nollan v. California Coastal Commission. . . .

More recently, in Horne v. Department of Agriculture, we observed that "people still do not expect their property, real or personal, to be actually occupied or taken away." 576 U.S., at 361. The physical appropriation by the government of the raisins in that case was a *per se* taking, even if a regulatory limit with the same economic impact would not have been. . . . "The Constitution," we explained, "is concerned with means as well as ends." 576 U.S., at 362.

The upshot of this line of precedent is that government-authorized invasions of property . . . are physical takings requiring just compensation. As in those cases, the government here has appropriated a right of access to the growers' property, allowing union organizers to traverse it at will for three hours a day, 120 days a year. The regulation appropriates a right to physically invade the growers' property—to literally "take access," as the regulation provides. . . . It is therefore a *per se* physical taking under our precedents. Accordingly, the growers' complaint states a claim for an uncompensated taking in violation of the Fifth and Fourteenth Amendments.

C

. . . [T]he Ninth Circuit took the view that the access regulation did not qualify as a *per se* taking because, although it grants a right to physically invade the growers' property, it does not allow for permanent and continuous access "24 hours a day, 365 days a year." . . . The dissent [concludes] likewise . . . . That position is insupportable as a matter of precedent and common sense. There is no reason the law should analyze an abrogation of the right to exclude in one manner if it extends for 365 days, but in an entirely different manner if it lasts for 364.

To begin with, we have held that a physical appropriation is a taking whether it is permanent or temporary. . . . The duration of an appropriation—just like the size of an appropriation, see *Loretto*, 458 U.S., at 436–437—bears only on the amount of compensation. . . .

. . .

Next, we have recognized that physical invasions constitute takings even if they are intermittent as opposed to continuous. *Causby* held that overflights of private property effected a taking, even though they occurred on only 4% of takeoffs and 7% of landings at the nearby airport. . . . The fact that a right to take access is exercised only from time to time does not make it any less a physical taking.

. . . [The Board's contention that] the access regulation . . . nevertheless fails to qualify as a *per se* taking because it "authorizes only limited and intermittent access for a narrow purpose[ ]" . . . is little more defensible . . . . The fact that the regulation grants access only to union organizers and only for a limited time does not transform it from a physical taking into a use restriction. . . .

The Board also takes issue with the growers' premise that the access regulation appropriates an easement. In the Board's estimation, the regulation does not exact a true easement in gross under California law because the access right may not be transferred, does not burden any particular parcel of property, and may not be recorded. This, the Board says, reinforces its conclusion that the regulation does not take a constitutionally protected property interest from the growers. The dissent agrees, suggesting that the access right cannot effect a *per se* taking because it does not require the growers to grant the union organizers an easement as defined by state property law.

These arguments misconstrue our physical takings doctrine. As a general matter, it is true that the property rights protected by the Takings Clause are creatures of state law. . . . But no one disputes that, without the access regulation, the growers would have had the right under California law to exclude union organizers from their property. . . . And no one disputes that the access regulation took that right from them. . . .

. . .

The Board and the dissent argue that PruneYard [Shopping Center v. Robins, 447 U.S. 74 (1980),] shows that limited rights of access to private property should be evaluated as regulatory rather than *per se* takings. We disagree. Unlike the growers' properties, the PruneYard was open to the public, welcoming some 25,000 patrons a day. . . . Limitations on how a business generally open to the public may treat individuals on the premises are readily distinguishable from regulations granting a right to invade property closed to the public. . . .

. . .

D

In its thoughtful opinion, the dissent advances a distinctive view of property rights. The dissent encourages readers to consider the issue "through the lens of ordinary English," and contends that, so viewed, the "regulation does not appropriate anything." Rather, the access regulation merely "*regulates* . . . the owners' right to exclude," so it must be assessed "under *Penn Central*'s fact-intensive test." . . . According to the dissent, . . . latitude toward temporary invasions is a practical necessity for governing in our complex modern world.

With respect, our own understanding of the role of property rights in our constitutional order is markedly different. In "ordinary English" "appropriation" means "*taking* as one's own," 1 Oxford English Dictionary 587 (2d ed. 1989) (emphasis added), and the regulation expressly grants to labor organizers the "right to *take* access," . . . . We cannot agree that the right to exclude is an empty formality, subject to modification at the government's pleasure. On the contrary, it is a "fundamental element of the property right," . . . that cannot be balanced away. Our cases establish that appropriations of a right to invade are *per se* physical takings, not use restrictions subject to *Penn Central* . . . . With regard to the complexities of modern society, we think they only reinforce the importance of safeguarding the basic property rights that help preserve individual liberty, as the Founders explained.

In the end, the dissent's permissive approach to property rights hearkens back to views expressed (in dissent) for decades. See, e.g., *Nollan*, 483 U.S., at 864 (Brennan, J., dissenting) . . .; *Loretto*, 458 U.S., at 455 (Blackmun, J., dissenting) . . .; *Causby*, 328 U.S., at 275 (Black, J., dissenting) . . . .

III

The Board, seconded by the dissent, warns that treating the access regulation as a *per se* physical taking will endanger a host of state and federal government activities involving entry onto private property. That fear is unfounded.

First, our holding does nothing to efface the distinction between trespass and takings. Isolated physical invasions, not undertaken pursuant to a granted right of access, are properly assessed as individual torts rather than appropriations of a property right. This basic distinction is firmly grounded in our precedent. . . .

. . .

Second, many government-authorized physical invasions will not amount to takings because they are consistent with longstanding background restrictions on property rights. As we explained in Lucas v. South Carolina Coastal Council, the government does not take a property interest when it merely asserts a "pre-existing limitation upon the land owner's title." . . . For example, the government owes a landowner no compensation for requiring him to abate a nuisance on his property, because he never had a right to engage in the nuisance in the first place. . . .

These background limitations also encompass traditional common law privileges to access private property. One such privilege allowed individuals to enter property in the event of public or private necessity. See Restatement (Second) of Torts § 196 (1964) (entry to avert an imminent public disaster); § 197 (entry to avert serious harm to a person, land, or chattels); . . . . The common law also recognized a privilege to enter property to effect an arrest or enforce the criminal law under certain circumstances. Restatement (Second) of Torts §§ 204–205. Because a property owner traditionally had no right to exclude an official engaged in a reasonable search, . . . government searches that are consistent with the Fourth Amendment and state law cannot be said to take any property right from landowners. . . .

Third, the government may require property owners to cede a right of access as a condition of receiving certain benefits, without causing a taking. In *Nollan*, we held that "a permit condition that serves the same legitimate police-power purpose as a refusal to issue the permit should not be found to be a taking if the refusal to issue the permit would not constitute a taking." 483 U.S., at 836. . . .

Under this framework, government health and safety inspection regimes will generally not constitute takings. . . . When the government conditions the grant of a benefit such as a permit, license, or registration on allowing access for reasonable health and safety inspections, both the nexus and rough proportionality requirements of the constitutional conditions framework should not be difficult to satisfy. . . .

None of these considerations undermine our determination that the access regulation here gives rise to a *per se* physical taking. Unlike a mere trespass, the regulation grants a formal entitlement to physically invade the growers' land. Unlike a law enforcement search, no traditional background principle of property law requires the growers to admit union organizers onto their premises. And unlike standard health and safety inspections, the access regulation is not germane to any benefit provided to agricultural employers or any risk posed to the public. . . . The access regulation amounts to simple appropriation of private property.

* * *

The access regulation grants labor organizations a right to invade the growers' property. It therefore constitutes a *per se* physical taking.

The judgment . . . is reversed . . . .[a]

■ JUSTICE BREYER, with whom JUSTICE SOTOMAYOR and JUSTICE KAGAN join, dissenting.

. . .

. . . [T]his regulation does not "appropriate" anything; it regulates the employers' right to exclude others. At the same time, our prior cases make clear that the regulation before us allows only a *temporary* invasion of a landowner's property and that this kind of temporary invasion amounts to a taking only if it goes "too far." . . . In my view, the

---

[a]   A concurring opinion by Justice Kavanaugh is omitted.

majority's conclusion threatens to make many ordinary forms of regulation unusually complex or impractical. And though the majority attempts to create exceptions to narrow its rule, the law's need for feasibility suggests that the majority's framework is wrong. . . .

I

. . .

A

Initially it may help to look at the legal problem . . . through the lens of ordinary English. The word "regulation" rather than "appropriation" fits this provision in both label and substance. It is contained in . . . the California Code of Regulations. It was adopted by a state regulatory board . . . in 1975. It is embedded in a set of related detailed regulations that describe and limit the access at issue. In addition to the hours of access . . ., it provides that union representatives can enter the property only "for the purpose of meeting and talking with employees and soliciting their support"; they have access only to "areas in which employees congregate before and after working" or "at such location or locations as the employees eat their lunch"; and they cannot engage in "conduct disruptive of the employer's property or agricultural operations, including injury to crops or machinery or interference with the process of boarding buses." §§ 20900(e), (e)(3), (e)(4)(C) (2021). From the employers' perspective, it restricts when and where they can exclude others from their property.

At the same time, the provision only awkwardly fits the terms "physical taking" and "physical appropriation." The "access" that it grants union organizers does not amount to any traditional property interest in land. . . .

The majority concludes that the regulation nonetheless amounts to a physical taking of property because, the majority says, it "appropriates" a "right to invade" or a "right to exclude" others. . . .

It is important to understand, however, that, technically speaking, the majority is wrong. The regulation does not *appropriate* anything. It does not take from the owners a right to invade (whatever that might mean). It does not give the union organizations the right to exclude anyone. It does not give the government the right to exclude anyone. What does it do? It gives union organizers the right temporarily to invade a portion of the property owners' land. It thereby limits the landowners' right to exclude certain others. The regulation *regulates* (but does not *appropriate*) the owners' right to exclude.

Why is it important to understand this technical point? Because only then can we understand the issue before us. That issue is whether a regulation that *temporarily* limits an owner's right to exclude others from property *automatically* amounts to a Fifth Amendment taking. Under our cases, it does not.

B

Our cases draw a distinction between regulations that provide permanent rights of access and regulations that provide nonpermanent rights of access. They either state or hold that the first type of regulation is a taking *per se*, but the second kind is a taking only if it goes "too far." . . .

. . .

. . . [T]he regulation here at issue provides access that is "temporary," not "permanent." Unlike the regulation in *Loretto*, it does not place a "fixed structure on land or real property." 458 U.S., at 437. The employers are not "forever denie[d]" "any power to control the use" of any particular portion of their property. *Id.*, at 436. And it does not totally reduce the value of any section of the property. *Ibid.* Unlike in *Nollan*, the public cannot walk over the land whenever it wishes; rather a subset of the public may enter a portion of the land three hours per day for four months per year (about 4% of the time). At bottom, the regulation here, unlike the regulations in *Loretto* and *Nollan*, is not "functionally equivalent to the classic taking in which government directly appropriates private property or ousts the owner from his domain." *Lingle*, 544 U.S., at 539.

At the same time, *PruneYard*'s holding that the taking was "temporary" (and hence not a *per se* taking) fits this case almost perfectly. There the regulation gave non-owners the right to enter privately owned property for the purpose of speaking generally to others, about matters of their choice, subject to reasonable time, place, and manner restrictions. . . . The regulation before us grants a far smaller group of people the right to enter landowners' property for far more limited times in order to speak about a specific subject. Employers have more power to control entry by setting work hours, lunch hours, and places of gathering. On the other hand, as the majority notes, the shopping center in *PruneYard* was open to the public generally. All these factors, however, are the stuff of which regulatory-balancing, not absolute *per se*, rules are made.

Our cases have recognized, as the majority says, that the right to exclude is a " 'fundamental element of the property right.' " For that reason, "[a] 'taking' may *more readily* be found when the interference with property can be characterized as a physical invasion by government." *Penn Central*, 438 U.S., at 124 (emphasis added) . . . . But a taking is not inevitably found just because the interference with property can be characterized as a physical invasion by the government, or, in other words, when it affects the right to exclude.

The majority refers to other cases. But those cases do not help its cause. That is because the Court in those cases . . . did not apply a *"per se* takings" approach. . . .

     . . .

If there is ambiguity in these cases, it concerns whether the Court considered the occupation at issue to be *temporary* (requiring *Penn Central*'s "too far" analysis) or *permanent* (automatically requiring compensation). Nothing in them suggests the majority's view, namely, that compensation is automatically required for a *temporary* right of access. Nor does anything in them support the distinction that the majority gleans between "trespass" and "takings."

The majority also refers to *Nollan* as support for its claim that the "fact that a right to take access is exercised only from time to time does not make it any less a physical taking." True. Here, however, unlike in *Nollan*, the right taken is not a right to have access to the property at any time (which access different persons "exercis[e] . . . from time to time"). Rather here we have a right that does not allow access at any time. It allows access only from "time to time." And that makes all the difference. A right to enter my woods whenever you wish is a right to use that property permanently, even if you exercise that right only on occasion. A right to enter my woods only on certain occasions is not a right to use the woods permanently. In the first case one might reasonably use the term *per se* taking. It is as if my woods are yours. In the second case it is a taking only if the regulation allowing it goes "too far," considering the factors we have laid out in *Penn Central*. That is what our cases say.

Finally, the majority says that *Nollan* would have come out the same way had it involved, similar to the regulation here, access short of 365 days a year. Perhaps so. But, if so, that likely would be because the Court would have viewed the access as an "easement," and therefore an appropriation. . . . Or, perhaps, the Court would have viewed the regulation as going "too far." I can assume, purely for argument's sake, that that is so. But the law is clear: A regulation that provides *temporary*, not *permanent*, access to a landowner's property, and that does not amount to a taking of a traditional property interest, is not a *per se* taking. That is, it does not automatically require compensation. Rather, a court must consider whether it goes "too far."

C

The . . . permanent/temporary distinction . . . serves an important purpose. We live together in communities. . . . Modern life in these communities requires different kinds of regulation. Some, perhaps many, forms of regulation require access to private property (for government officials or others) for different reasons and for varying periods of time. Most such temporary-entry regulations do not go "too far." And it is impractical to compensate every property owner for any brief use of their land. . . .

Consider the large numbers of ordinary regulations in a host of different fields that, for a variety of purposes, permit temporary entry onto (or an "invasion of") a property owner's land. They include activities ranging from examination of food products to inspections for compliance with preschool licensing requirements. . . .

The majority tries to deal with the adverse impact of treating these, and other, temporary invasions as if they were *per se* physical takings by creating a series of exceptions from its *per se* rule. . . . I suspect that the majority has substituted a new, complex legal scheme for a comparatively simpler old one.

As to the first exception, what will count as "isolated"? How is an "isolated physical invasion" different from a "temporary" invasion, sufficient under present law to invoke *Penn Central*? And where should one draw the line between trespass and takings? . . .

As to the second exception, a court must focus on "traditional common law privileges to access private property." Just what are they? . . .

As to the third, what is the scope of the phrase "certain benefits"? Does it include the benefit of being able to sell meat labeled "inspected" in interstate commerce? But see *Horne*, 576 U.S., at 366 (concluding that "[s]elling produce in interstate commerce" is "not a special governmental benefit"). What about the benefit of having electricity? Of sewage collection? Of internet accessibility? Myriad regulatory schemes based on just these sorts of benefits depend upon intermittent, temporary government entry onto private property.

Labor peace (brought about through union organizing) is one such benefit, at least in the view of elected representatives. They wrote laws that led to rules governing the organizing of agricultural workers. Many of them may well have believed that union organizing brings with it "benefits," including community health and educational benefits, higher standards of living, and (as I just said) labor peace. . . . A landowner, of course, may deny the existence of these benefits, but a landowner might do the same were a regulatory statute to permit brief access to verify proper preservation of wetlands or the habitat enjoyed by an endangered species or, for that matter, the safety of inspected meat. So, if a regulation authorizing temporary access for purposes of organizing agricultural workers falls outside of the Court's exceptions and is a *per se* taking, then to what other forms of regulation does the Court's *per se* conclusion also apply?

II

Finally, I touch briefly on remedies, which the majority does not address. . . . [T]he employers do not seek compensation. They seek only injunctive and declaratory relief.

Indeed, they did not allege any damages. . . . On remand, California should have the choice of foreclosing injunctive relief by providing compensation. . . .

. . .

2. PROTECTION OF PERSONAL LIBERTIES

C. PERSONAL AUTONOMY

Page 651. Add after National Institute of Family and Life Advocates v. Becerra, and omit Gonzales v. Carhart, Whole Woman's Health v. Hellerstedt, and June Medical Services L.L.C. v. Russo:

Dobbs v. Jackson Women's Health Organization

597 U.S. ___, 142 S.Ct. 2228 (2022).

■ JUSTICE ALITO delivered the opinion of the Court.

. . .

At the time of Roe [v. Wade in 1973], 30 States still prohibited abortion at all stages. In the years prior to that decision, about a third of the States had liberalized their laws, but *Roe* abruptly ended that political process. It . . . effectively struck down the abortion laws of every single State . . . [and] sparked a national controversy that has embittered our political culture for a half century.

. . . Planned Parenthood of Southeastern Pa. v. Casey, 505 U.S. 833 (1992), . . . revisited *Roe*, but the Members of the Court split three ways. . . . [T]he three . . . Justices . . . who jointly signed the controlling opinion . . . concluded that *stare decisis*, which calls for prior decisions to be followed in most instances, required adherence to what it called *Roe*'s "central holding"—that a State may not constitutionally protect fetal life before "viability"—even if that holding was wrong. Anything less, the opinion claimed, would undermine respect for this Court and the rule of law.

. . .

. . . [I]n this case, 26 States have expressly asked this Court to overrule *Roe* and *Casey* and allow the States to regulate or prohibit pre-viability abortions.

. . . Before us now is one such state law. The State of Mississippi asks us to uphold the constitutionality of a law that generally prohibits an abortion after the 15th week of pregnancy—several weeks before the point at which a fetus is now regarded as "viable" outside the womb. . . .

We hold that *Roe* and *Casey* must be overruled. The Constitution makes no reference to abortion, and no such right is implicitly protected by any constitutional provision, including the one on which the defenders of *Roe* and *Casey* now chiefly rely— the Due Process Clause of the Fourteenth Amendment. That provision has been held to guarantee some rights that are not mentioned in the Constitution, but any such right must be "deeply rooted in this Nation's history and tradition" and "implicit in the concept of ordered liberty." Washington v. Glucksberg, 521 U.S. 702, 721 (1997) . . . .

The right to abortion does not fall within this category. Until the latter part of the 20th century, such a right was entirely unknown in American law. Indeed, when the Fourteenth Amendment was adopted, three quarters of the States made abortion a crime at all stages of pregnancy. The abortion right is also critically different from any other right that this Court has held to fall within the Fourteenth Amendment's protection of "liberty." *Roe*'s defenders characterize the abortion right as similar to the rights recognized in past decisions involving matters such as intimate sexual relations, contraception, and marriage, but abortion is fundamentally different, as both *Roe* and *Casey* acknowledged, because it destroys what those decisions called "fetal life" and what the law now before us describes as an "unborn human being."

Stare decisis, . . . does not compel unending adherence to *Roe*'s abuse of judicial authority. *Roe* was egregiously wrong from the start. Its reasoning was exceptionally weak, and the decision has had damaging consequences. And far from bringing about a national settlement of the abortion issue, *Roe* and *Casey* have enflamed debate and deepened division.

It is time to heed the Constitution and return the issue of abortion to the people's elected representatives. . . . That is what the Constitution and the rule of law demand.

I

. . . Mississippi's Gestational Age Act, see Miss. Code Ann. § 41–41–191 (2018), contains this central provision: "Except in a medical emergency or in the case of a severe fetal abnormality, a person shall not intentionally or knowingly perform . . . or induce an abortion of an unborn human being if the probable gestational age of the unborn human being has been determined to be greater than fifteen (15) weeks." § 4(b).

To support this Act, the legislature made a series of factual findings. It began by noting that, at the time of enactment, only six countries besides the United States "permit[ted] nontherapeutic or elective abortion-on-demand after the twentieth week of gestation."15 § 2(a). The legislature then found that at 5 or 6 weeks' gestational age an "unborn human being's heart begins beating"; at 8 weeks the "unborn human being begins to move about in the womb"; at 9 weeks "all basic physiological functions are present"; at 10 weeks "vital organs begin to function," and "[h]air, fingernails, and toenails . . . begin to form"; at 11 weeks "an unborn human being's diaphragm is developing," and he or she may "move about freely in the womb"; and at 12 weeks the "unborn human being" has "taken on 'the human form' in all relevant respects." § 2(b)(i) (quoting Gonzales v. Carhart, 550 U.S. 124, 160 (2007)). It found that most abortions after 15 weeks employ "dilation and evacuation procedures which involve the use of surgical instruments to crush and tear the unborn child," and it concluded that the "intentional commitment of such acts for nontherapeutic or elective reasons is a barbaric practice, dangerous for the maternal patient, and demeaning to the medical profession." § 2(b)(i)(8).

[An abortion clinic, Jackson Women's Health Organization, and one of its doctors, successfully sued to enjoin enforcement of the Act, and the Fifth Circuit affirmed.]

II

. . .

. . . The Constitution makes no express reference to a right to obtain an abortion, and therefore those who claim that it protects such a right must show that the right is somehow implicit in the constitutional text.

Roe, however, was remarkably loose in its treatment of the constitutional text. It held that the abortion right, which is not mentioned in the Constitution, is part of a right to privacy, which is also not mentioned. . . . And that privacy right, *Roe* observed, had been found to spring from no fewer than five different constitutional provisions—the First, Fourth, Fifth, Ninth, and Fourteenth Amendments. . . .

. . . *Roe* expressed the "feel[ing]" that the Fourteenth Amendment was the provision that did the work, but its message seemed to be that the abortion right could be found somewhere in the Constitution and that specifying its exact location was not of paramount importance. The *Casey* Court did not defend this unfocused analysis and instead grounded its decision solely on the theory that the right to obtain an abortion is part of the "liberty" protected by the Fourteenth Amendment's Due Process Clause.

We discuss this theory in depth below, but before doing so, we briefly address one additional constitutional provision that some of respondents' *amici* have now offered as yet another potential home for the abortion right: the Fourteenth Amendment's Equal Protection Clause. . . . Neither *Roe* nor *Casey* saw fit to invoke this theory, and it is squarely foreclosed by our precedents, which establish that a State's regulation of abortion is not a sex-based classification and is thus not subject to the "heightened scrutiny" that applies to such classifications. The regulation of a medical procedure that only one sex can undergo does not trigger heightened constitutional scrutiny unless the regulation is a "mere pretex[t] designed to effect an invidious discrimination against members of one sex or the other." Geduldig v. Aiello, 417 U.S. 484, 496, n. 20 (1974). And . . . the "goal of preventing abortion" does not constitute "invidiously discriminatory animus" against women. Bray v. Alexandria Women's Health Clinic, 506 U.S. 263, 273–274 (1993) . . . . Accordingly, laws regulating or prohibiting abortion . . . are governed by the same standard of review as other health and safety measures.

. . .

The underlying theory . . . that the Fourteenth Amendment's Due Process Clause provides substantive, as well as procedural, protection for "liberty" . . . has long been controversial. But our decisions have held that the Due Process Clause protects two categories of substantive rights.

The first consists of rights guaranteed by the first eight Amendments. . . . The second . . .—the one in question here—comprises a select list of fundamental rights that are not mentioned anywhere in the Constitution.

In deciding whether a right falls into either of these categories, the Court has long asked whether the right is "deeply rooted in [our] history and tradition" and whether it is essential to our Nation's "scheme of ordered liberty." . . .

. . .

. . . [I]n *Glucksberg*, which held that the Due Process Clause does not confer a right to assisted suicide, the Court surveyed more than 700 years of "Anglo-American common law tradition," 521 U.S., at 711, and made clear that a fundamental right must be "objectively, deeply rooted in this Nation's history and tradition," id., at 720–721.

Historical inquiries of this nature are essential whenever we are asked to recognize a new component of the "liberty" protected by the Due Process Clause because the term "liberty" alone provides little guidance. . . .

In interpreting what is meant by the Fourteenth Amendment's reference to "liberty," we must guard against the natural human tendency to confuse what that Amendment protects with our own ardent views about the liberty that Americans should enjoy. . . .

On occasion, . . . the Court . . . has fallen into the freewheeling judicial policymaking that characterized discredited decisions such as Lochner v. New York, 198 U.S. 45 (1905). . . . [G]uided by the history and tradition that map the essential components of our Nation's concept of ordered liberty, we must ask what the *Fourteenth Amendment* means by the term "liberty." . . . [I]n the present case, the clear answer is that the Fourteenth Amendment does not protect the right to an abortion.

. . .

Until the latter part of the 20th century, there was no support in American law for a constitutional right to obtain an abortion. No state constitutional provision had recognized such a right. Until a few years before *Roe* was handed down, no federal or state court had recognized such a right. . .

Not only was there no support for such a constitutional right until shortly before *Roe*, but abortion had long been a crime in every single State. At common law, abortion was criminal in at least some stages of pregnancy and was regarded as unlawful and could have very serious consequences at all stages. American law followed the common law until a wave of statutory restrictions in the 1800s expanded criminal liability for abortions. By the time of the adoption of the Fourteenth Amendment, three-quarters of the States had made abortion a crime at any stage of pregnancy, and the remaining States would soon follow.

[Justice Alito's historical review included an assessment that at common law abortions after "quickening" were criminal; that "[a]lthough a pre-quickening abortion was not itself considered homicide, it does not follow that abortion was *permissible* at common law—much less that abortion was a legal *right*"; and that "we are aware of no common-law case or authority, and the parties have not pointed to any, that remotely suggests a positive *right* to procure an abortion at any stage of pregnancy." In this country, he determined that "by the 19th century, courts frequently explained that the common law made abortion of a quick child a crime." Whatever the "original ground for the quickening rule is of little importance for present purposes because the rule was abandoned in the 19th century" in any event. "By 1868, the year when the Fourteenth Amendment was ratified, three-quarters of the States, 28 out of 37, had enacted statutes making[abortion a crime even if it was performed before quickening[, and o]f the nine States that had not yet criminalized abortion at all stages, all but one did so by 1910." Similarly, of "the Territories that would become the last 13 States . . . [a]ll of them criminalized abortion at all stages of pregnancy between 1850 . . . and 1919 . . . ." Indeed, "[b]y the end of the 1950s, according to the *Roe* Court's own count, statutes in all but four States and the District of Columbia prohibited abortion 'however and whenever performed, unless done to save or preserve the life of the mother.' 410 U.S., at 139."]

The inescapable conclusion is that a right to abortion is not deeply rooted in the Nation's history and traditions. On the contrary, an unbroken tradition of prohibiting abortion on pain of criminal punishment persisted from the earliest days of the common law until 1973. . . .

. . .

Instead of seriously pressing the argument that the abortion right itself has deep roots, supporters of *Roe* and *Casey* contend that the abortion right is an integral part of a broader entrenched right. *Roe* termed this a right to privacy, 410 U.S., at 154, and *Casey* described it as the freedom to make "intimate and personal choices" that are "central to personal dignity and autonomy," 505 U.S., at 851. *Casey* elaborated: "At the heart of liberty is the right to define one's own concept of existence, of meaning, of the universe, and of the mystery of human life." Ibid.

. . . While individuals are certainly free *to think* and *to say* what they wish about "existence," "meaning," the "universe," and "the mystery of human life," they are not always free *to act* in accordance with those thoughts. License to act on the basis of such beliefs may correspond to one of the many understandings of "liberty," but it is certainly not "ordered liberty."

Ordered liberty sets limits and defines the boundary between competing interests. *Roe* and *Casey* each struck a particular balance between the interests of a woman who wants an abortion and the interests of what they termed "potential life." . . . But the people of the various States may evaluate those interests differently. . . . Our Nation's historical understanding of ordered liberty does not prevent the people's elected representatives from deciding how abortion should be regulated.

Nor does the right to obtain an abortion have a sound basis in precedent. *Casey* relied on cases involving the right to marry a person of a different race, Loving v. Virginia, 388 U.S. 1 (1967); the right to marry while in prison, Turner v. Safley, 482 U.S. 78 (1987); the right to obtain contraceptives, Griswold v. Connecticut, 381 U.S. 479 (1965), Eisenstadt v. Baird, 405 U.S. 438 (1972), Carey v. Population Services Int'l, 431 U.S. 678 (1977); the right to reside with relatives, Moore v. East Cleveland, 431 U.S. 494 (1977); the right to make decisions about the education of one's children, Pierce v. Society of Sisters, 268 U.S. 510 (1925), Meyer v. Nebraska, 262 U.S. 390 (1923); the right not to be sterilized without consent, Skinner v. Oklahoma ex rel. Williamson, 316 U.S. 535 (1942); and the right in certain circumstances not to undergo involuntary surgery, forced administration of drugs, or other substantially similar procedures, Winston v. Lee, 470 U.S. 753 (1985), Washington v. Harper, 494 U.S. 210 (1990), Rochin v. California, 342 U.S. 165 (1952). Respondents and the Solicitor General also rely on post-*Casey* decisions like Lawrence v. Texas, 539 U.S. 558 (2003) (right to engage in private, consensual sexual acts), and Obergefell v. Hodges, 576 U.S. 644 (2015) (right to marry a person of the same sex). . . .

These attempts to justify abortion through appeals to a broader right to autonomy and to define one's "concept of existence" prove too much. . . . Those criteria, at a high level of generality, could license fundamental rights to illicit drug use, prostitution, and the like. . . . None of these rights has any claim to being deeply rooted in history. . . .

What sharply distinguishes the abortion right from the rights recognized in the cases on which *Roe* and *Casey* rely is something that both those decisions acknowledged: Abortion destroys what those decisions call "potential life" and what the law at issue in this case regards as the life of an "unborn human being." See *Roe*, 410 U.S., at 159 (abortion is "inherently different"); *Casey*, 505 U.S., at 852 (abortion is "a unique act"). None of the other decisions cited by *Roe* and *Casey* involved the critical moral question posed by abortion. They are therefore inapposite. They do not support the right to obtain an abortion, and by the same token, our conclusion that the Constitution does not confer such a right does not undermine them in any way.

. . .

Defenders of *Roe* and *Casey* do not claim that any new scientific learning calls for a different answer to the underlying moral question, but they do contend that changes in society require the recognition of a constitutional right to obtain an abortion. Without the availability of abortion, they maintain, people will be inhibited from exercising their freedom to choose the types of relationships they desire, and women will be unable to compete with men in the workplace and in other endeavors.

Americans who believe that abortion should be restricted press countervailing arguments about modern developments. They note that attitudes about the pregnancy of unmarried women have changed drastically; that federal and state laws ban discrimination on the basis of pregnancy; that leave for pregnancy and childbirth are now guaranteed by law in many cases; that the costs of medical care associated with pregnancy are covered by insurance or government assistance; that States have increasingly adopted "safe haven" laws, which generally allow women to drop off babies anonymously; and that a woman who puts her newborn up for adoption today has little reason to fear that the baby will not find a suitable home. They also claim that many people now have a new appreciation of fetal life and that when prospective parents who want to have a child view a sonogram, they typically have no doubt that what they see is their daughter or son.

Both sides make important policy arguments, but . . . we . . . return the power to weigh those arguments to the people and their elected representatives.

> . . .

Because the dissent cannot argue that the abortion right is rooted in this Nation's history and tradition, it contends that the "constitutional tradition" is "not captured whole at a single moment," and that its "meaning gains content from the long sweep of our history and from successive judicial precedents." This vague formulation imposes no clear restraints on what Justice White called the "exercise of raw judicial power," *Roe*, 410 U.S., at 222 (dissenting opinion), and while the dissent claims that its standard "does not mean anything goes," any real restraints are hard to discern.

. . .[I]f the "long sweep of history" imposes any restraint on the recognition of unenumerated rights, then *Roe* was surely wrong, since abortion was never allowed (except to save the life of the mother) in a majority of States for over 100 years before that decision was handed down. Second, it is impossible to defend *Roe* based on prior precedent because all of the precedents *Roe* cited, including *Griswold* and *Eisenstadt*, were critically different for a reason that we have explained: None of those cases involved the destruction of what *Roe* called "potential life."

> . . .

The most striking feature of the dissent is the absence of any serious discussion of the legitimacy of the States' interest in protecting fetal life. . . .

. . . The dissent has much to say about the effects of pregnancy on women, the burdens of motherhood, and the difficulties faced by poor women. These are important concerns. However, the dissent evinces no similar regard for a State's interest in protecting prenatal life.

III

We next consider whether the doctrine of *stare decisis* counsels continued acceptance of *Roe* and *Casey*. . . .

. . . [W]hen one of our constitutional decisions goes astray, the country is usually stuck with the bad decision unless we correct our own mistake. . . .

Some of our most important constitutional decisions have overruled prior precedents. [Here, Justice Alito discussed Brown v. Board of Education, 347 U.S. 483 (1954), overruling "the infamous decision in Plessy v. Ferguson, 163 U.S. 537 (1896), along with six other Supreme Court precedents that had applied the separate-but-equal rule"; West Coast Hotel Co. v. Parrish, 300 U.S. 379 (1937), overruling "Adkins v. Children's Hospital of D. C., 261 U.S. 525 (1923), which had held that a law setting minimum wages for women violated the "liberty" protected by the Fifth Amendment's Due Process Clause"; and West Virginia Bd. of Ed. v. Barnette, 319 U.S. 624 (1943), which overruled Minersville School Dist. v. Gobitis, 310 U.S. 586 (1940), after only three years, and "held that public school students could not be compelled to salute the flag in violation of their sincere beliefs." (In a lengthy footnote, he listed many more "important constitutional decisions" the Court had overruled.)]

In this case, five factors weigh strongly in favor of overruling *Roe* and *Casey*: the nature of their error, the quality of their reasoning, the "workability" of the rules they imposed on the country, their disruptive effect on other areas of the law, and the absence of concrete reliance.

[First, *Plessy* was "egregiously wrong" on the day it was decided. "*Roe* was also egregiously wrong and deeply damaging. . . . [Its] constitutional analysis was far outside the bounds of any reasonable interpretation of the various constitutional provisions to which it vaguely pointed." *Casey* followed suit, and *West Coast Hotel* illustrated that "the Court has previously overruled decisions that wrongly removed an issue from the people and the democratic process."

[Second, "*Roe* . . . was more than just wrong. It stood on exceptionally weak grounds."]

Roe . . . failed to ground its decision in text, history, or precedent. It relied on an erroneous historical narrative; it devoted great attention to and presumably relied on matters that have no bearing on the meaning of the Constitution; it disregarded the fundamental difference between the precedents on which it relied and the question before the Court; it concocted an elaborate set of rules, with different restrictions for each trimester of pregnancy, but it did not explain how this veritable code could be teased out of anything in the Constitution, the history of abortion laws, prior precedent, or any other cited source; and its most important rule (that States cannot protect fetal life prior to "viability") was never raised by any party and has never been plausibly explained. *Roe*'s reasoning quickly drew scathing scholarly criticism, even from supporters of broad access to abortion.

The *Casey* plurality, while reaffirming *Roe*'s central holding, pointedly refrained from endorsing most of its reasoning. It revised the textual basis for the abortion right, silently abandoned *Roe*'s erroneous historical narrative, and jettisoned the trimester framework. But it replaced that scheme with an arbitrary "undue burden" test and relied on an exceptional version of *stare decisis* that . . . this Court had never before applied and has never invoked since.

. . .

. . . *Roe*'s failure even to note the overwhelming consensus of state laws in effect in 1868 is striking, and what it said about the common law was simply wrong. . . .

[According to Justice Alito, "none of" the substantive due process precedents on which *Roe* relied "involved what is distinctive about abortion: its effect on what *Roe* termed 'potential life.'" And the "scheme *Roe* produced *looked* like legislation, and the Court provided the sort of explanation that might be expected from a legislative body." In fact, "[w]hat *Roe* did not provide was any cogent justification for the lines it drew." A "glaring deficiency was *Roe*'s failure to justify the critical distinction it drew between pre- and post-viability abortions." Viability "is heavily dependent on factors that have nothing to do with the characteristics of a fetus[,]" such as the quality of available medical facilities and inevitable variability among different women and in different locations. "The viability line, which *Casey* termed *Roe*'s central rule, makes no sense, and it is telling that other countries almost uniformly eschew such a line."]

[As for the third *stare decisis* factor, *Casey*'s adoption of the "undue burden" test "proved to be unworkable[,]" as evidenced in part by how it "generated a long list of Circuit conflicts." With regard to the fourth factor, "*Roe* and *Casey* have led to the distortion of many important but unrelated legal doctrines, and that effect provides further support for overruling those decisions." On this score, Justice Alito said:]

The Court's abortion cases have diluted the strict standard for facial constitutional challenges. They have ignored the Court's third-party standing doctrine. They have disregarded standard *res judicata* principles. They have flouted the ordinary rules on the severability of unconstitutional provisions, as well as the rule that statutes should be read where possible to avoid unconstitutionality. And they have distorted First Amendment doctrines.

[Finally, regarding "reliance interests," "we agree with the *Casey* plurality that conventional, concrete reliance interests are not present here." Unlike that plurality, however, the Court here would not rest on "the novel and intangible form of reliance" on which *Casey* had relied, namely "that 'people [had] organized intimate relationships and made choices that define their views of themselves and their places in society . . . in reliance on the availability of abortion in the event that contraception should fail' and that '[t]he ability of women to participate equally in the economic and social life of the Nation has been facilitated by their ability to control their reproductive lives.' " Justice Alito said the following:]

. . . *Casey*'s notion of reliance . . . finds little support in our cases, which instead emphasize very concrete reliance interests, like those that develop in "cases involving property and contract rights." . . .

When a concrete reliance interest is asserted, courts are equipped to evaluate the claim, but assessing the novel and intangible form of reliance endorsed by the *Casey* plurality is another matter. That form of reliance depends on an empirical question that is hard for anyone—and in particular, for a court—to assess, namely, the effect of the abortion right on society and in particular on the lives of women. . . .

Our decision . . . allows women on both sides of the abortion issue to seek to affect the legislative process by influencing public opinion, lobbying legislators, voting, and running for office. Women are not without electoral or political power. It is noteworthy that the percentage of women who register to vote and cast ballots is consistently higher than the percentage of men who do so. . . .

Unable to show concrete reliance on *Roe* and *Casey* themselves, the Solicitor General suggests that overruling those decisions would "threaten the Court's precedents holding that the Due Process Clause protects other rights." Brief for United States 26 (citing *Obergefell*, 576 U.S. 644; *Lawrence*, 539 U.S. 558; *Griswold*, 381 U.S. 479). That is not correct for reasons we have already discussed. . . . And to ensure that our decision is not misunderstood or mischaracterized, we emphasize that our decision concerns the constitutional right to abortion and no other right. Nothing in this opinion should be understood to cast doubt on precedents that do not concern abortion.

IV

. . . [W]e must address one final argument that featured prominently in the *Casey* plurality opinion.

The argument . . . was essentially . . . [that t]here is a special danger that the public will perceive a decision as having been made for unprincipled reasons when the Court overrules a controversial "watershed" decision, such as *Roe*[,] . . . and therefore the preservation of public approval of the Court weighs heavily in favor of retaining *Roe*. . . .

. . . But we cannot exceed the scope of our authority under the Constitution, and we cannot allow our decisions to be affected by any extraneous influences such as concern about the public's reaction to our work. . . . That is true both when we initially decide a constitutional issue *and* when we consider whether to overrule a prior decision. . . .

. . . The Court has no authority to decree that an erroneous precedent is *permanently* exempt from evaluation under traditional *stare decisis* principles. . . .

The *Casey* plurality also misjudged the practical limits of this Court's influence. *Roe* certainly did not succeed in ending division on the issue of abortion. On the contrary, *Roe* "inflamed" a national issue that has remained bitterly divisive for the past half century. . . . And for the past 30 years, *Casey* has done the same.

Neither decision has ended debate over the issue of a constitutional right to obtain an abortion. . . . This Court cannot bring about the permanent resolution of a rancorous national controversy simply by dictating a settlement and telling the people to move on. . . .

We do not pretend to know how our political system or society will respond to today's decision overruling *Roe* and *Casey*. And even if we could foresee what will happen, we would have no authority to let that knowledge influence our decision. We can only do our job, which is to interpret the law, apply longstanding principles of *stare decisis*, and decide this case accordingly.

We therefore hold that the Constitution does not confer a right to abortion. *Roe* and *Casey* must be overruled, and the authority to regulate abortion must be returned to the people and their elected representatives.

V

The dissent argues that we have "abandon[ed]" *stare decisis*, but we have done no such thing . . . . The dissent's foundational contention is that the Court should never (or perhaps almost never) overrule an egregiously wrong constitutional precedent unless the Court can "poin[t] to major legal or factual changes undermining [the] decision's original basis." . . . Recognition that the cases [*Brown*] overruled were egregiously wrong on the day they were handed down was not enough.

The Court has never adopted this strange new version of *stare decisis*—and with good reason. Does the dissent really maintain that overruling *Plessy* was not justified until the country had experienced more than a half-century of state-sanctioned segregation and generations of Black school children had suffered all its effects?

. . . On the dissent's view, it must have been wrong for West Virginia Bd. of Ed. v. Barnette, 319 U.S. 624, to overrule Minersville School Dist. v. Gobitis, 310 U.S. 586, a bare three years after it was handed down. . . . The *Barnette* Court did not claim that its reexamination . . . was prompted by any intervening legal or factual developments . . .

Precedents should be respected, but sometimes the Court errs, and occasionally the Court issues an important decision that is egregiously wrong. When that happens, *stare decisis* is not a straitjacket. . . .

Even if the dissent were correct . . ., reexamination of *Roe* and *Casey* would be amply justified. . . . [P]ost-*Casey* developments [support that], but the most profound change may be the failure of the *Casey* plurality's call for "the contending sides" in the controversy about abortion "to end their national division," . . . .

The dissent . . . contends that the "very controversy surrounding *Roe* and *Casey*" is an important *stare decisis* consideration that requires upholding those precedents. But . . . *Casey* broke new ground when it treated the national controversy provoked by *Roe* as a ground for refusing to reconsider that decision, and no subsequent case has relied on that factor. . . .

Finally, the dissent suggests that our decision calls into question *Griswold*, *Eisenstadt*, *Lawrence*, and *Obergefell*. But we have stated unequivocally that "[n]othing in this opinion should be understood to cast doubt on precedents that do not concern abortion." . . . It is hard to see how we could be clearer. . . .

We now turn to the concurrence in the judgment, which reproves us for deciding whether *Roe* and *Casey* should be retained or overruled. . . .

. . . [B]oth parties and the Solicitor General have urged us either to reaffirm or overrule *Roe* and *Casey*. . . . What is more, the concurrence has not identified any of the more than 130 *amicus* briefs filed in this case that advocated its approach. . . .

The concurrence's most fundamental defect is its failure to offer any principled basis for its approach. The concurrence would "discar[d]" "the rule from *Roe* and *Casey* that a woman's right to terminate her pregnancy extends up to the point that the fetus is regarded as 'viable' outside the womb." But this rule was a critical component of the holdings in *Roe* and *Casey,* and *stare decisis* is "a doctrine of preservation, not transformation," . . . . [A] new rule that discards the viability rule cannot be defended on *stare decisis* grounds.

. . .

When the Court reconsidered *Roe* in *Casey,* it left no doubt about the importance of the viability rule. It described the rule as *Roe*'s "central holding," . . . .

Our subsequent cases have continued to recognize the centrality of the viability rule. . . .

. . .

. . . [S]*tare decisis* cannot justify the new "reasonable opportunity" rule propounded by the concurrence. If that rule is to become the law of the land, it must stand on its own, but the concurrence makes no attempt to show that this rule represents a correct interpretation of the Constitution. . . .

. . . If we held only that Mississippi's 15-week rule is constitutional, we would soon be called upon to pass on the constitutionality of a panoply of laws with shorter deadlines or no deadline at all. The "measured course" charted by the concurrence would be fraught with turmoil until the Court answered the question that the concurrence seeks to defer.

VI

We must now decide what standard will govern if state abortion regulations undergo constitutional challenge and whether the law before us satisfies the appropriate standard.

. . .

A law regulating abortion, like other health and welfare laws, is entitled to a "strong presumption of validity." Heller v. Doe, 509 U.S. 312, 319 (1993). It must be sustained if there is a rational basis on which the legislature could have thought that it would serve legitimate state interests. Id., at 320; FCC v. Beach Communications, Inc., 508 U.S. 307, 313 (1993) . . . . These legitimate interests include respect for and preservation of prenatal life at all stages of development . . .; the protection of maternal health and safety; the elimination of particularly gruesome or barbaric medical procedures; the preservation of the integrity of the medical profession; the mitigation of fetal pain; and the prevention of discrimination on the basis of race, sex, or disability.

. . . These legitimate interests provide a rational basis for the Gestational Age Act, and it follows that respondents' constitutional challenge must fail.

VII

. . . Abortion presents a profound moral question. The Constitution does not prohibit the citizens of each State from regulating or prohibiting abortion. *Roe* and *Casey* arrogated that authority. We now overrule those decisions and return that authority to the people and their elected representatives.

. . . [R]eversed . . . and remanded for further proceedings consistent with this opinion.

■ JUSTICE THOMAS, concurring.

. . .

I write separately to emphasize a second, more fundamental reason why there is no abortion guarantee lurking in the Due Process Clause. . . .

. . . Because the Due Process Clause does not secure *any* substantive rights, it does not secure a right to abortion.

The Court today declines to disturb substantive due process jurisprudence generally or the doctrine's application in other, specific contexts. Cases like Griswold v. Connecticut, . . . Lawrence v. Texas, . . . and Obergefell v. Hodges . . . are not at issue. The Court's abortion cases are unique . . . .

. . . [I]n future cases, we should reconsider all of this Court's substantive due process precedents, including *Griswold*, *Lawrence*, and *Obergefell*. . . . After overruling these demonstrably erroneous decisions, the question would remain whether other constitutional provisions guarantee the myriad rights that our substantive due process cases have generated. . . .

. . .

. . . Substantive due process . . . has harmed our country in many ways. Accordingly, we should eliminate it from our jurisprudence at the earliest opportunity.

■ JUSTICE KAVANAUGH, concurring.

I write separately to explain my additional views about why *Roe* was wrongly decided, why *Roe* should be overruled at this time, and the future implications of today's decision.

I

. . .

On the question of abortion, the Constitution is . . . neither pro-life nor pro-choice. The Constitution is neutral and leaves the issue for the people and their elected representatives to resolve through the democratic process in the States or Congress— like the numerous other difficult questions of American social and economic policy that the Constitution does not address.

Because the Constitution is neutral on the issue of abortion, this Court also must be scrupulously neutral. . . .

. . . The Constitution neither outlaws abortion nor legalizes abortion.

. . .

Today's decision therefore does not prevent the numerous States that readily allow abortion from continuing to readily allow abortion. . . .

. . .

. . . In my respectful view, the Court in *Roe* . . . erred by taking sides . . . .

II

The more difficult question in this case is *stare decisis* . . . .

. . .

... The history of *stare decisis* in this Court establishes that a constitutional precedent may be overruled only when (i) the prior decision is not just wrong, but is egregiously wrong, (ii) the prior decision has caused significant negative jurisprudential or real-world consequences, and (iii) overruling the prior decision would not unduly upset legitimate reliance interests. . . .

Applying those factors, I agree with the Court today that *Roe* should be overruled. . . .

Of course, the fact that a precedent is wrong, even egregiously wrong, does not alone mean that the precedent should be overruled. But as the Court today explains, *Roe* has caused significant negative jurisprudential and real-world consequences. By taking sides on a difficult and contentious issue on which the Constitution is neutral, *Roe* overreached and exceeded this Court's constitutional authority; gravely distorted the Nation's understanding of this Court's proper constitutional role; and caused significant harm to what *Roe* itself recognized as the State's "important and legitimate interest" in protecting fetal life. . . . All of that explains why tens of millions of Americans—and the 26 States that explicitly ask the Court to overrule *Roe*—do not accept *Roe* even 49 years later. Under the Court's longstanding *stare decisis* principles, *Roe* should be overruled.

But the *stare decisis* analysis here is somewhat more complicated because of *Casey*. . . .

. . .

But . . . *Casey*'s well-intentioned effort did not resolve the abortion debate. The national division has not ended. . . .

In short, *Casey*'s *stare decisis* analysis rested in part on a predictive judgment about the future development of state laws and of the people's views on the abortion issue. But that predictive judgment has not borne out. . . .

In any event, although *Casey* is relevant to the *stare decisis* analysis, the question of whether to overrule *Roe* cannot be dictated by *Casey* alone. . . .

III

. . . [T]he parties' arguments have raised other related questions, and I address some of them here.

First is . . . how this decision will affect other precedents involving issues such as contraception and marriage . . . . I emphasize what the Court today states: Overruling *Roe* does *not* mean the overruling of those precedents, and does *not* threaten or cast doubt on those precedents.

Second, as I see it, some of the other abortion-related legal questions raised by today's decision are not especially difficult as a constitutional matter. For example, may a State bar a resident of that State from traveling to another State to obtain an abortion? In my view, the answer is no based on the constitutional right to interstate travel. May a State retroactively impose liability or punishment for an abortion that occurred before today's decision takes effect? In my view, the answer is no based on the Due Process Clause or the *Ex Post Facto* Clause. . . .

. . .

■ CHIEF JUSTICE ROBERTS, concurring in the judgment.

. . .

. . . I would take a more measured course. I agree with the Court that the viability line established by *Roe* and *Casey* should be discarded under a straightforward *stare decisis* analysis. That line never made any sense. Our abortion precedents describe the right at issue as a woman's right to choose to terminate her pregnancy. That right should therefore extend far enough to ensure a reasonable opportunity to choose, but need not extend any further—certainly not all the way to viability. Mississippi's law allows a woman three months to obtain an abortion, well beyond the point at which it is considered "late" to discover a pregnancy. . . . I see no sound basis for questioning the adequacy of that opportunity.

But that is all I would say, out of adherence to a simple yet fundamental principle of judicial restraint: If it is not necessary to decide more to dispose of a case, then it is necessary *not* to decide more. . . . The Court's . . . dramatic and consequential ruling is unnecessary to decide the case before us.

. . .

. . . [T]he viability rule was created outside the ordinary course of litigation, is and always has been completely unreasoned, and fails to take account of state interests since recognized as legitimate. . . . The Court rightly rejects the arbitrary viability rule today.

II

None of this, however, requires that we also take the dramatic step of altogether eliminating the abortion right first recognized in *Roe*. Mississippi itself previously argued as much to this Court in this litigation.

. . .

[T]here is a clear path to deciding this case correctly without overruling *Roe* all the way down to the studs: recognize that the viability line must be discarded, as the majority rightly does, and leave for another day whether to reject any right to an abortion at all. . . .

Of course, such an approach would not be available if the rationale of *Roe* and *Casey* was inextricably entangled with and dependent upon the viability standard. It is not. . . . [T]here is nothing inherent in the right to choose that requires it to extend to viability or any other point, so long as a real choice is provided. . . .

To be sure, in reaffirming the right to an abortion, *Casey* termed the viability rule *Roe*'s "central holding." . . . But simply declaring it does not make it so. . . .

. . . The viability line is a separate rule fleshing out the metes and bounds of *Roe*'s core holding. Applying principles of *stare decisis*, I would excise that additional rule—and only that rule—from our jurisprudence.

. . . I agree that—whether it was originally holding or dictum—the viability line is clearly part of our "past precedent," and the Court has applied it as such in several cases since *Roe*. My point is that *Roe* adopted two distinct rules of constitutional law: one, that a woman has the right to choose to terminate a pregnancy; two, that such right may be overridden by the State's legitimate interests when the fetus is viable outside the womb. The latter is obviously distinct from the former. I would abandon that timing rule, but see no need in this case to consider the basic right.

. . .

Overruling the subsidiary rule is sufficient to resolve this case in Mississippi's favor. The law at issue allows abortions up through fifteen weeks, providing an adequate opportunity to exercise the right *Roe* protects. By the time a pregnant woman has reached that point, her pregnancy is well into the second trimester. . . .

III

. . . The Court says there is no "principled basis" for this approach, but in fact it is firmly grounded in basic principles of *stare decisis* and judicial restraint.

The Court's decision to overrule *Roe* and *Casey* is a serious jolt to the legal system—regardless of how you view those cases. A narrower decision rejecting the misguided viability line would be markedly less unsettling . . . .

. . . [R]espondents argue that generations of women have relied on the right to an abortion in organizing their relationships and planning their futures. . . . The Court questions whether these concerns are pertinent under our precedents, but the issue would not even arise with a decision rejecting only the viability line: It cannot reasonably be argued that women have shaped their lives in part on the assumption that they would be able to abort up to viability, as opposed to fifteen weeks.

. . . [T]he Court cites three seminal constitutional decisions that involved overruling prior precedents: Brown v. Board of Education, . . . West Virginia Bd. of Ed. v. Barnette, . . . and West Coast Hotel Co. v. Parrish . . . . The opinion in *Brown* was unanimous and eleven pages long; this one is neither. *Barnette* was decided only three years after the decision it overruled, three Justices having had second thoughts. And *West Coast Hotel* was issued against a backdrop of unprecedented economic despair that focused attention on the fundamental flaws of existing precedent. It also was part of a sea change in this Court's interpretation of the Constitution, "signal[ing] the demise of an entire line of important precedents"—a feature the Court expressly disclaims in today's decision, None of these leading cases, in short, provides a template for what the Court does today.

. . . [U]nder the narrower approach proposed here, state laws outlawing abortion altogether would still violate binding precedent. And to the extent States have laws that set the cutoff date earlier than fifteen weeks, any litigation over that timeframe would proceed free of the distorting effect that the viability rule has had on our constitutional debate. The same could be true . . . with respect to legislative consideration in the States. We would then be free to exercise our discretion in deciding whether and when to take up the issue, from a more informed perspective.

. . .

■ JUSTICE BREYER, JUSTICE SOTOMAYOR, and JUSTICE KAGAN, dissenting.

For half a century, Roe v. Wade, and Planned Parenthood of Southeastern Pa. v. Casey, have protected the liberty and equality of women. . . . *Roe* held, and *Casey* reaffirmed, that the Constitution safeguards a woman's right to decide for herself whether to bear a child. . . . Respecting a woman as an autonomous being, and granting her full equality, meant giving her substantial choice over this most personal and most consequential of all life decisions.

. . .

Today, the Court . . . says that from the very moment of fertilization, a woman has no rights to speak of. A State can force her to bring a pregnancy to term, even at the steepest personal and familial costs. . . . Some States . . . have passed laws without any exceptions for when the woman is the victim of rape or incest. Under those laws, a woman will have to bear her rapist's child or a young girl her father's—no matter if doing so will destroy her life. So too, after today's ruling, some States may compel women to carry to term a fetus with severe physical anomalies . . . . Across a vast array of circumstances, a State will be able to impose its moral choice on a woman and coerce her to give birth to a child.

. . .

. . . Above all others, women lacking financial resources will suffer from today's decision. In any event, interstate restrictions will also soon be in the offing. [S]ome States may block women from traveling out of State to obtain abortions, or even from receiving abortion medications from out of State. Some may criminalize efforts, including the provision of information or funding, to help women gain access to other States' abortion services. Most threatening of all, no language in today's decision stops the Federal Government from prohibiting abortions nationwide, once again from the moment of conception and without exceptions for rape or incest. . . .

Whatever the exact scope of the coming laws, one result of today's decision is certain: the curtailment of women's rights, and of their status as free and equal citizens. . . .

And no one should be confident that this majority is done with its work. The right *Roe* and *Casey* recognized . . . has [been] linked . . . for decades to other settled freedoms involving bodily integrity, familial relationships, and procreation. . . .—[and] more recently, to rights of same-sex intimacy and marriage. . . . They are all part of the same constitutional fabric, protecting autonomous decisionmaking over the most personal of life decisions. The majority (or to be more accurate, most of it) is eager to tell us today that nothing it does "cast[s] doubt on precedents that do not concern abortion.". . . But how could that be? The lone rationale for what the majority does today is that the right to elect an abortion is not "deeply rooted in history" . . . . The same could be said, though, of most of the rights the majority claims it is not tampering with. . . . So . . . [e]ither the majority does not really believe in its own reasoning. Or if it does, all rights that have no history stretching back to the mid-19th century are insecure. Either the mass of the majority's opinion is hypocrisy, or additional constitutional rights are under threat. It is one or the other.

. . . The majority has no good reason for the upheaval in law and society it sets off. *Roe* and *Casey* have been the law of the land for decades, shaping women's expectations of their choices when an unplanned pregnancy occurs. Women have relied on the availability of abortion both in structuring their relationships and in planning their lives. . . . No recent developments, in either law or fact, have eroded or cast doubt on those precedents. . . . *Casey* already found all of that to be true. *Casey* is a precedent about precedent. It reviewed the same arguments made here in support of overruling *Roe*, and it found that doing so was not warranted. The Court reverses course today for one reason and one reason only: because the composition of this Court has changed. . . . Today, the proclivities of individuals rule. The Court departs from its obligation to faithfully and impartially apply the law. We dissent.

I

. . . *Roe* and *Casey* were from the beginning, and are even more now, embedded in core constitutional concepts of individual freedom, and of the equal rights of citizens to decide on the shape of their lives. . . . Even in the face of public opposition, we uphold the right of individuals—yes, including women—to make their own choices and chart their own futures. Or at least, we did once.

. . .

We make one initial point . . . in light of the majority's insistence that *Roe* and *Casey*, and we in defending them, are dismissive of a "State's interest in protecting prenatal life." Nothing could get those decisions more wrong. . . . *Roe* and *Casey* invoked powerful state interests in that protection, operative at every stage of the pregnancy and overriding the woman's liberty after viability. The strength of those state interests is exactly why the Court allowed greater restrictions on the abortion right than on other rights deriving from the Fourteenth Amendment. But what *Roe* and *Casey* also recognized—which today's majority does not—is that a woman's freedom and equality are likewise involved. That fact—the presence of countervailing interests—is what made the abortion question hard, and what necessitated balancing.... To the majority "balance" is a dirty word, as moderation is a foreign concept. The majority would allow States to ban abortion from conception onward because it does not think forced childbirth at all implicates a woman's rights to equality and freedom. Today's Court, that is, does not think there is anything of constitutional significance attached to a woman's control of her body and the path of her life. *Roe* and *Casey* thought that one-sided view misguided. In some sense, that is the difference in a nutshell between our precedents and the majority opinion. The constitutional regime we have lived in for the last 50 years recognized competing interests, and sought a balance between them. The constitutional regime we enter today erases the woman's interest and recognizes only the State's (or the Federal Government's).

... The majority says (and with this much we agree) that ... [i]n 1868, there was no nationwide right to end a pregnancy, and no thought that the Fourteenth Amendment provided one.

. . .

The majority's core legal postulate ... is that we in the 21st century must read the Fourteenth Amendment just as its ratifiers did.... If the ratifiers did not understand something as central to freedom, then neither can we. Or said more particularly: If those people did not understand reproductive rights as part of the guarantee of liberty conferred in the Fourteenth Amendment, then those rights do not exist.

... [O]f course, "people" did not ratify the Fourteenth Amendment. Men did. So it is perhaps not so surprising that the ratifiers were not perfectly attuned to the importance of reproductive rights for women's liberty, or for their capacity to participate as equal members of our Nation. Indeed, the ratifiers—both in 1868 and when the original Constitution was approved in 1788—did not understand women as full members of the community embraced by the phrase "We the People." ... Those responsible for the original Constitution, including the Fourteenth Amendment, did not perceive women as equals, and did not recognize women's rights. When the majority says that we must read our foundational charter as viewed at the time of ratification ..., it consigns women to second-class citizenship.

. . .

... [T]his Court has rejected the majority's pinched view of how to read our Constitution.... The Framers (both in 1788 and 1868) understood that the world changes. So they did not define rights by reference to the specific practices existing at the time. Instead, the Framers defined rights in general terms, to permit future evolution in their scope and meaning. And over the course of our history, this Court has taken up the Framers' invitation. It has kept true to the Framers' principles by applying them in new ways, responsive to new societal understandings and conditions.

Nowhere has that approach been more prevalent than in construing the majestic but open-ended words of the Fourteenth Amendment—the guarantees of "liberty" and "equality" for all.... The Constitution does not freeze for all time the original view of what those rights guarantee, or how they apply.

That does not mean anything goes. The majority wishes people to think there are but two alternatives: (1) accept the original applications of the Fourteenth Amendment and no others, or (2) surrender to judges' "own ardent views," ungrounded in law, about the "liberty that Americans should enjoy." . . . [A]pplications of liberty and equality can evolve while remaining grounded in constitutional principles, constitutional history, and constitutional precedents. . . .

. . . *Casey* explicitly rejected the present majority's method. "[T]he specific practices of States at the time of the adoption of the Fourteenth Amendment," *Casey* stated, do not "mark[ ] the outer limits of the substantive sphere of liberty which the Fourteenth Amendment protects." 505 U.S., at 848. To hold otherwise—as the majority does today— "would be inconsistent with our law." *Id.*, at 847. . . . Whatever was true in 1868, "[i]t is settled now, as it was when the Court heard arguments in Roe v. Wade, that the Constitution places limits on a State's right to interfere with a person's most basic decisions about family and parenthood." *Id.*, at 849.

. . . It was settled at the time of *Roe*, settled at the time of *Casey*, and settled yesterday that the Constitution places limits on a State's power to assert control over an individual's body and most personal decisionmaking. A multitude of decisions supporting that principle led to *Roe*'s recognition and *Casey*'s reaffirmation of the right to choose; and *Roe* and *Casey* in turn supported additional protections for intimate and familial relations. . . . The Court's precedents about bodily autonomy, sexual and familial relations, and procreation are all interwoven—all part of the fabric of our constitutional law, and because that is so, of our lives. Especially women's lives, where they safeguard a right to self-determination.

And eliminating that right . . . is not taking a "neutral" position, as Justice Kavanaugh tries to argue. . . . [W]hen it comes to rights, the Court does not act "neutrally" when it leaves everything up to the States. Rather, the Court acts neutrally when it protects the right against all comers. . . . When the Court decimates a right women have held for 50 years, the Court is not being "scrupulously neutral." It is instead taking sides: against women who wish to exercise the right, and for States (like Mississippi) that want to bar them from doing so. Justice Kavanaugh['s] . . . position . . . is [a] brook-no-compromise refusal to recognize a woman's right to choose, from the first day of a pregnancy. . . .

[The dissenters examined "the line of this Court's cases protecting 'bodily integrity' "; noted that "an American woman is 14 times more likely to die by carrying a pregnancy to term than by having an abortion"; and observed that the "majority does not say—which is itself ominous—whether a State may prevent a woman from obtaining an abortion when she and her doctor have determined it is a needed medical treatment." They then emphasized that "*Roe* and *Casey* fit neatly into a long line of decisions protecting from government intrusion a wealth of private choices about family matters, child rearing, intimate relationships, and procreation."]

. . . Throughout our history, the sphere of protected liberty has expanded, bringing in individuals formerly excluded. In that way, the constitutional values of liberty and equality go hand in hand; they do not inhabit the hermetically sealed containers the majority portrays. . . .

Casey . . . understood, as the majority today does not, that the men who ratified the Fourteenth Amendment and wrote the state laws of the time did not view women as full and equal citizens. . . . And equal citizenship, *Casey* realized, was inescapably connected to reproductive rights. "The ability of women to participate equally" in the "life of the Nation"—in all its economic, social, political, and legal aspects—"has been facilitated by their ability to control their reproductive lives." . . . Without the ability to decide whether and when to have children, women could not—in the way men took for granted—

determine how they would live their lives, and how they would contribute to the society around them.

. . .

Faced with all these connections between *Roe/Casey* and judicial decisions recognizing other constitutional rights, the majority tells everyone . . . [i]t can . . . neatly extract the right to choose from the constitutional edifice without affecting any associated rights. . . .

. . .

Even placing the concurrence to the side, the assurance in today's opinion still does not work. . . . According to the majority, no liberty interest is present—because (and only because) the law offered no protection to the woman's choice in the 19th century. But here is the rub. The law also did not then (and would not for ages) protect a wealth of other things. It did not protect the rights recognized in *Lawrence* and *Obergefell* to same-sex intimacy and marriage. It did not protect the right recognized in *Loving* to marry across racial lines. It did not protect the right recognized in *Griswold* to contraceptive use. For that matter, it did not protect the right recognized in Skinner v. Oklahoma ex rel. Williamson, 316 U.S. 535 (1942), not to be sterilized without consent. So if the majority is right in its legal analysis, all those decisions were wrong, and all those matters properly belong to the States too—whatever the particular state interests involved. And if that is true, it is impossible to understand (as a matter of logic and principle) how the majority can say that its opinion today does not threaten—does not even "undermine"—any number of other constitutional rights.

. . .

. . . Our law . . . for decades upon decades . . . has considered fundamental constitutional principles, the whole course of the Nation's history and traditions, and the step-by-step evolution of the Court's precedents. It is disciplined but not static. It relies on accumulated judgments, not just the sentiments of one long-ago generation of men (who themselves believed, and drafted the Constitution to reflect, that the world progresses). And by doing so, it includes those excluded from that olden conversation, rather than perpetuating its bounds.

. . . Today's decision strips women of agency over what even the majority agrees is a contested and contestable moral issue. It forces her to carry out the State's will, whatever the circumstances and whatever the harm it will wreak on her and her family. In the Fourteenth Amendment's terms, it takes away her liberty. Even before we get to *stare decisis*, we dissent.

II

By overruling *Roe*, *Casey*, and more than 20 cases reaffirming or applying the constitutional right to abortion, the majority abandons *stare decisis*, a principle central to the rule of law. . . .

. . .

. . . Nothing—and in particular, no significant legal or factual change—supports overturning a half-century of settled law giving women control over their reproductive lives.

First, for all the reasons we have given, *Roe* and *Casey* were correct. . . . However divisive, a right is not at the people's mercy.

. . . *Casey* reached the only conclusion possible—that *stare decisis* operates powerfully here. It still does. The standards *Roe* and *Casey* set out are perfectly workable. No changes in either law or fact have eroded the two decisions. And tens of millions of American women have relied, and continue to rely, on the right to choose. So under traditional *stare decisis* principles, the majority has no special justification for the harm it causes.

. . . The majority has overruled *Roe* and *Casey* for one and only one reason: because it has always despised them, and now it has the votes to discard them. The majority thereby substitutes a rule by judges for the rule of law.

Contrary to the majority's view, there is nothing unworkable about *Casey's* "undue burden" standard. . . .

General standards, like the undue burden standard, are ubiquitous in the law, and particularly in constitutional adjudication. . . . So, for example, the Court asks about undue or substantial burdens on speech, on voting, and on interstate commerce. . . . The *Casey* undue burden standard is the same. . . .

. . .

When overruling constitutional precedent, the Court has almost always pointed to major legal or factual changes undermining a decision's original basis. . . . Certainly, that was so of the main examples the majority cites: Brown v. Board of Education, . . . and West Coast Hotel Co. v. Parrish . . . . The majority briefly invokes the current controversy over abortion. But it has to acknowledge that the same dispute has existed for decades: Conflict over abortion is not a change but a constant. . . .

Subsequent legal developments have only reinforced *Roe* and *Casey*. . . . *Roe* and *Casey* are inextricably interwoven with decades of precedent about the meaning of the Fourteenth Amendment. . . .

Moreover, no subsequent factual developments have undermined *Roe* and *Casey*. Women continue to experience unplanned pregnancies and unexpected developments in pregnancies. Pregnancies continue to have enormous physical, social, and economic consequences. . . . For some women, pregnancy and childbirth can mean life-altering physical ailments or even death. . . . Experts estimate that a ban on abortions increases maternal mortality by 21 percent, with white women facing a 13 percent increase in maternal mortality while black women face a 33 percent increase. Pregnancy and childbirth may also impose large-scale financial costs. The majority briefly refers to arguments about changes in laws relating to healthcare coverage, pregnancy discrimination, and family leave. Many women, however, still do not have adequate healthcare coverage before and after pregnancy; and, even when insurance coverage is available, healthcare services may be far away. Women also continue to face pregnancy discrimination that interferes with their ability to earn a living. Paid family leave remains inaccessible to many who need it most. . . .

The majority briefly notes the growing prevalence of safe haven laws and demand for adoption, but, to the degree that these are changes at all, they too are irrelevant. Neither reduces the health risks or financial costs of going through pregnancy and childbirth. Moreover, the choice to give up parental rights after giving birth is altogether different from the choice not to carry a pregnancy to term. The reality is that few women denied an abortion will choose adoption. The vast majority will continue, just as in *Roe* and *Casey's* time, to shoulder the costs of childrearing. Whether or not they choose to parent, they will experience the profound loss of autonomy and dignity that coerced pregnancy and birth always impose.

. . .

In sum, the majority can point to neither legal nor factual developments in support of its decision. . . .

. . . [T]he majority invokes . . . West Coast Hotel Co. v. Parrish and Brown v. Board of Education. But those decisions, unlike today's, responded to changed law and to changed facts and attitudes that had taken hold throughout society. As *Casey* recognized, the two cases are relevant only to show—by stark contrast—how unjustified overturning the right to choose is.

. . . In *West Coast Hotel*, the Court . . . recognize[ed] through the lens of experience the flaws of existing legal doctrine. . . . The havoc the Depression had worked on ordinary Americans, the Court noted, was "common knowledge through the length and breadth of the land." . . . And . . . the law had also changed. In several decisions, the Court had started to recognize the power of States to implement economic policies designed to enhance their citizens' economic well-being. . . .

. . . Whatever might have been thought in *Plessy*'s time, the *Brown* Court explained, both experience and "modern authority" showed the "detrimental effect[s]" of state-sanctioned segregation: It "affect[ed] [children's] hearts and minds in a way unlikely ever to be undone.". . . By that point, too, the law had begun to reflect that understanding. . . . Changed facts and changed law required *Plessy*'s end.

. . . [W]e are not saying that a decision can never be overruled just because it is terribly wrong. Take West Virginia Bd. of Ed. v. Barnette, . . . which the majority also relies on. That overruling took place just three years after the initial decision, before any notable reliance interests had developed. It happened as well because individual Justices changed their minds, not because a new majority wanted to undo the decisions of their predecessors. Both *Barnette* and *Brown*, moreover, share another feature setting them apart from the Court's ruling today. They protected individual rights with a strong basis in the Constitution's most fundamental commitments; they did not, as the majority does here, take away a right that individuals have held, and relied on, for 50 years. . . .

Casey itself addressed both *West Coast Hotel* and *Brown*, and found that neither supported *Roe*'s overruling. . . .

. . . *Roe* and *Casey* continue to reflect, not diverge from, broad trends in American society. It is, of course, true that many Americans, including many women, opposed those decisions when issued and do so now as well. Yet the fact remains: *Roe* and *Casey* were the product of a profound and ongoing change in women's roles in the latter part of the 20th century. . . . By 1992, when the Court decided *Casey*, the traditional view of a woman's role as only a wife and mother was "no longer consistent with our understanding of the family, the individual, or the Constitution." . . . Under that charter, *Casey* understood, women must take their place as full and equal citizens. And for that to happen, women must have control over their reproductive decisions. Nothing since *Casey*—no changed law, no changed fact—has undermined that promise.

The reasons for retaining *Roe* and *Casey* gain further strength from the overwhelming reliance interests those decisions have created. . . .

. . . [A]ll women now of childbearing age have grown up expecting that they would be able to avail themselves of *Roe*'s and *Casey*'s protections.

The disruption of overturning *Roe* and *Casey* will therefore be profound. Abortion is a common medical procedure and a familiar experience in women's lives. About 18 percent of pregnancies in this country end in abortion, and about one quarter of American women will have an abortion before the age of 45. Those numbers reflect the predictable and life-changing effects of carrying a pregnancy, giving birth, and becoming a parent. As *Casey* understood, people today rely on their ability to control and time pregnancies when making countless life decisions: where to live, whether and how to invest in education or careers, how to allocate financial resources, and how to approach intimate and family relationships. Women may count on abortion access for when contraception fails. They may count on abortion access for when contraception cannot be used, for example, if they were raped. They may count on abortion for when something changes in the midst of a pregnancy, whether it involves family or financial circumstances, unanticipated medical complications, or heartbreaking fetal diagnoses. Taking away the right to abortion, as the majority does today, destroys all those individual plans and expectations. In so doing, it diminishes women's opportunities to participate fully and equally in the Nation's political, social, and economic life. . . .

. . . The majority proclaims that " 'reproductive planning could take virtually immediate account of any sudden restoration of state authority to ban abortions.' " The facts are: 45 percent of pregnancies in the United States are unplanned. . . . Not all sexual activity is consensual . . . . The Mississippi law at issue here, for example, has no exception for rape or incest, even for underage women. Finally, the majority ignores . . . that some women decide to have an abortion because their circumstances change during a pregnancy. . . . Events can occur after conception, from unexpected medical risks to changes in family circumstances, which profoundly alter what it means to carry a pregnancy to term. . . . For those who will now have to undergo that pregnancy, the loss of *Roe* and *Casey* could be disastrous.

That is especially so for women without money. . . . Many will endure the costs and risks of pregnancy and giving birth against their wishes. Others will turn in desperation to illegal and unsafe abortions. . . .

Finally, the expectation of reproductive control is integral to many women's identity and their place in the Nation. . . .

. . . To allow a State to exert control over one of "the most intimate and personal choices" a woman may make is not only to affect the course of her life, monumental as those effects might be. . . . It is to alter her "views of [herself]" and her understanding of her "place[] in society" as someone with the recognized dignity and authority to make these choices. . . . Women have relied on *Roe* and *Casey* in this way for 50 years. . . . When *Roe* and *Casey* disappear, the loss of power, control, and dignity will be immense.

The Court's failure to perceive the whole swath of expectations *Roe* and *Casey* created reflects an impoverished view of reliance. . . .

. . .

. . . The majority's refusal even to consider the life-altering consequences of reversing *Roe* and *Casey* is a stunning indictment of its decision.

One last consideration counsels against the majority's ruling: the very controversy surrounding *Roe* and *Casey*. . . . *Casey* carefully assessed changed circumstances (none) and reliance interests (profound). . . . True enough that *Casey* took notice of the "national controversy" about abortion . . . . But *Casey*'s reason for acknowledging public conflict was the exact opposite of what the majority insinuates. *Casey* addressed the national controversy in order to emphasize how important it was, in that case of all cases, for the Court to stick to the law. Would that today's majority had done likewise.

. . .

. . . [A]s *Casey* recognized, weakening *stare decisis* in a hotly contested case like this one calls into question this Court's commitment to legal principle. It makes the

Court appear not restrained but aggressive, not modest but grasping. In all those ways, today's decision takes aim, we fear, at the rule of law.

. . .

. . . In overruling *Roe* and *Casey*, this Court betrays its guiding principles.

With sorrow—for this Court, but more, for the many millions of American women who have today lost a fundamental constitutional protection—we dissent.

3.   THE SECOND AMENDMENT AND PERSONAL LIBERTY

Page 709. Add at end of chapter:

New York State Rifle & Pistol Association, Inc. v. Bruen
597 U.S. ___, 142 S.Ct. 2111 (2022).

■ JUSTICE THOMAS delivered the opinion of the Court.

In District of Columbia v. Heller, 554 U.S. 570 (2008), and McDonald v. Chicago, 561 U.S. 742 (2010), we recognized that the Second and Fourteenth Amendments protect the right of an ordinary, law-abiding citizen to possess a handgun in the home for self-defense. In this case, petitioners and respondents agree that ordinary, law-abiding citizens have a similar right to carry handguns publicly for their self-defense. We too agree, and now hold . . . that the Second and Fourteenth Amendments protect an individual's right to carry a handgun for self-defense outside the home.

The parties nevertheless dispute whether New York's licensing regime respects th[at] constitutional right . . . . In 43 States, the government issues licenses to carry based on objective criteria. But in six States, including New York, the government further conditions issuance of a license to carry on a citizen's showing of some additional special need. Because . . . New York issues public-carry licenses only when an applicant demonstrates a special need for self-defense, we conclude that the State's licensing regime violates the Constitution.

I

A

[In 1911, New York's "Sullivan Law" imposed a criminal prohibition on "the possession of all handguns—concealed or otherwise—without a government-issued license." In 1913, the State clarified that "Magistrates could 'issue to [a] person a license to have and carry concealed a pistol or revolver without regard to employment or place of possessing such weapon' only if that person proved 'good moral character' and 'proper cause.' " The current licensing scheme is similar, criminalizing unlicensed possession of "any firearm" inside or outside the home, and providing in particular that "possessing a loaded firearm outside one's home or place of business without a license is a felony punishable by up to 15 years in prison." A license applicant who "wants to carry a firearm outside his home or place of business for self-defense . . . must obtain an unrestricted license to 'have and carry' a concealed 'pistol or revolver.' " That requires "prov[ing] that 'proper cause exists' to issue it." Otherwise, the applicant "can receive only a 'restricted' license for public carry, which allows him to carry a firearm for a limited purpose, such as hunting, target shooting, or employment."]

No New York statute defines "proper cause." But New York courts have held that an applicant shows proper cause only if he can "demonstrate a special need for self-protection distinguishable from that of the general community." E.g., In re Klenosky

.... This "special need" standard is demanding. For example, living or working in an area " 'noted for criminal activity' " does not suffice.... Rather, New York courts generally require evidence "of particular threats, attacks or other extraordinary danger to personal safety." ...

[Application denials by licensing officers (who are judicial or law enforcement officials) are subject to "limited" judicial review for "arbitrary and capricious" decisions.]

... [T]he vast majority of States—43 by our count—are "shall issue" jurisdictions, where authorities must issue concealed-carry licenses whenever applicants satisfy certain threshold requirements, without granting licensing officials discretion to deny licenses based on a perceived lack of need or suitability. Only six States and the District of Columbia have "may issue" licensing laws, under which authorities have discretion to deny concealed-carry licenses even when the applicant satisfies the statutory criteria, usually because the applicant has not demonstrated cause or suitability for the relevant license. Aside from New York, ... only California, the District of Columbia, Hawaii, Maryland, Massachusetts, and New Jersey have analogues to the "proper cause" standard. All ... have been upheld by the Courts of Appeals, save for the District of Columbia's ....

[Two law-abiding applicants from Rensselaer County were denied unrestricted licenses for failure to demonstrate the requisite "proper cause" (i.e., not establishing a "unique need for self-defense"), prompting this suit by them and the New York State Rifle & Pistol Association, Inc., a public-interest group organized to defend the Second Amendment rights of New Yorkers of which they are members. They sued "the superintendent of the New York State Police, who oversees the enforcement of the State's licensing laws, and a New York Supreme Court justice, who oversees the processing of licensing applications in Rensselaer County[,]" for violating their Second and Fourteenth Amendment rights. Both the District Court and the Court of Appeals rejected their challenge.]

II

... In the years since [*Heller* and *McDonald*], the Courts of Appeals have coalesced around a "two-step" framework for analyzing Second Amendment challenges that combines history with means-end scrutiny.

Today, we decline to adopt that two-part approach. In keeping with *Heller*, we hold that when the Second Amendment's plain text covers an individual's conduct, the Constitution presumptively protects that conduct. To justify its regulation, the government may not simply posit that the regulation promotes an important interest. Rather, the government must demonstrate that the regulation is consistent with this Nation's historical tradition of firearm regulation. Only if a firearm regulation is consistent with this Nation's historical tradition may a court conclude that the individual's conduct falls outside the Second Amendment's "unqualified command." Konigsberg v. State Bar of Cal., 366 U.S. 36, 50, n. 10 (1961).

. . .

Despite the popularity of this two-step approach, it is one step too many. Step one of the predominant framework is broadly consistent with *Heller*, which demands a test rooted in the Second Amendment's text, as informed by history. But *Heller* and *McDonald* do not support applying means-end scrutiny in the Second Amendment context. Instead, the government must affirmatively prove that its firearms regulation is part of the historical tradition that delimits the outer bounds of the right to keep and bear arms.

. . .

. . . *Heller*'s methodology centered on constitutional text and history. Whether it came to defining the character of the right (individual or militia dependent), suggesting the outer limits of the right, or assessing the constitutionality of a particular regulation, *Heller* relied on text and history. It did not invoke any means-end test such as strict or intermediate scrutiny.

. . .

Not only did *Heller* decline to engage in means-end scrutiny generally, but it also specifically ruled out the intermediate-scrutiny test that respondents and the United States now urge us to adopt. . . .

In sum, the Courts of Appeals' second step is inconsistent with *Heller*'s historical approach and its rejection of means-end scrutiny. We reiterate that the standard for applying the Second Amendment is as follows: When the Second Amendment's plain text covers an individual's conduct, the Constitution presumptively protects that conduct. The government must then justify its regulation by demonstrating that it is consistent with the Nation's historical tradition of firearm regulation. . . .

This Second Amendment standard accords with how we protect other constitutional rights. Take, for instance, the freedom of speech in the First Amendment, to which *Heller* repeatedly compared the right to keep and bear arms. . . .

. . . If a litigant asserts the right in court to "be confronted with the witnesses against him," U.S. Const., Amdt. 6, we require courts to consult history to determine the scope of that right. . . . Similarly, when a litigant claims a violation of his rights under the Establishment Clause, Members of this Court "loo[k] to history for guidance." American Legion v. American Humanist Assn., 588 U.S. ___, ___ (2019) (plurality opinion) (slip op., at 25). We adopt a similar approach here.

. . . [R]eliance on history to inform the meaning of constitutional text—especially text meant to codify a *pre-existing* right—is, in our view, more legitimate, and more administrable, than asking judges to "make difficult empirical judgments" about "the costs and benefits of firearms restrictions," especially given their "lack [of] expertise" in the field. . . .[6]

. . .

The test that we set forth in *Heller* and apply today requires courts to assess whether modern firearms regulations are consistent with the Second Amendment's text and historical understanding. In some cases, that inquiry will be fairly straightforward. For instance, when a challenged regulation addresses a general societal problem that has persisted since the 18th century, the lack of a distinctly similar historical regulation addressing that problem is relevant evidence that the challenged regulation is inconsistent with the Second Amendment. Likewise, if earlier generations addressed the societal problem, but did so through materially different means, that also could be

---

[6] The dissent claims that *Heller*'s text-and-history test will prove unworkable compared to means-end scrutiny in part because judges are relatively ill equipped to "resolv[e] difficult historical questions" or engage in "searching historical surveys." . . . We are unpersuaded. The job of judges is not to resolve historical questions in the abstract; it is to resolve legal questions presented in particular cases or controversies. That "legal inquiry is a refined subset" of a broader "historical inquiry," and it relies on "various evidentiary principles and default rules" to resolve uncertainties. W. Baude & S. Sachs, Originalism and the Law of the Past, 37 L. & Hist. Rev. 809, 810–811 (2019). For example, "[i]n our adversarial system of adjudication, we follow the principle of party presentation." United States v. Sineneng-Smith, . . .). Courts are thus entitled to decide a case based on the historical record compiled by the parties.

evidence that a modern regulation is unconstitutional. And if some jurisdictions actually attempted to enact analogous regulations during this timeframe, but those proposals were rejected on constitutional grounds, that rejection surely would provide some probative evidence of unconstitutionality.

. . .

New York's proper-cause requirement concerns the same alleged societal problem addressed in *Heller*: "handgun violence," primarily in "urban area[s]." . . . Following the course charted by *Heller*, we will consider whether "historical precedent" from before, during, and even after the founding evinces a comparable tradition of regulation. . . .[W]e find no such tradition in the historical materials that respondents and their *amici* have brought to bear on that question. See Part III-B, *infra*.

While the historical analogies here and in *Heller* are relatively simple to draw, other cases implicating unprecedented societal concerns or dramatic technological changes may require a more nuanced approach. The regulatory challenges posed by firearms today are not always the same as those that preoccupied the Founders in 1791 or the Reconstruction generation in 1868. . . . Although its meaning is fixed according to the understandings of those who ratified it, the Constitution can, and must, apply to circumstances beyond those the Founders specifically anticipated. . . .

. . . Thus, even though the Second Amendment's definition of "arms" is fixed according to its historical understanding, that general definition covers modern instruments that facilitate armed self-defense. . . .

Much like we use history to determine which modern "arms" are protected by the Second Amendment, so too does history guide our consideration of modern regulations that were unimaginable at the founding. When confronting such present-day firearm regulations, this historical inquiry that courts must conduct will often involve reasoning by analogy—a commonplace task for any lawyer or judge. Like all analogical reasoning, determining whether a historical regulation is a proper analogue for a distinctly modern firearm regulation requires a determination of whether the two regulations are "relevantly similar." . . .

While we do not now provide an exhaustive survey of the features that render regulations relevantly similar under the Second Amendment, we do think that *Heller* and *McDonald* point toward at least two metrics: how and why the regulations burden a law-abiding citizen's right to armed self-defense. . . . Therefore, whether modern and historical regulations impose a comparable burden on the right of armed self-defense and whether that burden is comparably justified are " *'central'* " considerations when engaging in an analogical inquiry. *McDonald*, ...

To be clear, analogical reasoning under the Second Amendment is neither a regulatory straightjacket nor a regulatory blank check. On the one hand, courts should not "uphold every modern law that remotely resembles a historical analogue," because doing so "risk[s] endorsing outliers that our ancestors would never have accepted." . . . On the other hand, analogical reasoning requires only that the government identify a well-established and representative historical *analogue*, not a historical *twin*. So even if a modern-day regulation is not a dead ringer for historical precursors, it still may be analogous enough to pass constitutional muster.

Consider, for example, *Heller*'s discussion of "longstanding" "laws forbidding the carrying of firearms in sensitive places such as schools and government buildings." . . . Although the historical record yields relatively few 18th- and 19th-century "sensitive places" where weapons were altogether prohibited—e.g., legislative assemblies, polling places, and courthouses—we are also aware of no disputes regarding the lawfulness of such prohibitions. . . . We therefore can assume it settled that these locations were "sensitive places" where arms carrying could be prohibited consistent with the Second Amendment. And courts can use analogies to those historical regulations of "sensitive places" to determine that modern regulations prohibiting the carry of firearms in new and analogous sensitive places are constitutionally permissible.

Although we have no occasion to comprehensively define "sensitive places" in this case, we do think respondents err in their attempt to characterize New York's proper-cause requirement as a "sensitive-place" law. In their view, "sensitive places" where the government may lawfully disarm law-abiding citizens include all "places where people typically congregate and where law-enforcement and other public-safety professionals are presumptively available." . . . It is true that people sometimes congregate in "sensitive places," and it is likewise true that law enforcement professionals are usually presumptively available in those locations. But expanding the category of "sensitive places" simply to all places of public congregation that are not isolated from law enforcement defines the category of "sensitive places" far too broadly. Respondents' argument would in effect exempt cities from the Second Amendment and would eviscerate the general right to publicly carry arms for self-defense that we discuss in detail below. See Part III-B, *infra*. Put simply, there is no historical basis for New York to effectively declare the island of Manhattan a "sensitive place" simply because it is crowded and protected generally by the New York City Police Department.

. . .

III

Having made the constitutional standard endorsed in *Heller* more explicit, we now apply [it.]

A

. . . We . . . turn to whether the plain text of the Second Amendment protects . . . carrying handguns publicly for self-defense.

We have little difficulty concluding that it does. Respondents do not dispute this. . . . Nor could they. Nothing in the Second Amendment's text draws a home/public distinction with respect to the right to keep and bear arms. . . .

Th[e] definition of "bear" naturally encompasses public carry. Most gun owners do not wear a holstered pistol at their hip in their bedroom or while sitting at the dinner table. Although individuals often "keep" firearms in their home, at the ready for self-defense, most do not "bear" (i.e., carry) them in the home beyond moments of actual confrontation. To confine the right to "bear" arms to the home would nullify half of the Second Amendment's operative protections.

Moreover, confining the right to "bear" arms to the home would make little sense given that self-defense is "the *central component* of the [Second Amendment] right itself." . . . After all, the Second Amendment guarantees an "individual right to possess and carry weapons in case of confrontation," *Heller*, . . . and confrontation can surely take place outside the home.

. . . Many Americans hazard greater danger outside the home than in it. . . . The text of the Second Amendment reflects that reality.

The Second Amendment's plain text thus presumptively guarantees . . . a right to "bear" arms in public for self-defense.

B

Conceding that the Second Amendment guarantees a general right to public carry, . . . respondents instead claim that the Amendment "permits a State to condition handgun carrying in areas 'frequented by the general public' on a showing of a non-speculative need for armed self-defense in those areas," . . . .[8] To support that claim, the burden falls on respondents to show that New York's proper-cause requirement is consistent with this Nation's historical tradition of firearm regulation. . . .

Respondents appeal to a variety of historical sources from the late 1200s to the early 1900s. We categorize these periods as follows: (1) medieval to early modern England; (2) the American Colonies and the early Republic; (3) antebellum America; (4) Reconstruction; and (5) the late-19th and early-20th centuries.

[Justice Thomas noted a number of considerations that might affect assessment of historical evidence and historical method related to proper understanding of the texts of the Second and Fourteenth Amendment rights at issue, but he also concluded that for the decision of this case "the public understanding of the right to keep and bear arms in both 1791 and 1868 was, for all relevant purposes, the same with respect to public carry."]

. . . Throughout modern Anglo-American history, the right to keep and bear arms in public has traditionally been subject to well-defined restrictions governing the intent for which one could carry arms, the manner of carry, or the exceptional circumstances under which one could not carry arms. But apart from a handful of late 19th-century jurisdictions, the historical record compiled by respondents does not demonstrate a tradition of broadly prohibiting the public carry of commonly used firearms for self-defense. Nor is there any such historical tradition limiting public carry only to those law-abiding citizens who demonstrate a special need for self-defense.[9] We conclude that respondents have failed to meet their burden to identify an American tradition justifying New York's proper-cause requirement. Under *Heller*'s text-and-history standard, the proper-cause requirement is therefore unconstitutional.

[Justice Thomas's lengthy analysis of the historical record included a number of observations and conclusions. He found "English history . . . ambiguous at best and . . . not sufficiently probative to defend New York's proper-cause requirement." The 1328 Statute of Northampton, which prohibited "go[ing] . . . armed" was not the sweeping restriction on public carry of self-defense weapons that would ultimately be adopted in Colonial America and justify "onerous public-carry regulations", as respondents argued, for it had "little bearing on the Second Amendment adopted in 1791" and respondents "point[ed] to no evidence suggesting the Statute applied to the smaller medieval weapons that strike us as most analogous to modern handguns." Moreover, "by the time

---

[8] The dissent claims that we cannot answer the question presented without giving respondents the opportunity to develop an evidentiary record fleshing out "how New York's law is administered in practice, how much discretion licensing officers in New York possess, or whether the proper cause standard differs across counties." We disagree. . . . [W]e conclude below that a State may not prevent law-abiding citizens from publicly carrying handguns because they have not demonstrated a special need for self-defense. . . . That conclusion does not depend upon any of the factual questions raised by the dissent. . . .

[9] To be clear, nothing in our analysis should be interpreted to suggest the unconstitutionality of the 43 States' "shall-issue" licensing regimes, under which "a general desire for self-defense is sufficient to obtain a [permit]." . . . [I]t appears that these shall-issue regimes, which often require applicants to undergo a background check or pass a firearms safety course, are designed to ensure only that those bearing arms in the jurisdiction are, in fact, "law-abiding, responsible citizens." . . . That said, because any permitting scheme can be put toward abusive ends, we do not rule out constitutional challenges to shall-issue regimes where, for example, lengthy wait times in processing license applications or exorbitant fees deny ordinary citizens their right to public carry.

Englishmen began to arrive in America in the early 1600s, the public carry of handguns was no longer widely proscribed." The Statute of Northampton "was no obstacle to public carry for self-defense in the decades leading to the founding." Ultimately, "we cannot conclude from this historical record that, by the time of the founding, English law would have justified restricting the right to publicly bear arms suited for self-defense only to those who demonstrate some special need for self-protection."

[With respect to "the history of the Colonies and early Republic, . . . there is little evidence of an early American practice of regulating public carry by the general public." Respondents "point to only three restrictions on public carry" in the colonial era—an insufficient showing of a tradition of public-carry regulation in any event—but also "[f]ar from banning the carrying of any class of firearms, they merely codified the existing common-law offense of bearing arms to terrorize the people, as had the Statute of Northampton itself." Besides, "[a]t most, respondents can show that colonial legislatures sometimes prohibited the carrying of 'dangerous and unusual weapons'—a fact we already acknowledged in *Heller*. . . . Drawing from this historical tradition, we explained there that the Second Amendment protects only the carrying of weapons that are those 'in common use at the time,' as opposed to those that 'are highly unusual in society at large.' " And "[w]hatever the likelihood that handguns were considered 'dangerous and unusual' during the colonial period, they are indisputably in 'common use' for self-defense today. . . . Thus, even if these colonial laws prohibited the carrying of handguns because they were considered 'dangerous and unusual weapons' in the 1690s, they provide no justification for laws restricting the public carry of weapons that are unquestionably in common use today." Especially since the three statutes cited have in common that they "prohibit bearing arms in a way that spreads 'fear' or 'terror' among the people[,]" all told, "in the century leading up to the Second Amendment and in the first decade after its adoption, there is no historical basis for concluding that the pre-existing right enshrined in the Second Amendment permitted broad prohibitions on all forms of public carry."

[After ratification of the Second Amendment, three categories of public-carry restrictions proliferated during the antebellum period—common-law offenses, statutory prohibitions, and "surety" statutes—but "[n]one of [them] imposed a substantial burden on public carry analogous to the burden created by New York's restrictive licensing regime." The common law offenses "of 'affray' or going armed 'to the terror of the people' continued to impose some limits on firearm carry in the antebellum period. But as with the earlier periods, there is no evidence indicating that these common-law limitations impaired the right of the general population to peaceable public carry." Similarly, interpretations of the statutory prohibitions revealed "a consensus that States could *not* ban public carry altogether." Finally, the surety statutes adopted by many jurisdictions in the mid-19th century "required certain individuals to post bond before carrying weapons in public." But they "were not bans on public carry, and they typically targeted only those threatening to do harm." Justice Thomas elaborated as follows:]

Contrary to respondents' position, these "reasonable-cause laws" in no way represented the "direct precursor" to the proper-cause requirement. . . . While New York presumes that individuals have no public carry right without a showing of heightened need, the surety statutes presumed that individuals had a right to public carry that could be burdened only if another could make out a specific showing of "reasonable cause to fear an injury, or breach of the peace." Mass. Rev. Stat., ch. 134, § 16 (1836). . . .

Thus, unlike New York's regime, a showing of special need was required only *after* an individual was reasonably accused of intending to injure another or breach the peace. And, even then, proving special need simply avoided a fee rather than a ban. . . .

[Justice Thomas further said that "we have little reason to think that the hypothetical possibility of posting a bond would have prevented anyone from carrying a firearm for self-defense in the 19th century[,]" and "[b]esides, respondents offer little evidence that authorities ever enforced surety laws." Then he offered this summary:]

The historical evidence from antebellum America does demonstrate that *the manner* of public carry was subject to reasonable regulation. Under the common law, individuals could not carry deadly weapons in a manner likely to terrorize others. Similarly, although surety statutes did not directly restrict public carry, they did provide financial incentives for responsible arms carrying. Finally, States could lawfully eliminate one kind of public carry—concealed carry—so long as they left open the option to carry openly.

None of these historical limitations on the right to bear arms approach New York's proper-cause requirement because none operated to prevent law-abiding citizens with ordinary self-defense needs from carrying arms in public for that purpose.

[As for the Reconstruction era, "[e]vidence from around the adoption of the Fourteenth Amendment also fails to support respondents' position." Justice Thomas referenced the congressionally created Freedmen's Bureau, which "regularly kept [Congress] abreast of the dangers to blacks and Union men in the postbellum South. The reports described how blacks used publicly carried weapons to defend themselves and their communities." He also noted that Congress's extension in 1868 of the 1866 Freedmen's Bureau Act "reaffirmed that freedmen were entitled to the 'full and equal benefit of all laws and proceedings concerning personal liberty [and] personal security . . . *including the constitutional right to keep and bear arms.*' " He conceded that "even during Reconstruction the right to keep and bear arms had limits. But those limits were consistent with a right of the public to peaceably carry handguns for self-defense." Finally, although he acknowledged that a Texas statute and "two late-19th-century cases in Texas" did "support New York's proper-cause requirement," the statute and those cases "are outliers. In fact, only one other State, West Virginia, adopted a similar public-carry statute before 1900." Still, "[i]n the end, while we recognize the support that postbellum Texas provides for respondents' view, we will not give disproportionate weight to a single state statute and a pair of state-court decisions."

[As for "the slight uptick in gun regulation during the late-19th century—principally in the Western Territories"—that evidence suffered from "several serious flaws even beyond their temporal distance from the founding." First, they represented only "a handful of temporary territorial laws that were enacted nearly a century after the Second Amendment's adoption, governed less than 1% of the American population, and also 'contradic[ted] the overwhelming weight' of other, more contemporaneous historical evidence. *Heller*, ..." Second, "because these territorial laws were rarely subject to judicial scrutiny, we do not know the basis of their perceived legality." Hence, "[a]bsent any evidence explaining *why* these unprecedented prohibitions on *all* public carry were understood to comport with the Second Amendment, we fail to see how they inform 'the origins and continuing significance of the Amendment.' " And finally, "these territorial restrictions deserve little weight because they were—consistent with the transitory nature of territorial government—short lived. Some were held unconstitutional shortly after passage. . . . Others did not survive a Territory's admission to the Union as a State." As a result, "they appear more as passing regulatory efforts by not-yet-mature jurisdictions on the way to statehood, rather than part of an enduring American tradition of state regulation."]

At the end of this long journey through the Anglo-American history of public carry, we conclude that respondents have not met their burden to identify an American tradition justifying the State's proper-cause requirement. The Second Amendment guaranteed to "all Americans" the right to bear commonly used arms in public subject to certain reasonable, well-defined restrictions. *Heller*, ... Those restrictions, for example, limited the intent for which one could carry arms, the manner by which one carried arms, or the exceptional circumstances under which one could not carry arms, such as before justices of the peace and other government officials. Apart from a few late-19th century outlier jurisdictions, American governments simply have not broadly prohibited the public carry of commonly used firearms for personal defense. Nor, subject to a few late-in-time outliers, have American governments required law-abiding, responsible citizens to "demonstrate a special need for self-protection distinguishable from that of the general community" in order to carry arms in public. *Klenosky*, ...

IV

... We know of no other constitutional right that an individual may exercise only after demonstrating to government officers some special need. That is not how the First Amendment works when it comes to unpopular speech or the free exercise of religion. It is not how the Sixth Amendment works when it comes to a defendant's right to confront the witnesses against him. And it is not how the Second Amendment works when it comes to public carry for self-defense.

... We ... reverse ... and remand ... for further proceedings consistent with this opinion.

■ JUSTICE ALITO, concurring.

. . .

... Our holding decides nothing about who may lawfully possess a firearm or the requirements that must be met to buy a gun. Nor does it decide anything about the kinds of weapons that people may possess. Nor have we disturbed anything that we said in *Heller* or *McDonald* ... about restrictions that may be imposed on the possession or carrying of guns.

In light of what we have actually held, it is hard to see what legitimate purpose can possibly be served by most of the dissent's lengthy introductory section. ...

. . .

... [W]hile the dissent seemingly thinks that the ubiquity of guns and our country's high level of gun violence provide reasons for sustaining the New York law, the dissent appears not to understand that it is these very facts that cause law-abiding citizens to feel the need to carry a gun for self-defense.

... The police cannot disarm every person who acquires a gun for use in criminal activity; nor can they provide bodyguard protection for the State's nearly 20 million residents or the 8.8 million people who live in New York City. Some of these people live in high-crime neighborhoods. Some must traverse dark and dangerous streets in order to reach their homes after work or other evening activities. Some are members of groups whose members feel especially vulnerable. And some of these people reasonably believe that unless they can brandish or, if necessary, use a handgun in the case of attack, they may be murdered, raped, or suffer some other serious injury.

. . .

My final point concerns the dissent's complaint that the Court relies too heavily on history and should instead approve the sort of "means-end" analysis employed in this case by the Second Circuit. Under that approach, a court, in most cases, assesses a law's burden on the Second Amendment right and the strength of the State's interest in imposing the challenged restriction. This mode of analysis places no firm limits on the ability of judges to sustain any law restricting the possession or use of a gun. . . .

. . .

Like [the] dissent in *Heller*, the real thrust of today's dissent is that guns are bad and that States and local jurisdictions should be free to restrict them essentially as they see fit. That argument was rejected in *Heller*, and while the dissent protests that it is not rearguing *Heller*, it proceeds to do just that. . . .

. . .

■ JUSTICE KAVANAUGH, with whom THE CHIEF JUSTICE joins, concurring.

. . .

I join the Court's opinion, and I write separately to underscore two important points about the limits of the Court's decision.

First, the Court's decision does not prohibit States from imposing licensing requirements for carrying a handgun for self-defense. In particular, the Court's decision does not affect the existing licensing regimes—known as "shall-issue" regimes—that are employed in 43 States.

The Court's decision addresses only the unusual discretionary licensing regimes, known as "may-issue" regimes . . .

. . . [The] shall-issue regimes may require a license applicant to undergo fingerprinting, a background check, a mental health records check, and training in firearms handling and in laws regarding the use of force, among other possible requirements. . . . As petitioners acknowledge, shall-issue licensing regimes are constitutionally permissible, subject of course to an as-applied challenge if a shall-issue licensing regime does not operate in that manner in practice. . . .

. . .

Second, . . . the Second Amendment allows a "variety" of gun regulations. *Heller*, . . . As Justice Scalia wrote . . . in *Heller*, and Justice Alito reiterated . . . in *McDonald*:

> "Like most rights, the right secured by the Second Amendment is not unlimited. From Blackstone through the 19th-century cases, commentators and courts routinely explained that the right was not a right to keep and carry any weapon whatsoever in any manner whatsoever and for whatever purpose. . . . [N]othing in our opinion should be taken to cast doubt on longstanding prohibitions on the possession of firearms by felons and the mentally ill, or laws forbidding the carrying of firearms in sensitive places such as schools and government buildings, or laws imposing conditions and qualifications on the commercial sale of arms. [Footnote 26: We identify these presumptively lawful regulatory measures only as examples; our list does not purport to be exhaustive.]

> "We also recognize another important limitation on the right to keep and carry arms. *Miller* said, as we have explained, that the sorts of weapons protected were those in common use at the time. We think that limitation is fairly supported by the historical tradition of prohibiting the carrying of dangerous and unusual weapons." . . .

. . .

■ JUSTICE BARRETT, concurring.

. . . I write separately to highlight two methodological points that the Court does not resolve. First, the Court does not conclusively determine the manner and circumstances in which post-ratification practice may bear on the original meaning of the Constitution. . . .

Second and relatedly, the Court avoids another "ongoing scholarly debate on whether courts should primarily rely on the prevailing understanding of an individual right when the Fourteenth Amendment was ratified in 1868" or when the Bill of Rights was ratified in 1791. Here, the lack of support for New York's law in either period makes it unnecessary to choose between them. . . . So today's decision should not be understood to endorse freewheeling reliance on historical practice from the mid-to-late 19th century to establish the original meaning of the Bill of Rights. . . .

■ JUSTICE BREYER, with whom JUSTICE SOTOMAYOR and JUSTICE KAGAN join, dissenting.

. . .

. . . The Court today severely burdens States' efforts to [address some of the dangers of gun violence by] strik[ing] down a New York law regulating the public carriage of concealed handguns. In my view, that decision rests upon several serious mistakes.

First, the Court decides this case on the basis of the pleadings, without the benefit of discovery or an evidentiary record. As a result, it may well rest its decision on a mistaken understanding of how New York's law operates in practice. Second, the Court wrongly limits its analysis to focus nearly exclusively on history. It refuses to consider the government interests that justify a challenged gun regulation, regardless of how compelling those interests may be. . . . Third, the Court itself demonstrates the practical problems with its history-only approach. In applying that approach to New York's law, the Court fails to correctly identify and analyze the relevant historical facts. Only by ignoring an abundance of historical evidence supporting regulations restricting the public carriage of firearms can the Court conclude that New York's law is not "consistent with the Nation's historical tradition of firearm regulation."

In my view, when courts interpret the Second Amendment, it is constitutionally proper, indeed often necessary, for them to consider the serious dangers and consequences of gun violence that lead States to regulate firearms. . . .

[Believing that the serious problem of gun violence is relevant to how the Second Amendment limitation on the power of democratically elected officials should be understood, Justice Breyer described the nearly 400 million firearms in the United States; the nation's "disproportionately high rate of firearm-related deaths" consisting of suicides, homicides, and unintentional injuries, totaling more than 45,000 in 2020; the disproportionate harm to "communities of color, and Black communities in particular"; and growing incidents of mass shootings, road rage, violent protests, domestic disputes, and interactions with police officers. He observed that while handguns may be the most popular weapon for self-defense in the home, they are also the "most popular weapon chosen by perpetrators of violent crime." He also noted this: "Firearm-related homicides and assaults are significantly more common in urban areas than rural ones."]

Justice Alito asks why I have begun my opinion by reviewing some of the dangers and challenges posed by gun violence and what relevance that has to today's case. All of the above considerations illustrate that the question of firearm regulation presents a complex problem—one that should be solved by legislatures rather than courts. . . . Different States . . . may face different challenges because of their different geographic and demographic compositions. . . . For a variety of reasons, States may also be willing to tolerate different degrees of risk and therefore choose to balance the competing benefits and dangers of firearms differently.

. . . The primary difference between the Court's view and mine is that I believe the Amendment allows States to take account of the serious problems posed by gun violence that I have just described. I fear that the Court's interpretation ignores these significant dangers and leaves States without the ability to address them.

. . .

In describing New York's law, the Court . . . suggests that New York's licensing regime gives licensing officers too much discretion and provides too "limited" judicial review of their decisions; that the proper cause standard is too "demanding"; and that these features make New York an outlier compared to the "vast majority of States." But . . . this case comes to us at the pleading stage. The parties have not had an opportunity to conduct discovery, and no evidentiary hearings have been held to develop the record. . . . Thus, at this point, there is no record to support the Court's negative characterizations, as we know very little about how the law has actually been applied on the ground.

. . .

. . . [T]he Court . . . provides an incomplete picture because it accounts for only the number of States with "may issue" regimes, not the number of people governed by those regimes. . . . Together, these seven jurisdictions comprise about 84.4 million people and account for over a quarter of the country's population. . . . Thus, "may issue" laws can hardly be described as a marginal or outdated regime.

And there are good reasons why these seven jurisdictions may have chosen not to follow other States in shifting toward "shall issue" regimes. The seven remaining "may issue" jurisdictions are among the most densely populated in the United States . . . . New York City, for example, has a population of about 8.5 million people, making it more populous than 38 States, and it squeezes that population into just over 300 square miles. . . .

. . . [D]ensely populated urban areas face different kinds and degrees of dangers from gun violence than rural areas. It is thus easy to see why the seven "may issue" jurisdictions might choose to regulate firearm carriage more strictly than other States. . . .

New York and its *amici* present substantial data justifying the State's decision to retain a "may issue" licensing regime. The data show that stricter gun regulations are associated with lower rates of firearm-related death and injury. . . . In particular, studies have shown that "may issue" licensing regimes, like New York's, are associated with lower homicide rates and lower violent crime rates than "shall issue" licensing regimes. . . .

Justice Alito points to competing empirical evidence that arrives at a different conclusion. But these types of disagreements are exactly the sort that are better addressed by legislatures than courts. . . .

III

A

[Aside from arguing that *Heller* did not abandon means-end scrutiny, Justice Breyer contended that "the Court today is wrong when it says that its rejection of means-end scrutiny and near-exclusive focus on history 'accords with how we protect other constitutional rights.'. . . [I]f conduct falls within a category of protected speech, we then use means-end scrutiny to determine whether a challenged regulation unconstitutionally burdens that speech." And "beyond the right to freedom of speech, we regularly use means-end scrutiny in cases involving other constitutional provisions[,]" such as free exercise of religion and equal protection.]

The upshot is that applying means-end scrutiny to laws that regulate the Second Amendment right to bear arms would not create a constitutional anomaly. Rather, it is the Court's rejection of means-end scrutiny and adoption of a rigid history-only approach that is anomalous.

B

The Court's near-exclusive reliance on history . . . is deeply impractical. It imposes a task on the lower courts that judges cannot easily accomplish. . . . Legal experts typically have little experience answering contested historical questions or applying those answers to resolve contemporary problems.

. . . Do lower courts have the research resources necessary to conduct exhaustive historical analyses in every Second Amendment case? What historical regulations and decisions qualify as representative analogues to modern laws? How will judges determine which historians have the better view of close historical questions? Will the meaning of the Second Amendment change if or when new historical evidence becomes available? And, most importantly, will the Court's approach permit judges to reach the outcomes they prefer and then cloak those outcomes in the language of history? . . .

. . .

. . . [S]cholars have continued to write books and articles arguing that the Court's decision in *Heller* misread the text and history of the Second Amendment. . . .

. . . I do not cite these arguments in order to relitigate *Heller*. I wish only to illustrate the difficulties that may befall lawyers and judges when they attempt to rely *solely* on history to interpret the Constitution. . . .

. . .

. . . [T]he Court's opinion today . . . gives the lower courts precious little guidance regarding how to resolve modern constitutional questions based almost solely on history. . . . Ironically, the only two "relevan[t]" metrics that the Court does identify are "how and why" a gun control regulation "burden[s the] right to armed self-defense." In other words, the Court believes that the most relevant metrics of comparison are a regulation's means (how) and ends (why)—even as it rejects the utility of means-end scrutiny.

What the Court offers instead is a laundry list of reasons to discount seemingly relevant historical evidence. The Court believes that some historical laws and decisions cannot justify upholding modern regulations because, it says, they were outliers. It explains that just two court decisions or three colonial laws are not enough to satisfy its test. But the Court does not say how many cases or laws would suffice "to show a tradition of public-carry regulation." Other laws are irrelevant, the Court claims, because they are too dissimilar from New York's concealed-carry licensing regime. But the Court does not say what "representative historical analogue," short of a "twin" or a "dead ringer," would suffice. Indeed, the Court offers many and varied reasons to reject potential representative analogues, but very few reasons to accept them. At best, the numerous justifications that the Court finds for rejecting historical evidence give judges ample tools to pick their friends out of history's crowd. At worst, they create a one-way ratchet that will disqualify virtually any "representative historical analogue" and make it nearly impossible to sustain common-sense regulations necessary to our Nation's safety and security.

[E]ven under ideal conditions, historical evidence will often fail to provide clear answers to difficult questions. . . .

. . . I fear that history will be an especially inadequate tool when it comes to modern cases presenting modern problems. . . . Small founding-era towns are unlikely to have faced the same degrees and types of risks from gun violence as major metropolitan areas do today, so the types of regulations they adopted are unlikely to address modern needs. . . .

. . . How can we expect laws and cases that are over a century old to dictate the legality of regulations targeting "ghost guns" constructed with the aid of a three-dimensional printer? . . . Or modern laws requiring all gun shops to offer smart guns, which can only be fired by authorized users? . . . Or laws imposing additional criminal penalties for the use of bullets capable of piercing body armor? . . .

The Court's answer is that judges will simply have to employ "analogical reasoning." . . .

Although I hope—fervently—that future courts will be able to identify historical analogues supporting the validity of regulations that address new technologies, I fear that it will often prove difficult to identify analogous technological and social problems from Medieval England, the founding era, or the time period in which the Fourteenth Amendment was ratified. . . .

IV

Indeed, the Court's application of its history-only test in this case demonstrates the very pitfalls described above. The historical evidence reveals a 700-year Anglo-American tradition of regulating the public carriage of firearms in general, and concealed or concealable firearms in particular. The Court spends more than half of its opinion trying to discredit this tradition. But, in my view, the robust evidence of such a tradition cannot be so easily explained away. Laws regulating the public carriage of weapons existed in England as early as the 13th century and on this Continent since before the founding. Similar laws remained on the books through the ratifications of the Second and Fourteenth Amendments through to the present day. Many of those historical regulations imposed significantly stricter restrictions on public carriage than New York's licensing requirements do today. Thus, even applying the Court's history-only analysis, New York's law must be upheld because "historical precedent from before, during, and . . . after the founding evinces a comparable tradition of regulation."

[Justice Breyer divided his review of the historical precedent into six parts. First, he thought that "[l]ike New York's law, . . . early [English] edicts prohibited public carriage absent special governmental permission and enforced that prohibition on pain of punishment." His reading included that "the most significant pre-firearm regulation of public carriage—the Statute of Northampton—was in fact applied to guns once they appeared in England[,]" making it "a criminal offense to carry arms without the King's authorization"; that "[t]he statute . . . remained in force for hundreds of years, well into the 18th century"; and that the Court's belief "that, by the end of the 17th century, [it] was understood to contain an extratextual intent element: the intent to cause terror in others" was refuted by sources indicating that "terror was the natural consequence—not an additional element—of the crime." Thus, "the better reading of the Statute of Northampton [is] as a broad prohibition on the public carriage of firearms and other weapons, without an intent-to-terrify requirement or exception for self-defense."

[Second, the "American Colonies continued the English tradition of regulating public carriage..." Though "these laws were only enacted in three colonies[,] ... that does not mean that they may be dismissed as outliers. They were successors to several centuries of comparable laws in England and predecessors to numerous similar (in some cases, materially identical) laws enacted by the States after the founding." Furthermore, "while it may be true that these laws applied only to 'dangerous and unusual weapons,' that category almost certainly included guns ...."

[Third, the "tradition of regulations restricting public carriage of firearms ... continued into the founding era." These laws, "modeled on the Statute of Northampton, ... appear to have been understood to set forth a broad prohibition on public carriage of firearms without any intent-to-terrify requirement."

[Fourth, regarding "the 19th century, States began to innovate on the Statute of Northampton in at least two ways. First, many States and Territories passed bans on concealed carriage or on any carriage, concealed or otherwise, of certain concealable weapons." These bans "were stricter than New York's law," which "permits concealed carriage with a lawfully obtained license." And the "second 19th-century innovation, adopted in a number of States, was surety laws[,]" which "like New York's proper cause requirement, ... conditioned public carriage in at least some circumstances on a special showing of need." All told, "[t]he surety laws and broader bans on concealed carriage enacted in the 19th century demonstrate that even relatively stringent restrictions on public carriage have long been understood to be consistent with the Second Amendment and its state equivalents."

[Fifth, "in the postbellum period, States continued to enact generally applicable restrictions on public carriage, many ... even more restrictive than their predecessors.... Most notably, many States [notably Texas] and Western Territories enacted stringent regulations that prohibited *any* public carriage of firearms, with only limited exceptions." When challenged, "these laws were generally upheld."

[Sixth, and finally, though the "Court disregards '20th-century historical evidence[,]' " ... it is worth noting that the law the Court strikes down today is well over 100 years old ...." And "unlike Justice Kavanaugh, I find the disconnect between *Heller*'s treatment of laws prohibiting, for example, firearms possession by felons or the mentally ill, and the Court's treatment of New York's licensing regime, hard to square. The inconsistency suggests that the Court today takes either an unnecessarily cramped view of the relevant historical record or a needlessly rigid approach to analogical reasoning."]

... At a minimum, the laws I have recounted *resembled* New York's law, similarly restricting the right to publicly carry weapons and serving roughly similar purposes. That is all that the Court's test, which allows and even encourages "analogical reasoning," purports to require.

In each instance, the Court finds a reason to discount the historical evidence's persuasive force. Some of the laws New York has identified are too old. But others are too recent. Still others did not last long enough. Some applied to too few people. Some were enacted for the wrong reasons. Some may have been based on a constitutional rationale that is now impossible to identify. Some arose in historically unique circumstances. And some are not sufficiently analogous to the licensing regime at issue here. But if the examples discussed above, taken together, do not show a tradition and history of regulation that supports the validity of New York's law, what could? Sadly, I do not know the answer to that question. What is worse, the Court appears to have no answer either.

. . .

. . . To the extent that any uncertainty remains between the Court's view of the history and mine, that uncertainty counsels against relying on history alone. In my view, it is appropriate in such circumstances to look beyond the history and engage in what the Court calls means-end scrutiny. Courts must be permitted to consider the State's interest in preventing gun violence, the effectiveness of the contested law in achieving that interest, the degree to which the law burdens the Second Amendment right, and, if appropriate, any less restrictive alternatives.

The Second Circuit has previously done just that, and it held that New York's law does not violate the Second Amendment. . . I would affirm that holding.

PART 4

Constitutional Protection of Expression and Conscience

CHAPTER 14

RESTRICTIONS ON TIME, PLACE, OR MANNER OF EXPRESSION

3. SPEECH ON PRIVATE PREMISES

Page 1518. Add after Reed v. Town of Gilbert:

City of Austin v. Reagan National Advertising of Austin
596 U.S. ___, 142 S.Ct. 1464 (2022).

The City of Austin—like tens of thousands of municipalities nationwide after the federal Highway Beautification Act of 1965 had "directed States receiving federal highway funding to regulate outdoor signs in proximity to federal highways, in part by limiting off-premises signs"—chose to regulate off-premises signs (those, mostly billboards, that advertise things not located on the same premises as the sign) more strictly than signs that advertise goods or services available on the same premises where the sign is located (on-premises signs). Reagan, an outdoor advertising company that was denied a permit to digitize some of its grandfathered pre-existing off-premises billboards in Austin, challenged the permit denial as a Free Speech violation subject to strict scrutiny analysis under Reed v. Gilbert, *supra*, because on-premises signs were allowed to be digitized.

The Supreme Court reversed the judgment of the Court of Appeals, which had understood *Reed* to require the application of strict scrutiny to the on-/off-premises distinction, which it considered content-based. The Court determined instead that the distinction was not facially content based and then remanded for determinations whether nonetheless there was evidence that an impermissible purpose or justification underpinned this "facially content-neutral distinction" and whether the distinction in any event might fail to satisfy intermediate scrutiny. Justice Sotomayor's majority opinion said in relevant part:

"A regulation of speech is facially content based under the First Amendment if it 'target[s] speech based on its communicative content'—that is, if it 'applies to particular speech because of the topic discussed or the idea or message expressed.' *Reed*, ... The Court of Appeals interpreted *Reed* to mean that if '[a] reader must ask: who is the speaker and what is the speaker saying' to apply a regulation, then the regulation is automatically content based.... This rule, which holds that a regulation cannot be content neutral if it requires reading the sign at issue, is too extreme an interpretation of this Court's precedent. Unlike the regulations at issue in *Reed*, the City's off-premises distinction requires an examination of speech only in service of drawing neutral, location-based lines. It is agnostic as to content. Thus, absent a content-based purpose or justification, the City's distinction is content neutral and does not warrant the application of strict scrutiny.

"...

"In this case, enforcing the City's challenged sign code provisions requires reading a billboard to determine whether it directs readers to the property on which it stands or to some other, offsite location. Unlike the sign code at issue in *Reed*, however, the City's provisions at issue here do not single out any topic or subject matter for differential treatment. A sign's substantive message itself is irrelevant to the application of the provisions; there are no content-discriminatory classifications for political messages, ideological messages, or directional messages concerning specific events, including those sponsored by religious and nonprofit organizations. Rather, the City's provisions distinguish based on location: A given sign is treated differently based solely on whether it is located on the same premises as the thing being discussed or not. The message on the sign matters only to the extent that it informs the sign's relative location. The on-/off-premises distinction is therefore similar to ordinary time, place, or manner restrictions. *Reed* does not require the application of strict scrutiny to this kind of location-based regulation. . . .

     " . . .

     "[Previous precedents] reject[ed] the view that *any* examination of speech or expression inherently triggers heightened First Amendment concern. Rather, it is regulations that discriminate based on 'the topic discussed or the idea or message expressed' that are content based. *Reed*, ... The sign code provisions challenged here do not discriminate on those bases.

     " . . .

     " . . . [A] regulation of speech cannot escape classification as facially content based simply by swapping an obvious subject-matter distinction for a 'function or purpose' proxy that achieves the same result. That does not mean that any classification that considers function or purpose is *always* content based. Such a reading of 'function or purpose' would contravene numerous precedents . . . . *Reed* did not purport to cast doubt on these cases.

     "Nor did *Reed* cast doubt on the Nation's history of regulating off-premises signs. Off-premises billboards of the sort that predominate today were not present in the founding era, but as large outdoor advertisements proliferated in the 1800s, regulation followed. As early as 1932, the Court had already approved a location-based differential for advertising signs. . . . Thereafter, for the last 50-plus years, federal, state, and local jurisdictions have repeatedly relied upon on-/off-premises distinctions to address the distinct safety and esthetic challenges posed by billboards and other methods of outdoor advertising. . . . The unbroken tradition of on-/off-premises distinctions counsels against the adoption of Reagan's novel rule. . . ."

     Justice Breyer wrote a separate concurring opinion to reiterate his continued "belie[f] that the Court's reasoning in *Reed* was wrong" and to add that "*Reed*'s strict formalism can sometimes disserve the very First Amendment interests it was designed to protect." Justice Alito concurred in the judgment in part, and dissented in part. He reasoned that the "distinction between a digitized and non-digitized sign is not based on content, topic, or subject matter[,]" but he also said this:

     "Today's decision . . . holds flatly that '[t]he sign code provisions challenged here do not discriminate' on the basis of ' "the topic discussed or the idea or message expressed," ' and that categorical statement is incorrect. The provisions defining on- and off-premises signs clearly discriminate on those grounds, and at least as applied in some situations, strict scrutiny should be required.

     "As the Court notes, under the provisions in effect when petitioner's applications were denied, a sign was considered to be off-premises if it 'advertis[ed],' among other things, a 'person, activity, . . . or servic[e] not located on the site where the sign is installed' or if it 'direct[ed] persons to any location not on that site.' Austin, Tex., City Code § 25–10–3(11). Consider what this definition would mean as applied to signs posted in the front window of a commercial establishment, say, a little coffee shop. If the owner put up a sign advertising a new coffee drink, the sign would be classified as on-premises, but suppose the owner instead mounted a sign in the same location saying: 'Contribute to X's legal defense fund' or 'Free COVID tests available at Y pharmacy' or 'Attend City Council meeting to speak up about Z.' All those signs would appear to fall within the definition of an off-premises sign and would thus be disallowed. . . . Providing disparate treatment for the sign about a new drink and the signs about social and political matters constitutes discrimination on the basis of topic or subject matter. . .

". . . I would simply hold that the provisions at issue are not facially unconstitutional, and I would refrain from making any broader pronouncements."

Finally, Justice Thomas's dissent, joined by Justices Gorsuch and Barrett, contained these passages:

"The Court . . . misinterprets *Reed*'s clear rule for content-based restrictions and replaces it with an incoherent and malleable standard. In so doing, the majority's reasoning is reminiscent of this Court's erroneous decision in Hill v. Colorado, 530 U.S. 703 (2000), which upheld a blatantly content-based prohibition on 'counseling' near abortion clinics on the ground that it discriminated against 'an extremely broad category of communications.' Id., at 723. Because I would adhere to *Reed* rather than echo *Hill*'s long-discredited approach, I respectfully dissent.

". . .

". . . A sign that conveys a message about off-premises activities is restricted, while one that conveys a message about on-premises activities is not. . . . And, per *Reed*, it does not matter that Austin's code 'defin[es] regulated speech by its function or purpose'—i.e., advertising or directing passersby elsewhere. . . . .[A]ll that matters is that the regulation 'draws distinctions based on' a sign's 'communicative content,' which the off-premises restriction plainly does.

"This conclusion is not undermined because the off-premises sign restriction depends in part on a content-neutral element: the location of the sign. Much like in *Reed*, that an Austin official applying the sign code must know *where* the sign is does not negate the fact that he also must know *what* the sign says. Take, for instance, a sign outside a Catholic bookstore. If the sign says, 'Visit the Holy Land,' it is likely an off-premises sign because it conveys a message directing people elsewhere . . . . But if the sign instead says, 'Buy More Books,' it is likely a permissible on-premises sign . . . . Finally, suppose the sign says, 'Go to Confession.' After examining the sign's message, an official would need to inquire whether a priest ever hears confessions at that location. If one does, the sign could convey a permissible 'on-premises' message. If not, the sign conveys an impermissible off-premises message. Because enforcing the sign code in any of these instances 'requires [Austin] officials to determine whether a sign' conveys a particular message, the sign code is content based under *Reed*. . . .

"In sum, the off-premises rule is content based and thus invalid unless Austin can satisfy strict scrutiny. . . . Because Austin has offered nothing to make that showing, the Court of Appeals did not err in holding that the off-premises rule violates the First Amendment.

". . .

". . . [T]he majority . . . finds the sign code to be content neutral by recasting facially content-based restrictions as only those that target sufficiently specific categories of communicative content and not as those that depend on communicative content *simpliciter.*

"...

"... Only by jettisoning *Reed*'s 'commonsense' definition of what it means to be content based can the majority assert that the off-premises rule is strictly 'location-based' and 'agnostic as to content,' even though the law undeniably depends on *both* location *and* communicative content.

"...

"We have defined content-based restrictions to include *all* content-based distinctions because any other rule would be incoherent. After all, off-premises advertising could be considered a 'subject' or a 'topic' as those words are ordinarily used. . . . And, in any event, there is no principled way to decide whether a category of communicative content is 'substantive' or 'specific' enough for the majority to deem it a 'topic' or 'subject' worthy of heightened protection. . . . The majority offers only its own *ipse dixit* to explain why off-premises advertising is insufficiently specific to qualify as content based under *Reed*. Worse still, the majority does not explain how courts should draw the line between a sufficiently substantive or specific content-based classification and one that is insufficiently substantive or specific.

"...

"Near the end of its analysis, the majority invokes an allegedly 'unbroken tradition of on-/off-premises distinctions' that it claims 'counsels against' faithful application of *Reed*. . . .

"Ultimately, the majority's only 'historical' support is that regulations like Austin's 'proliferated following the enactment of the Highway Beautification Act of 1965.' The majority's suggestion that the First Amendment should yield to a speech restriction that 'proliferated'—under pressure from the Federal Government—some two centuries after the founding is both 'startling and dangerous.'. . . Regardless, even if this allegedly 'unbroken tradition' did not fall short by a century or two, the majority offers no explanation why historical regulation is relevant to the question whether the off-premises restriction is content based under *Reed* and our modern content-neutrality jurisprudence. If Austin had met its burden of identifying a historical tradition of analogous regulation—as can be done, say, for obscenity or defamation—that would not make the off-premises rule content neutral. It might simply mean that the off-premises rule is a constitutional form of content-based discrimination. But content neutrality under *Reed* is an empirical question, not a historical one. Thus, the majority's historical argument is not only meritless but misguided.

"...

"... [A]rbitrary carveouts from *Reed* undermine the 'clear and firm rule governing content neutrality' that we understood to be 'an essential means of protecting the freedom of speech.' 576 U.S., at 171. The majority's deviation from that 'clear and firm rule' poses two serious threats to the First Amendment's protections.

"First, transforming *Reed*'s clear definition of 'content based regulation' back into an opaque and malleable 'term of art' turns the concept of content neutrality into a 'vehicl[e] for the implementation of individual judges' policy preferences.'. . .

"Second, sanctioning certain content-based classifications but not others ignores that even seemingly reasonable content-based restrictions are ready tools for those who would 'suppress disfavored speech.' . . . That danger only grows when the content-based distinctions are 'by no means clear,' giving more leeway for government officials to punish disfavored speakers and ideas. . . .

"...

"Because *Reed* provided a clear and neutral rule that protected the freedom of speech from governmental caprice and viewpoint discrimination, I would adhere to that precedent rather than risk resuscitating *Hill*. I respectfully dissent."

4. SPEECH IN THE PUBLIC SCHOOLS

Page 1541. Add after Morse v. Frederick:

Mahanoy Area School District v. B. L.

594 U.S. ___, 141 S.Ct. 2038, 210 L.Ed.2d 403 (2021).

■ JUSTICE BREYER delivered the opinion of the Court.

A public high school student used, and transmitted to her Snapchat friends, vulgar language and gestures criticizing both the school and the school's cheerleading team. The student's speech took place outside of school hours and away from the school's campus. In response, the school suspended the student for a year from the cheerleading team. . . . Although we do not agree with the reasoning of the Third Circuit panel's majority, we do agree with its conclusion that the school's disciplinary action violated the First Amendment.

I

A

[B.L. unsuccessfully tried out for the school's varsity cheerleading squad at the end of her freshman year, though she was offered a spot on the junior varsity team. Still upset that weekend, especially since an entering freshman made the squad, at a convenience store (the Cocoa Hut) with a friend, she "used her smartphone to post two photos on Snapchat, a social media application that allows users to post photos and videos that disappear after a set period of time." Any of her roughly 250 friends in her "friend" group could "view the images for a 24 hour period."]

The first image B. L. posted showed B. L. and a friend with middle fingers raised; it bore the caption: "Fuck school fuck softball fuck cheer fuck everything." . . . The second image was blank but for a caption, which read: "Love how me and [another student] get told we need a year of jv before we make varsity but tha[t] doesn't matter to anyone else?" The caption also contained an upside-down smileyface emoji.

[Some of her Snapchat "friends" were on the squad, and at least one took pictures of her posts and shared them with other cheer squad members. In turn, one of them shared the posts with her mother, a cheerleading squad coach. As the images spread,] several cheerleaders and other students approached the . . . coaches "visibly upset" about [them]. . . . Questions about the posts persisted during an Algebra class taught by one of the two coaches. . . .

After discussing the matter with the school principal, the coaches decided that because the posts used profanity in connection with a school extracurricular activity, they violated team and school rules. As a result, the coaches suspended B. L. from the junior varsity cheerleading squad for the upcoming year. B. L.'s subsequent apologies did not move school officials. The school's athletic director, principal, superintendent, and school board, all affirmed B. L.'s suspension from the team. In response, B. L., together with her parents, filed this lawsuit in Federal District Court.

[The District Court found in B. L.'s favor. The Third Circuit affirmed, a majority of the panel concluding that because her "speech took place off campus, . . . *Tinker* . . . did not apply and the school consequently could not discipline B. L. for engaging in a form of pure speech."]

. . .

II

We have made clear that students do not "shed their constitutional rights to freedom of speech or expression," even "at the school house gate." *Tinker*, . . . [but] we [also] have stressed . . . that schools at times stand *in loco parentis, i.e.,* in the place of parents. See Bethel School Dist. No. 403 v. Fraser, 478 U.S. 675, 684 (1986).

This Court has previously outlined three specific categories of student speech that schools may regulate in certain circumstances: (1) "indecent," "lewd," or "vulgar" speech uttered during a school assembly on school grounds, see *id.,* at 685; (2) speech, uttered during a class trip, that promotes "illegal drug use," see Morse v. Frederick, 551 U.S. 393, 409 (2007); and (3) speech that others may reasonably perceive as "bear[ing] the imprimatur of the school," such as that appearing in a school-sponsored newspaper, see *Kuhlmeier,* 484 U.S., at 271. Finally, in *Tinker*, we said schools have a special interest in regulating speech that "materially disrupts classwork or involves substantial disorder or invasion of the rights of others." 393 U.S., at 513. These special characteristics call for special leeway when schools regulate speech that occurs under its supervision.

Unlike the Third Circuit, we do not believe the special characteristics that give schools additional license to regulate student speech always disappear when a school regulates speech that takes place off campus. The school's regulatory interests remain significant in some off-campus circumstances. The parties' briefs, and those of *amici,* list several types of off-campus behavior that may call for school regulation. These include serious or severe bullying or harassment targeting particular individuals; threats aimed at teachers or other students; the failure to follow rules concerning lessons, the writing of papers, the use of computers, or participation in other online school activities; and breaches of school security devices, including material maintained within school computers.

Even B. L. herself and the *amici* supporting her would redefine the Third Circuit's off-campus/on-campus distinction, treating as on campus: all times when the school is responsible for the student; the school's immediate surroundings; travel en route to and from the school; all speech taking place over school laptops or on a school's website; speech taking place during remote learning; activities taken for school credit; and communications to school email accounts or phones. . . . And it may be that speech related to extracurricular activities, such as team sports, would also receive special treatment under B. L.'s proposed rule. . . .

We are uncertain as to the length or content of any such list of appropriate exceptions or carveouts to the Third Circuit majority's rule. . . . Particularly given the advent of computer-based learning, we hesitate to determine precisely which of many school-related off-campus activities belong on such a list. Neither do we now know how such a list might vary, depending upon a student's age, the nature of the school's off-campus activity, or the impact upon the school itself. Thus, we do not now set forth a broad, highly general First Amendment rule stating just what counts as "off campus" speech and whether or how ordinary First Amendment standards must give way off campus to a school's special need to prevent, e.g., substantial disruption of learning-related activities or the protection of those who make up a school community.

We can, however, mention three features of off-campus speech that often, even if not always, distinguish schools' efforts to regulate that speech from their efforts to regulate on-campus speech. Those features diminish the strength of the unique educational characteristics that might call for special First Amendment leeway.

First, a school, in relation to off-campus speech, will rarely stand *in loco parentis.* . . . Geographically speaking, off-campus speech will normally fall within the zone of parental, rather than school-related, responsibility.

Second, from the student speaker's perspective, regulations of off-campus speech, when coupled with regulations of on-campus speech, include all the speech a student utters during the full 24-hour day. That means courts must be more skeptical of a school's efforts to regulate off-campus speech, for doing so may mean the student cannot engage in that kind of speech at all. When it comes to political or religious speech that occurs outside school or a school program or activity, the school will have a heavy burden to justify intervention.

Third, the school itself has an interest in protecting a student's unpopular expression, especially when the expression takes place off campus. America's public schools are the nurseries of democracy. Our representative democracy only works if we protect the "marketplace of ideas." This free exchange facilitates an informed public opinion, which, when transmitted to lawmakers, helps produce laws that reflect the People's will. That protection must include the protection of unpopular ideas, for popular ideas have less need for protection. . . .

. . . Taken together, these three features of much off-campus speech mean that the leeway the First Amendment grants to schools in light of their special characteristics is diminished. We leave for future cases to decide where, when, and how these features mean the speaker's off-campus location will make the critical difference. This case can, however, provide one example.

III

Consider B. L.'s speech. Putting aside the vulgar language, the listener would hear criticism, of the team, the team's coaches, and the school—in a word or two, criticism of the rules of a community of which B. L. forms a part. This criticism did not involve features that would place it outside the First Amendment's ordinary protection. . . . To the contrary, B. L. uttered the kind of pure speech to which, were she an adult, the First Amendment would provide strong protection. . . .

Consider too when, where, and how B. L. spoke. Her posts appeared outside of school hours from a location outside the school. She did not identify the school in her posts or target any member of the school community with vulgar or abusive language. B. L. also transmitted her speech through a personal cellphone, to an audience consisting of her private circle of Snapchat friends. These features of her speech, while risking transmission to the school itself, nonetheless . . . diminish the school's interest in punishing B. L.'s utterance.

But what about the school's interest, here primarily an interest in prohibiting students from using vulgar language to criticize a school team or its coaches—at least when that criticism might well be transmitted to other students, team members, coaches, and faculty? We can break that general interest into three parts.

First, we consider the school's interest in teaching good manners and consequently in punishing the use of vulgar language aimed at part of the school community. . . . The strength of this anti-vulgarity interest is weakened considerably by the fact that B. L. spoke outside the school on her own time. . . .

B. L. spoke under circumstances where the school did not stand *in loco parentis.* And there is no reason to believe B. L.'s parents had delegated to school officials their own control of B. L.'s behavior at the Cocoa Hut. Moreover, the vulgarity in B. L.'s posts encompassed a message, an expression of B. L.'s irritation with, and criticism of, the school and cheerleading communities. Further, the school has presented no evidence of any general effort to prevent students from using vulgarity outside the classroom. Together, these facts convince us that the school's interest in teaching good manners is not sufficient, in this case, to overcome B. L.'s interest in free expression.

Second, the school argues that it was trying to prevent disruption, if not within the classroom, then within the bounds of a school-sponsored extracurricular activity. But we can find no evidence in the record of the sort of "substantial disruption" of a school activity or a threatened harm to the rights of others that might justify the school's action. *Tinker*, 393 U.S., at 514. Rather, the record shows that discussion of the matter took, at most, 5 to 10 minutes of an Algebra class "for just a couple of days" and that some members of the cheerleading team were "upset" about the content of B. L.'s Snapchats. . . . But when one of B. L.'s coaches was asked directly if she had "any reason to think that this particular incident would disrupt class or school activities other than the fact that kids kept asking . . . about it," she responded simply, "No." . . . As we said in *Tinker*, "for the State in the person of school officials to justify prohibition of a particular expression of opinion, it must be able to show that its action was caused by something more than a mere desire to avoid the discomfort and unpleasantness that always accompany an unpopular viewpoint." 393 U.S., at 509. The alleged disturbance here does not meet *Tinker*'s demanding standard.

Third, the school presented some evidence that expresses (at least indirectly) a concern for team morale. One of the coaches testified that the school decided to suspend B. L., not because of any specific negative impact upon a particular member of the school community, but "based on the fact that there was negativity put out there that could impact students in the school." . . . There is little else, however, that suggests any serious decline in team morale—to the point where it could create a substantial interference in, or disruption of, the school's efforts to maintain team cohesion. As we have previously said, simple "undifferentiated fear or apprehension . . . is not enough to overcome the right to freedom of expression." *Tinker*, 393 U.S., at 508.

It might be tempting to dismiss B. L.'s words as unworthy of the robust First Amendment protections discussed herein. But sometimes it is necessary to protect the superfluous in order to preserve the necessary. . . .

. . . The judgment . . . is . . . affirmed.

■ JUSTICE ALITO, with whom JUSTICE GORSUCH joins, concurring.

I join the opinion of the Court but write separately to explain my understanding of the Court's decision and the framework within which I think cases like this should be analyzed. . . .

. . .

. . . [W]hen a public school regulates what students say or write when they are not on school grounds and are not participating in a school program, the school has the obligation to answer the question . . .: Why should enrollment in a public school result in the diminution of a student's free-speech rights?

The only plausible answer . . . must be that by enrolling a child in a public school, parents consent on behalf of the child to the relinquishment of some of the child's free-speech rights.

. . .

When it comes to children, courts in this country have analyzed the issue of consent by adapting the common-law doctrine of *in loco parentis*. . . .

. . .

If *in loco parentis* is transplanted from Blackstone's England to the 21st century United States, what it amounts to is simply a doctrine of inferred parental consent to a public school's exercise of a degree of authority that is commensurate with the task that the parents ask the school to perform. Because public school students attend school for only part of the day and continue to live at home, the degree of authority conferred is obviously less than that delegated to the head of a late-18th century boarding school, but because public school students are taught outside the home, the authority conferred may be greater in at least some respects than that enjoyed by a tutor of Blackstone's time.

So how much authority to regulate speech do parents implicitly delegate when they enroll a child at a public school? The answer must be that parents are treated as having relinquished the measure of authority that the schools must be able to exercise in order to carry out their state-mandated educational mission, as well as the authority to perform any other functions to which parents expressly or implicitly agree—for example, by giving permission for a child to participate in an extracurricular activity or to go on a school trip.

III

. . . During the entire school day, a school must have the authority to protect everyone on its premises, and therefore schools must be able to prohibit threatening and harassing speech. . . . But even when students are on school premises during regular school hours, they are not stripped of their free-speech rights. *Tinker* teaches that expression that does not interfere with a class . . . cannot be suppressed unless it "involves substantial disorder or invasion of the rights of others." 393 U.S., at 513.

IV

A

A public school's regulation of off-premises student speech is a different matter. [T]he decision to enroll a student in a public school . . . cannot be treated as a complete transfer of parental authority over a student's speech. In our society, parents, not the State, have the primary authority and duty to raise, educate, and form the character of their children. . . . Parents do not implicitly relinquish all that authority when they send their children to a public school. . . .

B

The degree to which enrollment in a public school can be regarded as a delegation of authority over off-campus speech depends on the nature of the speech and the circumstances under which it occurs. . . . [W]ith respect to speech in each of [a few basic] groups, the question that courts must ask is whether parents who enroll their children in a public school can reasonably be understood to have delegated to the school the authority to regulate the speech in question.

One category of off-premises student speech falls easily within the scope of the authority that parents implicitly or explicitly provide. This category includes speech that takes place during or as part of what amounts to a temporal or spatial extension of the regular school program, e.g., online instruction at home, assigned essays or other homework, and transportation to and from school. Also included are statements made during other school activities in which students participate with their parents' consent, such as school trips, school sports and other extracurricular activities that may take place after regular school hours or off school premises, and after-school programs for students who would otherwise be without adult supervision during that time. Abusive speech that occurs while students are walking to and from school may also fall into this category on the theory that it is school attendance that puts students on that route and in the company of the fellow students who engage in the abuse. The imperatives that justify the regulation of student speech while in school—the need for orderly and effective instruction and student protection—apply more or less equally to these off-premises activities.

. . .

At the other end of the spectrum, there is a category of speech that is almost always beyond the regulatory authority of a public school. This is student speech that is not expressly and specifically directed at the school, school administrators, teachers, or fellow students and that addresses matters of public concern, including sensitive subjects like politics, religion, and social relations. Speech on such matters lies at the heart of the First Amendment's protection . . . .

. . .

This is true even if the student's off-premises speech on a matter of public concern is intemperate and crude. When a student engages in oral or written communication of this nature, the student is subject to whatever restraints the student's parents impose, but the student enjoys the same First Amendment protection against government regulation as all other members of the public. . . .

Between these two extremes (i.e., off-premises speech that is tantamount to on-campus speech and general statements made off premises on matters of public concern) lie the categories of off-premises student speech that appear to have given rise to the most litigation. . . .

One group of cases involves perceived threats to school administrators, teachers, other staff members, or students. Laws that apply to everyone prohibit defined categories of threats, . . . but schools have claimed that their duties demand broader authority.

Another common category involves speech that criticizes or derides school administrators, teachers, or other staff members. Schools may assert that parents who send their children to a public school implicitly authorize the school to demand that the child exhibit the respect that is required for orderly and effective instruction, but parents surely do not relinquish their children's ability to complain in an appropriate manner about wrongdoing, dereliction, or even plain incompetence. . . .

Perhaps the most difficult category involves criticism or hurtful remarks about other students. Bullying and severe harassment are serious (and age-old) problems, but these concepts are not easy to define with the precision required for a regulation of speech. . . .

V

The present case does not fall into any of these categories. Instead, it simply involves criticism (albeit in a crude manner) of the school and an extracurricular activity. Unflattering speech about a school or one of its programs is different from speech that criticizes or derides particular individuals, and for the reasons detailed by the Court . . ., the school's justifications for punishing B. L.'s speech were weak. . . .

The school did not claim that the messages caused any significant disruption of classes. . . .

. . .

. . . [F]inally, . . . whatever B. L.'s parents thought about what she did, it is not reasonable to infer that they gave the school the authority to regulate her choice of language when she was off school premises and not engaged in any school activity. And B. L.'s school does not claim that it possesses or makes any effort to exercise the authority to regulate the vocabulary and gestures of all its students 24 hours a day and 365 days a year.

. . . The overwhelming majority of school administrators, teachers, and coaches are men and women who are deeply dedicated to the best interests of their students, but it is predictable that there will be occasions when some will get carried away, as did the school officials in the case at hand. If today's decision teaches any lesson, it must be that the regulation of many types of off-premises student speech raises serious First Amendment concerns, and school officials should proceed cautiously before venturing into this territory.

■ JUSTICE THOMAS, dissenting.

. . .

. . . [S]chools historically could discipline students in circumstances like those presented here. Because the majority does not attempt to explain why we should not apply this historical rule and does not attempt to tether its approach to anything stable, I respectfully dissent.

. . .

. . . [According to Justice Thomas, 19th century cases followed this rule:] A school can regulate speech when it occurs off campus, so long as it has a proximate tendency to harm the school, its faculty or students, or its programs.

. . .

The majority . . . acknowledges that schools act *in loco parentis* when students speak on campus. But the majority fails to address the historical contours of that doctrine, whether the doctrine applies to off-campus speech, or why the Court has abandoned it.

. . . Unlike *Tinker*, . . . this case involves speech made in one location but capable of being received in countless others—an issue that has been aggravated exponentially by recent technological advances. The Court's decision not to create a solid foundation in *Tinker*, and now here not to consult the relevant history, predictably causes the majority to ignore relevant analysis.

First, the majority gives little apparent significance to B. L.'s decision to participate in an extracurricular activity. But the historical test suggests that authority of schools over off-campus speech may be greater when students participate in extracurricular programs. . . . [S]tudents like B. L. who are active in extracurricular programs have a greater potential, by virtue of their participation, to harm those programs. . . .

Second, the majority fails to consider whether schools often will have *more* authority, not less, to discipline students who transmit speech through social media. Because off-campus speech made through social media can be received on campus (and can spread rapidly to countless people), it often will have a greater proximate tendency to harm the school environment than will an off-campus in-person conversation.

Third, and relatedly, the majority uncritically adopts the assumption that B. L.'s speech, in fact, was off campus. But, the location of her speech is a much trickier question than the majority acknowledges. Because speech travels, schools sometimes may be able to treat speech as on campus even though it originates off campus. . . . [W]here it is foreseeable and likely that speech will travel onto campus, a school has a stronger claim to treating the speech as on-campus speech.

Here, it makes sense to treat B. L.'s speech as off-campus speech. There is little evidence that B. L.'s speech was received on campus. . . . But, the majority . . . bypasses this relevant inquiry.

* * *

The Court . . . states just one rule: Schools can regulate speech less often when that speech occurs off campus. . . . But . . . courts (and schools) will almost certainly be at a loss as to what exactly the Court's opinion today means.

. . .

5. Government Subsidies to Speech

Page 1572. Add after Matal v. Tam:

Shurtleff v. City of Boston, Massachusetts
596 U.S. ___, 142 S.Ct. 1583 (2022).

The Court held that Boston had not engaged in permissible viewpoint discriminatory government speech, but rather had engaged in impermissible viewpoint discrimination against private speech, when it denied a request from Camp Constitution, an organization seeking to "commemorate the civic and social contributions of the Christian community" on the 7-acre City Hall Plaza, in part by flying on one of three 83-foot city flagpoles located near the front of City Hall a "Christian flag" consisting of a red cross on a blue field against a white background. Two of Boston's flagpoles fly the American and Massachusetts flags, respectively, and the third normally flies Boston's city flag, but at least from 2005 until 2017 Boston had allowed all the other private group applicants to hoist in the aggregate about 50 unique flags, raised at 284 ceremonies, in lieu of the city flag for the duration of their accompanying events. "Most [of these] ceremonies . . . involved the flags of other countries . . . marking the national holidays of Bostonians' many countries of origin. But several [were] associated with other kinds of groups or causes, such as Pride Week, emergency medical service workers, and a community bank."

Justice Breyer's majority opinion contained this analysis:

"The boundary between government speech and private expression can blur when, as here, a government invites the people to participate in a program. In those situations, when does government-public engagement transmit the government's own message? And when does it instead create a forum for the expression of private speakers' views?

"In answering these questions, we conduct a holistic inquiry designed to determine whether the government intends to speak for itself or to regulate private expression. Our review is not mechanical; it is driven by a case's context rather than the rote application of rigid factors. Our past cases have looked to several types of evidence to guide the analysis, including: the history of the expression at issue; the public's likely perception as to who (the government or a private person) is speaking; and the extent to which the government has actively shaped or controlled the expression. See *Walker*, 576 U.S., at 209–214.

". . .

"... [S]ome evidence favors Boston, and other evidence favors Shurtleff.

"To begin, we look to the history of flag flying, particularly at the seat of government. Were we to consider only that general history, we would find that it supports Boston.

"...

"Not just the content of a flag, but also its presence and position have long conveyed important messages about government. . . .

"The flying of a flag other than a government's own can also convey a governmental message. A foreign flag outside Blair House, across the street from the White House, signals that a foreign leader is visiting and the residence has 'becom[e] a de facto diplomatic mission of the guest's home nation.' . . .

"Keeping with this tradition, flags on Boston's City Hall Plaza usually convey the city's messages. On a typical day, the American flag, the Massachusetts flag, and the City of Boston's flag wave from three flagpoles. Boston's flag, when flying there at full mast, symbolizes the city. When flying at halfstaff, it conveys a community message of sympathy or somber remembrance. . . .

"While this history favors Boston, it is only our starting point. The question remains whether, on the 20 or so times a year when Boston allowed private groups to raise their own flags, those flags, too, expressed the city's message. . . .

"Next, then, we consider whether the public would tend to view the speech at issue as the government's. In this case, the circumstantial evidence does not tip the scale. . . .

"... [E]ven if the public would ordinarily associate a flag's message with Boston, that is not necessarily true for the flags at issue here. [So,] evidence of the public's perception does not resolve whether Boston conveyed a city message with these flags.

"Finally, we look at the extent to which Boston actively controlled these flag raisings and shaped the messages the flags sent. The answer, it seems, is not at all. And that is the most salient feature of this case.

"...

"... Boston told the public that it sought 'to accommodate all applicants' who wished to hold events at Boston's 'public forums,' including on City Hall Plaza. . . . The application form asked only for contact information and a brief description of the event, with proposed dates and times. The city employee who handled applications testified by deposition that he had previously 'never requested to review a flag or requested changes to a flag in connection with approval'; nor did he even see flags before the events. . . . The city's practice was to approve flag raisings, without exception. It has no record of denying a request until Shurtleff's. . . . [T]he city had nothing—no written policies or clear internal guidance—about what flags groups could fly and what those flags would communicate.

"... In *Summum*, we emphasized that Pleasant Grove City always selected which monuments it would place in its park (whether or not the government funded those monuments), and it typically took ownership over them. . . . In *Walker*, a state board 'maintain[ed] direct control' over license plate designs by 'actively' reviewing every proposal and rejecting at least a dozen. . . . Boston has no comparable record.

"The facts of this case are much closer to Matal v. Tam. . . .

"...

"All told, while the historical practice of flag flying at government buildings favors Boston, the city's lack of meaningful involvement in the selection of flags or the crafting of their messages leads us to classify the flag raisings as private, not government, speech—though nothing prevents Boston from changing its policies going forward."

Finally, because Boston was not engaged in government speech and it "concede[d] that it denied Shurtleff 's request solely because the Christian flag he asked to raise 'promot[ed] a specific religion[,]' . . . [u]nder our precedents, and in view of our government-speech holding here, that refusal discriminated based on religious viewpoint and violated the Free Speech Clause."

Justice Kavanaugh concurred to observe that this "dispute arose only because of a government official's mistaken understanding of the Establishment Clause." A government "does not violate the Establishment Clause merely because it treats religious persons, organizations, and speech equally with secular persons, organizations, and speech in public programs, benefits, facilities, and the like." Rather, "a government may not treat religious persons, religious organizations, or religious speech as second-class."

Concurring in the judgment only, Justice Alito, joined by Justices Thomas and Gorsuch, objected at length to "the Court's decision to analyze this case in terms of the triad of factors—history, the public's perception of who is speaking, and the extent to which the government has exercised control over speech . . . ." Instead, he argued that "treating those factors as a test obscures the real question in government-speech cases: whether the government is *speaking* instead of regulating private expression." Because the "ultimate question is whether the government is actually expressing its own views or the real speaker is a private party and the government is surreptitiously engaged in the 'regulation of private speech.' *Summum*, . . . each of the factors mentioned in [*Walker* and *Summum*] could be relevant only insofar as it sheds light on the identity of the speaker." Otherwise, "considered in isolation from that inquiry, the factors central to *Walker* and *Summum* can lead a court astray."

First, "neither 'control' nor 'final approval authority' can in itself distinguish government speech from censorship of private speech, and analyzing that factor in isolation from speaker identity flattens the distinction between government speech and speech tolerated by the censor. And it is not as though 'actively' exercising control over the 'nature and content' of private expression makes a difference, as the Court suggests. Censorship is not made constitutional by aggressive and direct application."

Second, although "[h]istorical practice can establish that a means of expression 'typically represent[s] government speech[,]' *Summum*, . . . in determining whether speech is the government's, the real question is not whether a form of expression is *usually* linked with the government but whether the speech *at issue* expresses the government's own message. Governments can put public resources to novel uses. And when governments allow private parties to use a resource normally devoted to government speech to express their own messages, the government cannot rely on historical expectations to pass off private speech as its own."

Third, "[f]ocusing on public perception encourages courts to categorize private expression as government speech in circumstances in which the public is liable to misattribute that speech to the government." Justice Alito continued in part:

"The factors relied upon by the Court are thus an uncertain guide to speaker identity. But beyond that, treating these factors as a freestanding test for the existence of government speech artificially separates the question whether the government is speaking from whether the government is facilitating or regulating private speech.

Under the Court's factorized approach, government speech occurs when the government exercises a 'sufficient' degree of control over speech that occurs in a setting connected with government speech in the eyes of history and the contemporary public, regardless of whether the government is actually merely facilitating private speech. This approach allows governments to exploit public expectations to mask censorship."

Instead, Justice Alito's view was that "government speech occurs if—but only if—a government purposefully expresses a message of its own through persons authorized to speak on its behalf, and in doing so, does not rely on a means that abridges private speech." Among other things, he cautioned that "government speech in the literal sense is not exempt from First Amendment attack if it uses a means that restricts private expression in a way that 'abridges' the freedom of speech, as is the case with compelled speech." Hence, "to establish that expression constitutes government speech exempt from First Amendment attack, the government must satisfy two conditions. First, it must show that the challenged activity constitutes government speech in the literal sense—purposeful communication of a governmentally determined message by a person acting within the scope of a power to speak for the government. Second, the government must establish it did not rely on a means that abridges the speech of persons acting in a private capacity."

Government communication "that relies on private parties can constitute government speech" in two ways. One is "by deputizing private persons as its agents. . . . So long as this responsibility is voluntarily assumed, speech by a private party within the scope of his power to speak for the government constitutes government speech." The other allows the "government [to] 'adop[t]' a medium of expression created by a private party and use it to express a government message. *Summum* . . . . For the adopted expression to qualify as the government's, the private party must alienate control over the medium of expression to the government. And government actors must put the medium to use to intentionally express a government message." Importantly, "to avoid running afoul of the prohibition on compelled speech, that alienation must be voluntary."

Applying his framework in this case, "the flag displays were plainly private speech within a forum created by the City, not government speech." The "City's application materials . . . characterized the flagpoles as one of the City's 'public forums[,]' " and "the City [had] never [before] rejected any request to raise a flag submitted by any private party"—even though "private speakers accounted for 78% of the flag-raising applicants." Moreover, the "City did nothing to indicate an intent to communicate a message. . . . Nor did it deputize private speakers or appropriate private-party expressive content." Accordingly, the "City's policy and practice . . . squarely indicate[d] an intent to open a public forum for any private speakers who met the City's basic criteria."

Justice Gorsuch, joined by Justice Thomas, also authored a separate opinion concurring in the judgment, in order to identify "the real problem in this case" as stemming not "from Boston's mistake about the scope of the government speech doctrine or its error in applying our public forum precedents." Rather, the deeper problem was Boston's mistaken view, which no member of the Court "seeks to defend[,]" that "a municipal policy allowing all groups to fly their flags, secular and religious alike, would offend the Establishment Clause." He suggested that much of the blame for that "traces back to Lemon v. Kurtzman, 403 U.S. 602 (1971)[,]" and he devoted the rest of his lengthy opinion to elaborating why in his view that precedent should be overruled.

CHAPTER 15

PROTECTION OF PENUMBRAL FIRST AMENDMENT RIGHTS

2. FREEDOM OF ASSOCIATION

A. INTRODUCTION

Page 1598. Add after NAACP v. Alabama:

Americans for Prosperity Foundation v. Bonta
594 U.S. ___, 141 S.Ct. 2373, 210 L.Ed.2d 716 (2021).

■ CHIEF JUSTICE ROBERTS delivered the opinion of the Court, except as to Part II-B-1.

To solicit contributions in California, charitable organizations must disclose to the state Attorney General's Office the identities of their major donors. The State contends that having this information on hand makes it easier to police misconduct by charities. We must decide whether California's disclosure requirement violates the First Amendment right to free association.

I

The California Attorney General's Office is responsible for statewide law enforcement, including the supervision and regulation of charitable fundraising. Under state law, the Attorney General is authorized to "establish and maintain a register" of charitable organizations and to obtain "whatever information, copies of instruments, reports, and records are needed for the establishment and maintenance of the register." Cal. Govt. Code Ann. § 12584 (West 2018). In order to operate and raise funds in California, charities generally must register with the Attorney General and renew their registrations annually.... Over 100,000 charities are currently registered in the State, and roughly 60,000 renew their registrations each year.

California law empowers the Attorney General to make rules and regulations regarding the registration and renewal process.... Pursuant to this regulatory authority, the Attorney General requires charities renewing their registrations to file copies of their Internal Revenue Service Form 990, along with any attachments and schedules.... Form 990 contains information regarding tax-exempt organizations' mission, leadership, and finances. Schedule B to Form 990—the document that gives rise to the present dispute—requires organizations to disclose the names and addresses of donors who have contributed more than $5,000 in a particular tax year (or, in some cases, who have given more than 2 percent of an organization's total contributions)....

The petitioners are tax-exempt charities that solicit contributions in California and are subject to the Attorney General's registration and renewal requirements. Americans for Prosperity Foundation is a public charity that is "devoted to education and training about the principles of a free and open society, including free markets, civil liberties, immigration reform, and constitutionally limited government." ... Thomas More Law Center is a public interest law firm whose "mission is to protect religious freedom, free speech, family values, and the sanctity of human life." ... Since 2001, each petitioner has renewed its registration and has filed a copy of its Form 990 with the Attorney General, as required by [California law]. Out of concern for their donors' anonymity, however, the petitioners have declined to file their Schedule Bs (or have filed only redacted versions) with the State.

For many years, the petitioners' reluctance to turn over donor information presented no problem because the Attorney General was not particularly zealous about collecting Schedule Bs. That changed in 2010, when the California Department of Justice "ramped up its efforts to enforce charities' Schedule B obligations, sending thousands of deficiency letters to charities that had not complied with the Schedule B requirement." . . . The Law Center and the Foundation received deficiency letters in 2012 and 2013, respectively. When they continued to resist disclosing their contributors' identities, the Attorney General threatened to suspend their registrations and fine their directors and officers.

The petitioners each responded by filing suit in the Central District of California. In their complaints, they alleged that the Attorney General had violated their First Amendment rights and the rights of their donors. The petitioners alleged that disclosure of their Schedule Bs would make their donors less likely to contribute and would subject them to the risk of reprisals. Both organizations challenged the disclosure requirement on its face and as applied to them.

In each case, the District Court granted preliminary injunctive relief prohibiting the Attorney General from collecting their Schedule B information. . . . The Ninth Circuit vacated and remanded. . . . The court held that it was bound by Circuit precedent to reject the petitioners' facial challenge. . . . And reviewing the petitioners' as-applied claims under an "exacting scrutiny" standard, the panel narrowed the injunction, allowing the Attorney General to collect the petitioners' Schedule Bs so long as he did not publicly disclose them. . . .

On remand, the District Court held bench trials in both cases, after which it entered judgment for the petitioners and permanently enjoined the Attorney General from collecting their Schedule Bs. . . . Applying exacting scrutiny, the District Court held that disclosure of Schedule Bs was not narrowly tailored to the State's interest in investigating charitable misconduct. The court credited testimony from California officials that Schedule Bs were rarely used to audit or investigate charities. And it found that even where Schedule B information was used, that information could be obtained from other sources.

The court also determined that the disclosure regime burdened the associational rights of donors. In both cases, the court found that the petitioners had suffered from threats and harassment in the past, and that donors were likely to face similar retaliation in the future if their affiliations became publicly known. For example, the CEO of the Foundation testified that a technology contractor working at the Foundation's headquarters had posted online that he was "inside the belly of the beast" and "could easily walk into [the CEO's] office and slit his throat." . . . And the Law Center introduced evidence that it had received "threats, harassing calls, intimidating and obscene emails, and even pornographic letters." . . .

The District Court also found that California was unable to ensure the confidentiality of donors' information. During the course of litigation, the Foundation identified nearly 2,000 confidential Schedule Bs that had been inadvertently posted to the Attorney General's website, including dozens that were found the day before trial. One of the Foundation's expert witnesses also discovered that he was able to access hundreds of thousands of confidential documents on the website simply by changing a digit in the URL. The court found after trial that "the amount of careless mistakes made by the Attorney General's Registry is shocking." . . . And although California subsequently codified a policy prohibiting disclosure . . .—an effort the District Court described as "commendable"—the court determined that "[d]onors and potential donors would be reasonably justified in a fear of disclosure given such a context" of past breaches. . . .

The Ninth Circuit again vacated the District Court's injunctions, and this time reversed the judgments and remanded for entry of judgment in favor of the Attorney General. . . . The court held that the District Court had erred by imposing a narrow tailoring requirement. . . . And it reasoned that the disclosure regime satisfied exacting scrutiny because the up-front collection of charities' Schedule Bs promoted investigative efficiency and effectiveness. . . . The panel also found that the disclosure of Schedule Bs would not meaningfully burden donors' associational rights, in part because the Attorney General had taken remedial security measures to fix the confidentiality breaches identified at trial. . . .

. . .

We granted certiorari. . . .

II

A

The First Amendment prohibits government from "abridging the freedom of speech, or of the press; or the right of the people peaceably to assemble, and to petition the Government for a redress of grievances." This Court has "long understood as implicit in the right to engage in activities protected by the First Amendment a corresponding right to associate with others." Roberts v. United States Jaycees, 468 U.S. 609, 622 (1984). Protected association furthers "a wide variety of political, social, economic, educational, religious, and cultural ends," and "is especially important in preserving political and cultural diversity and in shielding dissident expression from suppression by the majority." *Ibid.* Government infringement of this freedom "can take a number of forms." *Ibid.* We have held, for example, that the freedom of association may be violated where a group is required to take in members it does not want, see *id.*, at 623, where individuals are punished for their political affiliation, see Elrod v. Burns, 427 U.S. 347, 355 (1976) (plurality opinion), or where members of an organization are denied benefits based on the organization's message, see Healy v. James, 408 U.S. 169, 181–182 (1972).

We have also noted that "[i]t is hardly a novel perception that compelled disclosure of affiliation with groups engaged in advocacy may constitute as effective a restraint on freedom of association as [other] forms of governmental action." NAACP v. Alabama ex rel. Patterson, 357 U.S. 449, 462 (1958). NAACP v. Alabama involved this chilling effect in its starkest form. The NAACP opened an Alabama office that supported racial integration in higher education and public transportation. . . . In response, NAACP members were threatened with economic reprisals and violence. . . . As part of an effort to oust the organization from the State, the Alabama Attorney General sought the group's membership lists. . . . We held that the First Amendment prohibited such compelled disclosure. . . . We explained that "[e]ffective advocacy of both public and private points of view, particularly controversial ones, is undeniably enhanced by group association," *id.*, at 460, and we noted "the vital relationship between freedom to associate and privacy in one's associations," *id.*, at 462. Because NAACP members faced a risk of reprisals if their affiliation with the organization became known—and because Alabama had demonstrated no offsetting interest "sufficient to justify the deterrent effect" of disclosure . . .—we concluded that the State's demand violated the First Amendment.

B

1

NAACP v. Alabama did not phrase in precise terms the standard of review that applies to First Amendment challenges to compelled disclosure. We have since settled on a standard referred to as "exacting scrutiny." Buckley v. Valeo, 424 U.S. 1, 64 (1976) (*per curiam*). Under that standard, there must be "a substantial relation between the disclosure requirement and a sufficiently important governmental interest." Doe v. Reed, 561 U.S. 186 (2010) (internal quotation marks omitted). "To withstand this scrutiny, the strength of the governmental interest must reflect the seriousness of the actual burden on First Amendment rights." . . . (internal quotation marks omitted). Such scrutiny, we have held, is appropriate given the "deterrent effect on the exercise of First Amendment rights" that arises as an "inevitable result of the government's conduct in requiring disclosure." *Buckley*, 424 U.S., at 65.

The Law Center (but not the Foundation) argues that we should apply strict scrutiny, not exacting scrutiny. Under strict scrutiny, the government must adopt "the least restrictive means of achieving a compelling state interest," McCullen v. Coakley, 573 U.S. 464, 478 (2014), rather than a means substantially related to a sufficiently important interest. The Law Center contends that only strict scrutiny adequately protects the associational rights of charities. And although the Law Center acknowledges that we have applied exacting scrutiny in prior disclosure cases, it argues that those cases arose in the electoral context, where the government's important interests justify less searching review.

It is true that we first enunciated the exacting scrutiny standard in a campaign finance case. See *Buckley*, 424 U.S., at 64–68. And we have since invoked it in other election-related settings. See, *e.g.*, Citizens United v. Federal Election Comm'n, 558 U.S. 310, 366–367 (2010); Davis v. Federal Election Comm'n, 554 U.S. 724, 744 (2008). But exacting scrutiny is not unique to electoral disclosure regimes. To the contrary, *Buckley* derived the test from NAACP v. Alabama itself, as well as other nonelection cases. See 424 U.S., at 64 [citations omitted]. As we explained in NAACP v. Alabama, "it is immaterial" to the level of scrutiny "whether the beliefs sought to be advanced by association pertain to political, economic, religious or cultural matters." 357 U.S., at 460–461. Regardless of the type of association, compelled disclosure requirements are reviewed under exacting scrutiny.

2

The Law Center (now joined by the Foundation) argues in the alternative that even if exacting scrutiny applies, such review incorporates a least restrictive means test similar to the one imposed by strict scrutiny. The United States and the Attorney General respond that exacting scrutiny demands no additional tailoring beyond the "substantial relation" requirement noted above. We think that the answer lies between those two positions. While exacting scrutiny does not require that disclosure regimes be the least restrictive means of achieving their ends, it does require that they be narrowly tailored to the government's asserted interest.

The need for narrow tailoring was set forth early in our compelled disclosure cases. In Shelton v. Tucker, we considered an Arkansas statute that required teachers to disclose every organization to which they belonged or contributed. 364 U.S., at 480. We acknowledged the importance of "the right of a State to investigate the competence and fitness of those whom it hires to teach in its schools." *Id.*, at 485. On that basis, we distinguished prior decisions in which we had found "no substantially relevant correlation between the governmental interest asserted and the State's effort to compel disclosure." *Ibid.* But we nevertheless held that the Arkansas statute was invalid because even a "legitimate and substantial" governmental interest "cannot be pursued by means that broadly stifle fundamental personal liberties when the end can be more narrowly achieved." . . .; see also Louisiana ex rel. Gremillion v. NAACP, 366 U.S. 293, 296 (1961) (quoting same).

Shelton stands for the proposition that a substantial relation to an important interest is not enough to save a disclosure regime that is insufficiently tailored. This requirement makes sense. Narrow tailoring is crucial where First Amendment activity is chilled—even if indirectly—"[b]ecause First Amendment freedoms need breathing space to survive." . . .

Our more recent decisions confirm the need for tailoring. In McCutcheon v. Federal Election Commission, 572 U.S. 185 (2014), for example, a plurality of the Court explained:

> "In the First Amendment context, fit matters. Even when the Court is not applying strict scrutiny, we still require a fit that is not necessarily perfect, but reasonable; that represents not necessarily the single best disposition but one whose scope is in proportion to the interest served, that employs not necessarily the least restrictive means but a means narrowly tailored to achieve the desired objective." *Id.*, at 218 (internal quotation marks and alterations omitted).

McCutcheon is instructive here. A substantial relation is necessary but not sufficient to ensure that the government adequately considers the potential for First Amendment harms before requiring that organizations reveal sensitive information about their members and supporters. Where exacting scrutiny applies, the challenged requirement must be narrowly tailored to the interest it promotes, even if it is not the least restrictive means of achieving that end.

. . .

III

. . .

A

As explained, exacting scrutiny requires that there be "a substantial relation between the disclosure requirement and a sufficiently important governmental interest," . . . and that the disclosure requirement be narrowly tailored to the interest it promotes. . . . The Ninth Circuit found that there was a substantial relation between the Attorney General's demand for Schedule Bs and a sufficiently strong governmental interest. . . . Of particular relevance, the court found that California had such an interest in preventing charitable fraud and self-dealing, and that "the up-front collection of Schedule B information improves the efficiency and efficacy of the Attorney General's important regulatory efforts." . . . The court did not apply a narrow tailoring requirement, however, because it did not read our cases to mandate any such inquiry. . . . That was error. And properly applied, the narrow tailoring requirement is not satisfied by the disclosure regime.

We do not doubt that California has an important interest in preventing wrongdoing by charitable organizations. It goes without saying that there is a "substantial governmental interest[ ] in protecting the public from fraud." . . . The Attorney General receives complaints each month that identify a range of misconduct, from "misuse, misappropriation, and diversion of charitable assets," to "false and misleading charitable solicitations," to other "improper activities by charities soliciting charitable donations." . . . Such offenses cause serious social harms. And the Attorney General is the primary law enforcement officer charged with combating them under California law. . . .

There is a dramatic mismatch, however, between the interest that the Attorney General seeks to promote and the disclosure regime that he has implemented in service of that end. Recall that 60,000 charities renew their registrations each year, and nearly all are required to file a Schedule B. Each Schedule B, in turn, contains information about a charity's top donors—a small handful of individuals in some cases, but hundreds in others. . . . This information includes donors' names and the total contributions they have made to the charity, as well as their addresses.

Given the amount and sensitivity of this information harvested by the State, one would expect Schedule B collection to form an integral part of California's fraud detection efforts. It does not. To the contrary, the record amply supports the District Court's finding that there was not "a single, concrete instance in which pre-investigation collection of a Schedule B did anything to advance the Attorney General's investigative, regulatory or enforcement efforts.". . .

. . .

The Attorney General and the dissent contend that alternative means of obtaining Schedule B information—such as a subpoena or audit letter—are inefficient and ineffective compared to up-front collection. . . . It became clear at trial, however, that the Office had not even considered alternatives to the current disclosure requirement. . . . The Attorney General and the dissent also argue that a targeted request for Schedule B information could tip a charity off, causing it to "hide or tamper with evidence." . . . But again, the States' witnesses failed to substantiate that concern. . . . Furthermore, even if tipoff were a concern in some cases, the State's indiscriminate collection of Schedule Bs in all cases would not be justified.

The upshot is that California casts a dragnet for sensitive donor information from tens of thousands of charities each year, even though that information will become relevant in only a small number of cases involving filed complaints. . . . California does not rely on Schedule Bs to initiate investigations, and in all events, there are multiple alternative mechanisms through which the Attorney General can obtain Schedule B information after initiating an investigation. The need for up-front collection is particularly dubious given that California—one of only three States to impose such a requirement . . .—did not rigorously enforce the disclosure obligation until 2010. . . .

In reality, then, California's interest is less in investigating fraud and more in ease of administration. This interest, however, cannot justify the disclosure requirement. The Attorney General may well prefer to have every charity's information close at hand, just in case. But "the prime objective of the First Amendment is not efficiency." . . . Mere administrative convenience does not remotely "reflect the seriousness of the actual burden" that the demand for Schedule Bs imposes on donors' association rights. . . .

B

The foregoing discussion also makes clear why a facial challenge is appropriate in these cases. Normally, a plaintiff bringing a facial challenge must "establish that no set of circumstances exists under which the [law] would be valid,", . . . or show that the law lacks "a plainly legitimate sweep," . . . In the First Amendment context, however, we have recognized "a second type of facial challenge, whereby a law may be invalidated as overbroad if a substantial number of its applications are unconstitutional, judged in relation to the statute's plainly legitimate sweep." . . . . We have no trouble concluding here that the Attorney General's disclosure requirement is overbroad. The lack of tailoring to the State's investigative goals is categorical—present in every case—as is the weakness of the State's interest in administrative convenience. Every demand that might chill association therefore fails exacting scrutiny.

The Attorney General tries to downplay the burden on donors, arguing that "there is no basis on which to conclude that California's requirement results in any broad-based chill." He emphasizes that "California's Schedule B requirement is confidential," and he suggests that certain donors—like those who give to noncontroversial charities—are unlikely to be deterred from contributing. . . . He also contends that disclosure to his office imposes no added burdens on donors because tax-exempt charities already provide their Schedule Bs to the IRS. . . .

We are unpersuaded. Our cases have said that disclosure requirements can chill association "[e]ven if there [is] no disclosure to the general public." . . . In *Shelton*, for example, we noted the "constant and heavy" pressure teachers would experience simply by disclosing their associational ties to their schools. . . . Exacting scrutiny is triggered by "state action which *may* have the effect of curtailing the freedom to associate," and by the "*possible* deterrent effect" of disclosure. NAACP v. Alabama, 357 U.S., at 460–461 (emphasis added); see Talley v. California, 362 U.S. 60, 65 (1960) ("identification and fear of reprisal *might* deter perfectly peaceful discussions of public matters of importance" (emphasis added)). While assurances of confidentiality may reduce the burden of disclosure to the State, they do not eliminate it.

It is irrelevant, moreover, that some donors might not mind—or might even prefer—the disclosure of their identities to the State. The disclosure requirement "creates an unnecessary risk of chilling" in violation of the First Amendment, . . ., indiscriminately sweeping up the information of *every* major donor with reason to remain anonymous. The petitioners here, for example, introduced evidence that they and their supporters have been subjected to bomb threats, protests, stalking, and physical violence. . . . Such risks are heightened in the 21st century and seem to grow with each passing year, as "anyone with access to a computer [can] compile a wealth of information about" anyone else, including such sensitive details as a person's home address or the school attended by his children. . . .

The gravity of the privacy concerns in this context is further underscored by the filings of hundreds of organizations as *amici curiae* in support of the petitioners. Far from representing uniquely sensitive causes, these organizations span the ideological spectrum, and indeed the full range of human endeavors: from the American Civil Liberties Union to the Proposition 8 Legal Defense Fund; from the Council on American-Islamic Relations to the Zionist Organization of America; from Feeding America—Eastern Wisconsin to PBS Reno. The deterrent effect feared by these organizations is real and pervasive, even if their concerns are not shared by every single charity operating or raising funds in California.

. . .

Finally, California's demand for Schedule Bs cannot be saved by the fact that donor information is already disclosed to the IRS as a condition of federal tax-exempt status. For one thing, each governmental demand for disclosure brings with it an additional risk of chill. For another, revenue collection efforts and conferral of tax-exempt status may raise issues not presented by California's disclosure requirement, which can prevent charities from operating in the State altogether. . . .

. . .

The District Court correctly entered judgment in favor of the petitioners and permanently enjoined the Attorney General from collecting their Schedule Bs. The Ninth Circuit erred by vacating those injunctions and directing entry of judgment for the Attorney General. The judgment of the Ninth Circuit is reversed, and the cases are remanded for further proceedings consistent with this opinion.

It is so ordered.

■ JUSTICE THOMAS, concurring in Parts I, II-A, II-B-2, and III-A, and concurring in the judgment.

The Court correctly holds that California's disclosure requirement violates the First Amendment. It also correctly concludes that the District Court properly enjoined California's attorney general from collecting the forms at issue, which contain sensitive donor information. But, while I agree with much of the Court's opinion, I would approach three issues differently.

First, the bulk of "our precedents . . . require application of strict scrutiny to laws that compel disclosure of protected First Amendment association." . . .

Second, the Court holds the law "overbroad" and, thus, invalid in all circumstances. . . . But I continue to have "doubts about [the] origins and application" of our "overbreadth doctrine." . . .

Third, and relatedly, this Court also lacks the power "to 'pronounce that the statute is unconstitutional in *all* applications,'" even if the Court suspects that the law will likely be unconstitutional in every future application as opposed to just a substantial number of its applications. . . . A declaration that the law is "facially" unconstitutional "seems to me no more than an advisory opinion—which a federal court should never issue at all." . . . Courts cannot "strike down statutory text" or resolve the legal rights of litigants not before them. . . .

Despite the Court's use of the term "facially unconstitutional," I join Part III-A, which finds that California's law fails exacting scrutiny, because the Court does not say that it is "provid[ing] relief beyond the parties to the case." . . .

With those points of difference clarified, I join Parts I, II-A, II-B-2, and III-A of the majority's opinion and concur in the judgment.

■ JUSTICE ALITO, with whom JUSTICE GORSUCH joins, concurring in Parts I, II-A, II-B-2, and III, and concurring in the judgment.

I am pleased to join most of THE CHIEF JUSTICE'S opinion. In particular, I agree that the exacting scrutiny standard drawn from our election-law jurisprudence has real teeth. It requires both narrow tailoring and consideration of alternative means of obtaining the sought-after information. . . . For the reasons THE CHIEF JUSTICE explains, California's blunderbuss approach to charitable disclosures fails exacting scrutiny and is facially unconstitutional. . . . The question is not even close. And for the same reasons, California's approach necessarily fails strict scrutiny.

THE CHIEF JUSTICE would hold that the particular exacting scrutiny standard in our election-law jurisprudence applies categorically "to First Amendment challenges to compelled disclosure." . . . JUSTICE THOMAS, by contrast, would hold that strict scrutiny applies in all such cases. . . . I am not prepared at this time to hold that a single standard applies to all disclosure requirements. And I do not read our cases to have broadly resolved the question in favor of exacting scrutiny. . . .

Because the choice between exacting and strict scrutiny has no effect on the decision in these cases, I see no need to decide which standard should be applied here or whether the same level of scrutiny should apply in all cases in which the compelled disclosure of associations is challenged under the First Amendment.

■ JUSTICE SOTOMAYOR, with whom JUSTICE BREYER and JUSTICE KAGAN join, dissenting.

Although this Court is protective of First Amendment rights, it typically requires that plaintiffs demonstrate an actual First Amendment burden before demanding that a law be narrowly tailored to the government's interests, never mind striking the law down in its entirety. Not so today. Today, the Court holds that reporting and disclosure requirements must be narrowly tailored even if a plaintiff demonstrates no burden at all. The same scrutiny the Court applied when NAACP members in the Jim Crow South did not want to disclose their membership for fear of reprisals and violence now applies equally in the case of donors only too happy to publicize their names across the websites and walls of the organizations they support.

California oversees nearly a quarter of this Nation's charitable assets. As part of that oversight, it investigates and prosecutes charitable fraud, relying in part on a registry where it collects and keeps charitable organizations' tax forms. The majority holds that a California regulation requiring charitable organizations to disclose tax forms containing the names and contributions of their top donors unconstitutionally burdens the right to associate even if the forms are not publicly disclosed.

In so holding, the Court discards its decades-long requirement that, to establish a cognizable burden on their associational rights, plaintiffs must plead and prove that disclosure will likely expose them to objective harms, such as threats, harassment, or reprisals. It also departs from the traditional, nuanced approach to First Amendment challenges, whereby the degree of means-end tailoring required is commensurate to the actual burdens on associational rights. Finally, it recklessly holds a state regulation facially invalid despite petitioners' failure to show that a substantial proportion of those affected would prefer anonymity, much less that they are objectively burdened by the loss of it.

Today's analysis marks reporting and disclosure requirements with a bull's-eye. Regulated entities who wish to avoid their obligations can do so by vaguely waving toward First Amendment "privacy concerns." ... It does not matter if not a single individual risks experiencing a single reprisal from disclosure, or if the vast majority of those affected would happily comply. That is all irrelevant to the Court's determination that California's Schedule B requirement is facially unconstitutional. Neither precedent nor common sense supports such a result. I respectfully dissent.

. . .

4. APPLICATION OF THE FIRST AMENDMENT TO GOVERNMENT REGULATION OF ELECTIONS

B. POLITICAL FUNDRAISING AND EXPENDITURES

Page 1671. Add the following new section directly before the report of Citizens United v. Federal Election Commission:

Repayment Restrictions

Candidates often loan money to their campaigns. To repay these and other campaign debts, campaigns may continue to receive contributions after election day. But the terms of § 304 of the Bipartisan Campaign Reform Act of 2002 (BCRA) restrict the use of post-election contributions by limiting the amount that a candidate may be repaid from such funds to $250,000. In Federal Election Commission v. Cruz, ___ U.S. ___, 142 S.Ct. 1638 (2022), the Court (with Justice Kagan, joined by Justices Breyer and Sotomayor, dissenting) invalidated these repayment limits in § 304 because it burdens core political speech without sufficient justification. The Court reasoned that the loan-repayment limitation abridges First Amendment rights by burdening candidates who wish to make expenditures on behalf of their own candidacy through personal loans. Restricting the sources of funds that campaigns may use to repay candidate loans increases the risk that such loans will not be repaid in full, which, in turn, deters candidates from loaning money to their campaigns. This burden, the Court concluded, is no small matter since debt is a ubiquitous tool for financing electoral campaigns, especially for new candidates and challengers. By inhibiting a candidate from using this critical source of campaign funding, § 304 raises a barrier to entry—thus abridging political speech. The Government argued that the post-election contributions at issue raised a heightened risk of corruption because they are used to repay a candidate's personal loans. But given that these contributions are already capped at $2,900 per election in order to prevent corruption or its appearance, the approach of adding an additional layer of regulation is a significant indicator that the regulation may not be necessary for the interest it seeks to protect. And the Government, the Court found, was unable to identify a single case of quid pro quo corruption in this context, even though most States do not impose a limit on the use of post-election contributions to repay candidate loans.

5. SPEECH AND ASSOCIATION OF RIGHTS OF GOVERNMENT EMPLOYEES

Page 1723. Add after Lane v. Franks:

Kennedy v. Bremerton School District
597 U.S. ___, 142 S.Ct. 2407 (2022).

[The report of this case appears *infra*, p. 137.]

Page 1732. Add after Note and discussion of Nevada Commission on Ethics v. Carrigan:

To be sure, while a legislator's casting of a vote is not *itself* protected speech, the Court recently confirmed in Houston Community College System v. Wilson, ___ U.S. ___, 142 S.Ct. 1253 (2022), that legislators may still claim First Amendment protection for other forms of speech regarding legislative actions. The Court considered whether the College System's Board of Trustees violated the First Amendment when the Board verbally censured David Wilson, one of its own members, for both publicly criticizing and bringing multiple lawsuits challenging various Board actions. The Court rejected Wilson's challenge, holding narrowly that "a censure of one member of an elected body by other members of the same body" without additional material consequences does not constitute an "adverse action" triggering First Amendment protection. The Court reached this conclusion both because of a long and early history of similar censures in this country and because the mere censure could not "have materially deterred an elected official like Mr. Wilson from exercising his own right to speak." As this latter formulation suggests, the Court clearly characterized Wilson's censure-provoking challenges to Board conduct as "his speech" rather than unprotected official conduct. While the act of voting itself is not protected speech, "[t]he First Amendment surely promises an elected representative like Mr. Wilson the right to speak freely on questions of government policy."

CHAPTER 17

RELIGION AND THE CONSTITUTION

1. THE ESTABLISHMENT CLAUSE

B. GOVERNMENT RELIGIOUS EXERCISES, CEREMONIES, DISPLAYS, AND PRACTICES

1. PUBLIC SCHOOLS

Page 1779. Add before Elk Grove Unified School District v. Newdow:

Kennedy v. Bremerton School District
597 U.S. ___, 142 S.Ct. 2407 (2022).

Without complaint for over seven years, Kennedy, a junior varsity football coach at Bremerton High School from 2008–2015, prayed on the school's playing field after each game by taking a knee at the 50-yard line and praying quietly for about 30 seconds. Initially he prayed on his own, but over time "some players asked whether they could pray alongside him[,]" which he allowed. Most of the team eventually joined him after some games, and they sometimes "invited opposing players to join." When he was not praying alone, the coach "began incorporating short motivational speeches with his prayer[.]" Separately, in a "school tradition" that predated his tenure, "the team at times engaged in pregame or postgame prayers in the locker room." Kennedy reportedly "never told any student that it was important they participate in any religious activity" and he "never pressured or encouraged any student to join" his postgame midfield prayers.

When the District learned about these practices, its superintendent sent Kennedy a letter on September 17, 2015. Instructing him to avoid motivational talks with students that included religious expression and "to avoid 'suggest[ing], encourag[ing] (or discourage[ing]), or supervis[ing]' any prayers of students, which students remained free to 'engage in.'" The district also informed him that any religious activity on his part had to be "'nondemonstrative (i.e., not outwardly discernible as religious activity)' if 'students are also engaged in religious conduct' in order to 'avoid the perception of endorsement.'" The District explained that "an employee's free exercise rights 'must yield so far as necessary to avoid school endorsement of religious activities.'"

In response, Kennedy "ended the tradition, predating him, of offering locker-room prayers[,]" and he "also ended his practice of incorporating religious references or prayer into his postgame motivational talks to his team on the field." But his lawyer on October 14 "sent a letter to school officials informing them that, because of his 'sincerely-held religious beliefs,' he felt 'compelled' to offer a 'post-game personal prayer' of thanks at midfield[, and] ask[ing] the District to allow him to continue that 'private religious expression' alone." The District acknowledged that he "had complied" with its September directives, but forbade him "from engaging in 'any overt actions' that could 'appea[r] to a reasonable observer to endorse ... prayer ... while he is on duty as a District-paid coach.'"

After the game on October 16, Kennedy started praying alone at midfield, but "players from the other team and members of the community joined him before he finished." That spurred media coverage, subsequent District efforts to prevent public access to the field, and another letter before the game on October 23, which offered him only the option "to pray after a game in a 'private location' behind closed doors and 'not observable to students or the public.'" Kennedy did kneel and bow his head for a brief, quiet prayer at midfield after that game, however, though no one joined him. After another game on October 26, he "again knelt alone to offer a brief prayer as the players engaged in postgame traditions[,]" though "other adults gathered around him on the field." Then he "rejoined his players for a postgame talk, after they had finished singing the school fight song."

Soon thereafter, the District placed Kennedy on administrative leave. In a "document provided to the public, the District admitted that it possessed 'no evidence that students have been directly coerced to pray with Kennedy'" and "acknowledged that [he] 'ha[d] complied' with the District's instruction to refrain from his 'prior practices of leading players in a pre-game prayer in the locker room or leading players in a post-game prayer immediately following games[,]'" but the District said it "could not allow [him] to 'engage in a public religious display'" without "'violat[ing] the . . . Establishment Clause' because 'reasonable . . . students and attendees' might perceive the 'district [as] endors[ing] . . . religion.'" About a month later, the District for the first time "gave him a poor performance evaluation . . . advis[ing] against rehiring" him for "'fail[ure] to follow district policy' regarding religious expression and 'fail[ure] to supervise student-athletes after games.'" Kennedy did not return for the next season.

Kennedy then sued, alleging violations of his rights to free speech and free exercise of religion. On cross-motions for summary judgment, the district court "found that the '"sole reason"' for the District's decision to suspend Mr. Kennedy was its perceived 'risk of constitutional liability' under the Establishment Clause for his 'religious conduct' after the October 16, 23, and 26 games." But it ruled against him, holding that "any speech he uttered was offered in his capacity as a government employee and unprotected by the First Amendment"; that "even if [his] speech qualified as private speech," it was properly suppressed, because otherwise the District would have invited "an Establishment Clause violation"; and that his free exercise claim failed for the same reason. The Ninth Circuit affirmed, essentially for the same reasons, and an en banc rehearing was denied "over the dissents of 11 judges."

The Supreme Court reversed, 6–3. Justice Gorsuch's majority opinion first concluded that Kennedy had carried the respective burdens demonstrating "an infringement of his rights under the Free Exercise and Free Speech Clauses[,]" which required "the defendant to show that its actions were nonetheless justified and tailored consistent with the demands of our case law. See, e.g., Fulton v. Philadelphia, 593 U.S. ___, ___–___, ___ (2021)." He then held that the District's Establishment Clause concerns did not justify those infringements.

Justice Gorsuch began by noting that "the Free Exercise and Free Speech Clauses work in tandem. Where the Free Exercise Clause protects religious exercises, whether communicative or not, the Free Speech Clause provides overlapping protection for expressive religious activities. See, e.g., Widmar v. Vincent, 454 U.S. 263, 269, n. 6 (1981); Rosenberger v. Rector and Visitors of Univ. of Va., 515 U.S. 819, 841 (1995)."

Regarding the free exercise claim, "a plaintiff may carry the burden of proving a free exercise violation in various ways, including by showing that a government entity has burdened his sincere religious practice pursuant to a policy that is not 'neutral' or 'generally applicable.' " If that showing is made, "this Court will find a First Amendment violation unless the government can satisfy 'strict scrutiny' by demonstrating its course was justified by a compelling state interest and was narrowly tailored in pursuit of that interest." Here, that "Kennedy has discharged his burdens is effectively undisputed. No one questions that he seeks to engage in a sincerely motivated religious exercise." Further, his "contested exercise . . . does not involve leading prayers with the team or before any other captive audience[, and t]he District disciplined him *only* for his decision to persist in praying quietly without his players after three games in October 2015." No one questioned "that, in forbidding Mr. Kennedy's brief prayer, the District failed to act pursuant to a neutral and generally applicable rule."

Government action is "not . . . neutral if it is 'specifically directed at . . . religious practice[,]" and the District "candidly acknowledged" that prohibiting Kennedy's religious practice was the "unquestioned 'object' " of its policies, "conceding that [those] policies were 'not neutral' toward religion." In addition, its policies "fail[ed] the general applicability test[,]" because the performance evaluation advising against his rehiring on the basis of failure to supervise student athletes after games "was not applied in an evenhanded, across-the-board way[,]" given that the "District permitted other members of the coaching staff to forgo supervising students briefly after the game to do things like visit with friends or take personal phone calls."

The free speech analysis was more complex, because "[i]n addition to being private citizens, teachers and coaches are also government employees paid in part to speak on the government's behalf and convey its intended messages." The "Court's decisions . . . suggest proceeding in two steps. The first step involves a threshold inquiry into the nature of the speech at issue[:] If a public employee speaks 'pursuant to [his or her] official duties,' . . . the Free Speech Clause generally will not shield the individual from an employer's control and discipline because that kind of speech is—for constitutional purposes at least—the government's own speech." But if "an employee 'speaks as a citizen addressing a matter of public concern,'. . . courts should proceed to a second step" and "engage in 'a delicate balancing of the competing interests surrounding the speech and its consequences.' " Here, both sides "agree that Mr. Kennedy's speech implicates a matter of public concern."

The Court concluded that "it seems clear to us that Mr. Kennedy has demonstrated that his speech was private speech, not government speech. When Mr. Kennedy uttered the three prayers that resulted in his suspension, he was not engaged in speech 'ordinarily within the scope' of his duties as a coach. . . . He did not speak pursuant to government policy." When he prayed after games, "coaches were free to attend briefly to personal matters." And it was not "dispositive" that his prayers took place "on the field of play[,]" for "what matters is whether Mr. Kennedy offered his prayers while acting within the scope of his duties as a coach." Thus, "[t]aken together, both the substance of [his] speech and the circumstances surrounding it point to the conclusion that he did not." That "as a coach, [he] served as a role model[,]" and that he "remained on duty after games[,]" did not compel a contrary conclusion, because his "actual job description left time for a private moment after the game" just like [o]thers working for the District [who] were free to engage briefly in personal speech and activity." That he "chose to use the same time to pray does not transform his speech into government speech. To hold differently would be to treat religious expression as second-class speech and eviscerate this Court's repeated promise that teachers do not 'shed their constitutional rights to freedom of speech or expression at the schoolhouse gate.' "

That his "prayers represented his own private speech" showed only that he "has carried his threshold burden[,]" leaving the second step "where the government may seek to prove that its interests as employer outweigh even an employee's private speech on a matter of public concern." Having made out a sufficient case under the Free Exercise of Free Speech Clause to shift the burden to the District, however, the Court indicated that "strict scrutiny" would normally be required. The District asked the Court to apply the "more lenient second-step" involving balancing of interests "or alternatively intermediate scrutiny[,]" but the Court said that "it does not matter which standard we apply[, as t]he District cannot sustain its burden under any of them."

That led to the most contested part of the case—the District's position "that its suspension of Mr. Kennedy was essential to avoid a violation of the Establishment Clause." Justice Gorsuch responded in significant part as follows:

"The District . . . began with the premise that the Establishment Clause is offended whenever a 'reasonable observer' could conclude that the government has 'endorse[d]' religion. . . . The District then took the view that a 'reasonable observer' could think it 'endorsed Kennedy's religious activity by not stopping the practice.' . . . On the District's account, it did not matter whether the Free Exercise Clause protected Mr. Kennedy's prayer. It did not matter if his expression was private speech protected by the Free Speech Clause. It did not matter that the District never actually endorsed Mr. Kennedy's prayer, no one complained that it had, and a strong public reaction only followed after the District sought to ban Mr. Kennedy's prayer. Because a reasonable observer could (mistakenly) infer that by allowing the prayer the District endorsed Mr. Kennedy's message, the District felt it had to act, even if that meant suppressing otherwise protected First Amendment activities. . . ."

The "District relied on Lemon [v. Kurtzman, 403 U.S. 602 (1971),] and its progeny." *Lemon* "called for an examination of a law's purposes, effects, and potential for entanglement with religion. . . . In time, the approach also came to involve estimations about whether a 'reasonable observer' would consider the government's challenged action an 'endorsement' of religion. See, e.g., County of Allegheny v. American Civil Liberties Union, Greater Pittsburgh Chapter, 492 U.S. 573, 593 (1989) . . . ."

"What the District and the Ninth Circuit overlooked, however, is that the 'shortcomings' associated with this 'ambitiou[s],' abstract, and ahistorical approach to the Establishment Clause became so 'apparent' that this Court long ago abandoned *Lemon* and its endorsement test offshoot. *American Legion*, . . . (plurality opinion) . . . . The Court has explained that these tests 'invited chaos' in lower courts, led to 'differing results' in materially identical cases, and created a 'minefield' for legislators. *Pinette*, . . . (plurality opinion) . . . . This Court has since made plain, too, that the Establishment Clause does not include anything like a 'modified heckler's veto, in which . . . religious activity can be proscribed' based on ' "perceptions" ' or ' "discomfort." ' Good News Club v. Milford Central School, 533 U.S. 98, 119 (2001). An Establishment Clause violation does not automatically follow whenever a public school or other government entity 'fail[s] to censor' private religious speech. Board of Ed. Of Westside Community Schools (Dist. 66) v. Mergens, 496 U.S. 226, 250 (1990) (plurality opinion). Nor does the Clause 'compel the government to purge from the public sphere' anything an objective observer could reasonably infer endorses or 'partakes of the religious.' Van Orden v. Perry, 545 U.S. 677, 699 (2005) (Breyer, J., concurring in judgment). . . .

"In place of *Lemon* and the endorsement test, this Court has instructed that the Establishment Clause must be interpreted by ' "reference to historical practices and understandings." ' *Town of Greece*, 572 U.S., at 576 . . . . An analysis focused on original meaning and history, this Court has stressed, has long represented the rule rather than some ' "exception" ' within the 'Court's Establishment Clause jurisprudence.' . . .

". . . [T]he District . . . offers a backup argument . . . [that] it was justified in suppressing Mr. Kennedy's religious activity because otherwise it would have been guilty of coercing students to pray. . . .

". . . [H]owever, . . . [t]he evidence cannot sustain [this theory]. . . . Members of this Court have sometimes disagreed on what exactly qualifies as impermissible coercion in light of the original meaning of the Establishment Clause. . . . But in this case Mr. Kennedy's private religious exercise did not come close to crossing any line one might imagine separating protected private expression from impermissible government coercion.

". . . [T]he District's . . . correspondence with Mr. Kennedy . . . never raised coercion concerns. To the contrary, the District conceded in a public 2015 document that there was 'no evidence that students [were] directly coerced to pray with Kennedy.' . . .

". . . Kennedy did not seek to direct any prayers to students or require anyone else to participate. . . .

"Naturally, Mr. Kennedy's proposal to pray quietly by himself on the field would have meant some people would have seen his religious exercise. Those close at hand might have heard him too. But learning how to tolerate speech or prayer of all kinds is 'part of learning how to live in a pluralistic society,' a trait of character essential to 'a tolerant citizenry.' *Lee*, 505 U.S., at 590. This Court has long recognized as well that 'secondary school students are mature enough . . . to understand that a school does not endorse,' let alone coerce them to participate in, 'speech that it merely permits on a nondiscriminatory basis.' *Mergens*, 496 U.S., at 250 (plurality opinion). Of course, some will take offense to certain forms of speech or prayer they are sure to encounter in a society where those activities enjoy such robust constitutional protection. But '[o]ffense . . . does not equate to coercion.' *Town of Greece*, 572 U.S., at 589 (plurality opinion).

"The District responds that . . . students might have felt compelled to pray alongside him. . . .

"This reply fails too. . . . There is no indication in the record that anyone expressed any coercion concerns to the District about the quiet, postgame prayers that Mr. Kennedy asked to continue and that led to his suspension. Nor is there any record evidence that students felt pressured to participate in these prayers. To the contrary, . . . not a single Bremerton student joined Mr. Kennedy's quiet prayers following the three October 2015 games for which he was disciplined. . . .

". . . [T]he District suggests that *any* visible religious conduct by a teacher or coach should be deemed—without more and as a matter of law—impermissibly coercive on students. . . . [T]he District[ ] suggest[s] not only that it *may* prohibit teachers from engaging in any demonstrative religious activity, but that it *must* do so in order to conform to the Constitution.

"Such a rule would be a sure sign that our Establishment Clause jurisprudence had gone off the rails. In the name of protecting religious liberty, the District would have us suppress it. Rather than respect the First Amendment's double protection for religious expression, it would have us preference secular activity. Not only could schools fire teachers for praying quietly over their lunch, for wearing a yarmulke to school, or for offering a midday prayer during a break before practice. Under the District's rule, a school would be *required* to do so. . . . We are aware of no historically sound understanding of the Establishment Clause that begins to 'mak[e] it necessary for government to be hostile to religion' in this way. . . .

"... [T]here is no evidence anyone sought to persuade or force students to participate, and there is no formal school program accommodating the religious activity at issue.

"[T]his case looks very different from those in which this Court has found prayer involving public school students to be problematically coercive. In *Lee*, this Court held that school officials violated the Establishment Clause by 'including [a] clerical membe[r]' who publicly recited prayers 'as part of [an] official school graduation ceremony' because the school had 'in every practical sense compelled attendance and participation in' a 'religious exercise.' ... In Santa Fe Independent School Dist. v. Doe, the Court held that a school district violated the Establishment Clause by broadcasting a prayer 'over the public address system' before each football game. ... The Court observed that, while students generally were not required to attend games, attendance was required for 'cheerleaders, members of the band, and, of course, the team members themselves.' ... None of that is true here. The prayers for which Mr. Kennedy was disciplined were not publicly broadcast or recited to a captive audience. Students were not required or expected to participate. And, in fact, none of Mr. Kennedy's students did participate in any of the three October 2015 prayers that resulted in Mr. Kennedy's discipline. ...

"... [T]here is no conflict between the constitutional commands before us. There is only the 'mere shadow' of a conflict, a false choice premised on a misconstruction of the Establishment Clause. ... And in no world may a government entity's concerns about phantom constitutional violations justify actual violations of an individual's First Amendment rights. ...

"... Here, a government entity sought to punish an individual for engaging in a brief, quiet, personal religious observance doubly protected by the Free Exercise and Free Speech Clauses of the First Amendment. And the only meaningful justification the government offered for its reprisal rested on a mistaken view that it had a duty to ferret out and suppress religious observances even as it allows comparable secular speech. The Constitution neither mandates nor tolerates that kind of discrimination. Mr. Kennedy is entitled to summary judgment on his First Amendment claims."[a]

Justice Sotomayor, joined by Justices Breyer and Kagan, dissented. She objected that the Court "yet again pay[s] almost exclusive attention to the Free Exercise Clause's protection for individual religious exercise while giving short shrift to the Establishment Clause's prohibition on state establishment of religion." She elaborated in part as follows:

"... To the degree the Court portrays petitioner['s] prayers as private and quiet, it misconstrues the facts. The record reveals that Kennedy had a longstanding practice of conducting demonstrative prayers on the 50-yard line of the football field. Kennedy consistently invited others to join his prayers and for years led student athletes in prayer at the same time and location. The Court ignores this history. The Court also ignores the severe disruption to school events caused by Kennedy's conduct, viewing it as irrelevant because the ... District ... stated that it was suspending Kennedy to avoid it being viewed as endorsing religion. Under the Court's analysis, presumably this would be a different case if the District had cited Kennedy's repeated disruptions of school programming and violations of school policy regarding public access to the field as grounds for suspending him. As the District did not articulate those grounds, the Court

---

[a]   Brief, individual concurring opinions by Justices Thomas and Alito are omitted.

assesses only the District's Establishment Clause concerns. It errs by assessing them divorced from the context and history of Kennedy's prayer practice.

". . . [B]eyond . . . misreading the record[, t]he Court overrules Lemon v. Kurtzman . . . and calls into question decades of subsequent precedents that it deems 'offshoot[s]' of that decision. In the process, the Court rejects longstanding concerns surrounding government endorsement of religion and replaces the standard for reviewing such questions with a new 'history and tradition' test. In addition, while the Court reaffirms that the Establishment Clause prohibits the government from coercing participation in religious exercise, it applies a nearly toothless version of the coercion analysis, failing to acknowledge the unique pressures faced by students when participating in school-sponsored activities. . . ."

Justice Sotomayor supplemented the facts delineated by the majority by noting and emphasizing that Kennedy's "duties encompassed 'supervising student activities immediately following the completion of the game' until the students were released to their parents or otherwise allowed to leave"; that he was "responsible for interacting with members of the community"; and that he was required to adhere to "the District's policy on 'Religious-Related Activities and Practices[, which]' provided that '[s]chool staff shall neither encourage or discourage a student from engaging in non-disruptive oral or silent prayer or any other form of devotional activity' and that '[r]eligious services, programs or assemblies shall not be conducted in school facilities during school hours or in connection with any school sponsored or school related activity.' " The District's inquiry into whether that policy had been violated uncovered that over time "a majority of the team" joined Kennedy when he prayed on the field; that his "practice evolved into postgame talks in which Kennedy would hold aloft student helmets and deliver speeches with 'overtly religious references,' which Kennedy described as prayers, while the players kneeled around him"; and that the school's athletic director told him at a September 11 game "that he should not be conducting prayers with players[,]" but after the game, "while the athletic director watched, Kennedy led a prayer out loud, holding up a player's helmet as the players kneeled around him." The District's September 17 letter "emphasized that 'school staff may not indirectly encourage students to engage in religious activity' or 'endors[e]' religious activity" and "that 'all District staff are free to engage in religious activity, including prayer, so long as it does not interfere with job responsibilities.' " After Kennedy's attorney sent the District his letter, and before the October 16 "homecoming game, Kennedy made multiple media appearances to publicize his plans to pray at the 50-yard line," which led to the District "receiving a large number of emails, letters, and calls, many of them threatening." After that game, Kennedy knelt to pray and:

"He quickly was joined by coaches and players from the opposing team. Television news cameras surrounded the group. Members of the public rushed the field to join Kennedy, jumping fences to access the field and knocking over student band members. After the game, the District received calls from Satanists who ' "intended to conduct ceremonies on the field after football games if others were allowed to." ' . . . To secure the field and enable subsequent games to continue safely, the District was forced to make security arrangements with the local police and to post signs near the field and place robocalls to parents reiterating that the field was not open to the public."

The letter the District sent after that game, on October 23, besides informing Kennedy that "his conduct at the October 16 game was inconsistent with the District's requirements[,]" also "emphasized that it was happy to accommodate Kennedy's desire to pray on the job in a way that did not interfere with his duties or risk perceptions of endorsement." Rather than respond to the District's invitation to "discuss accommodations that might be mutually satisfactory," Kennedy's "attorneys told the media that he would accept only demonstrative prayer on the 50-yard line immediately after games." Although at "the October 23 game, Kennedy kneeled on the field alone with players standing nearby[, a]t the October 26 game, [he] prayed surrounded by members of the public, including state representatives who attended the game to support" him. And "several parents reached out to the District saying that their children had participated in Kennedy's prayers solely to avoid separating themselves from the rest of the team." Finally, there was this:

"In Kennedy's annual review, the head coach of the varsity team recommended Kennedy not be rehired because he 'failed to follow district policy,' 'demonstrated a lack of cooperation with administration,' 'contributed to negative relations between parents, students, community members, coaches, and the school district,' and 'failed to supervise student-athletes after games due to his interactions with media and community' members. . . . The head coach himself also resigned after 11 years in that position, expressing fears that he or his staff would be shot from the crowd or otherwise attacked because of the turmoil created by Kennedy's media appearances. Three of five other assistant coaches did not reapply."

Justice Sotomayor then engaged in analysis of what she perceived to be the relevant law:

II

Properly understood, this case is not about the limits on an individual's ability to engage in private prayer at work. This case is about whether a school district is required to allow one of its employees to incorporate a public, communicative display of the employee's personal religious beliefs into a school event, where that display is recognizable as part of a longstanding practice of the employee ministering religion to students as the public watched. A school district is not required to permit such conduct; in fact, the Establishment Clause prohibits it from doing so.

. . .

. . . "The Court has been particularly vigilant in monitoring compliance with the Establishment Clause in elementary and secondary schools." Edwards v. Aguillard, 482 U.S. 578, 583–584 (1987). The reasons motivating this vigilance inhere in the nature of schools themselves and the young people they serve. Two are relevant here.

First, government neutrality toward religion is particularly important in the public school context given the role public schools play in our society. . . . [T]he Establishment Clause "proscribes public schools from 'conveying or attempting to convey a message that religion or a particular religious belief is favored or preferred'" or otherwise endorsing religious beliefs. Lee, 505 U.S., at 604–605 (Blackmun, J., concurring) . . . .

Second, schools face a higher risk of unconstitutionally "coerc[ing] . . . support or participat[ion] in religion or its exercise" than other government entities. . . . The State "exerts great authority and coercive power" in schools as a general matter "through mandatory attendance requirements." Edwards . . . . Moreover, the State exercises that great authority over children, who are uniquely susceptible to "subtle coercive pressure." Lee, ...

Given the twin Establishment Clause concerns of endorsement and coercion, it is unsurprising that the Court has consistently held integrating prayer into public school activities to be unconstitutional, including when student participation is not a formal requirement or prayer is silent. . . . [And] this Court has held that including prayers in student football games is unconstitutional, even when delivered by students rather than staff and even when students themselves initiated the prayer. Santa Fe Independent School Dist. v. Doe, 530 U.S. 290 (2000).

Under these precedents, the Establishment Clause violation at hand is clear. . . . Kennedy was on the job as a school official "on government property" when he incorporated a public, demonstrative prayer into "government-sponsored school-related events" as a regularly scheduled feature of those events. *Santa Fe*, 530 U.S., at 302.

Kennedy's tradition of a 50-yard line prayer thus strikes at the heart of the Establishment Clause's concerns about endorsement. For students and community members at the game, Coach Kennedy was the face and the voice of the District during football games. . . . Although the football game itself had ended, the football game events had not; Kennedy himself acknowledged that his responsibilities continued until the players went home. Kennedy's postgame responsibilities were what placed Kennedy on the 50-yard line in the first place; that was, after all, where he met the opposing team to shake hands after the game. Permitting a school coach to lead students and others he invited onto the field in prayer at a predictable time after each game could only be viewed as a postgame tradition occurring "with the approval of the school administration." . . .

Kennedy's prayer practice also implicated the coercion concerns at the center of this Court's Establishment Clause jurisprudence. This Court has previously recognized a heightened potential for coercion where school officials are involved . . . . [S]tudents face immense social pressure. Students look up to their teachers and coaches as role models and seek their approval. Students also depend on this approval for tangible benefits. Players recognize that gaining the coach's approval may pay dividends small and large, from extra playing time to a stronger letter of recommendation to additional support in college athletic recruiting. In addition to these pressures[,] . . . players face "immense social pressure" from their peers in the "extracurricular event that is American high school football." *Santa Fe* . . . .

. . . [T]he Court accepts . . . that [Kennedy's] highly visible and demonstrative prayer at the last three games before his suspension did not violate the Establishment Clause because these prayers were quiet and thus private. This Court's precedents, however, do not permit isolating government actions from their context in determining whether they violate the Establishment Clause. . . .

. . . Kennedy's "changed" prayers at these last three games were a clear continuation of a "long-established tradition of sanctioning" school official involvement in student prayers. *Ibid.* Students at the three games following Kennedy's changed practice witnessed Kennedy kneeling at the same time and place where he had led them in prayer for years. They witnessed their peers from opposing teams joining Kennedy, just as they had when Kennedy was leading joint team prayers. They witnessed members of the public and state representatives going onto the field to support Kennedy's cause and pray with him. Kennedy did nothing to stop this unauthorized access to the field, a clear dereliction of his duties. The BHS players in fact joined the crowd around Kennedy after he stood up from praying at the last game. That BHS students did not join Kennedy in these last three specific prayers did not make those events compliant with the Establishment Clause. The coercion to do so was evident. . . .

Finally, Kennedy stresses that he never formally required students to join him in his prayers. But existing precedents do not require coercion to be explicit, particularly when children are involved. . . .

. . .

... Under [our] precedents, the District's interest in avoiding an Establishment Clause violation justified both its time and place restrictions on Kennedy's speech and his exercise of religion.

First, as to Kennedy's free speech claim, Kennedy "accept[ed] certain limitations" on his freedom of speech when he accepted government employment. Garcetti v. Ceballos, 547 U.S. 410, 418 (2006). . . .

... [T]he District has a strong argument that Kennedy's speech, formally integrated into the center of a District event, was speech in his official capacity as an employee that is not entitled to First Amendment protections at all. . . . It is unnecessary to resolve this question, however, because, even assuming that Kennedy's speech was in his capacity as a private citizen, the District's responsibilities under the Establishment Clause provided "adequate justification" for restricting it. . . .

Similarly, Kennedy's free exercise claim must be considered in light of the fact that he is a school official and, as such, his participation in religious exercise can create Establishment Clause conflicts. . . .

Here, the District's directive prohibiting Kennedy's demonstrative speech at the 50-yard line was narrowly tailored to avoid an Establishment Clause violation. The District's suspension of Kennedy followed a long history. The last three games proved that Kennedy did not intend to pray silently, but to thrust the District into incorporating a religious ceremony into its events, as he invited others to join his prayer and anticipated in his communications with the District that students would want to join as well. Notably, the District repeatedly sought to work with Kennedy to develop an accommodation to permit him to engage in religious exercise during or after his game-related responsibilities. Kennedy, however, ultimately refused to respond to the District's suggestions and declined to communicate with the District, except through media appearances. Because the District's valid Establishment Clause concerns satisfy strict scrutiny, Kennedy's free exercise claim fails as well.

III

... The Court relies on an assortment of pluralities, concurrences, and dissents by Members of the current majority to effect fundamental changes in this Court's Religion Clauses jurisprudence, all the while proclaiming that nothing has changed at all.

. . .

... [T]he First Amendment's protections for religion diverge from those for speech because of the Establishment Clause, which provides a "specific prohibition on forms of state intervention in religious affairs with no precise counterpart in the speech provisions." . . . Therefore, while our Constitution "counsel[s] mutual respect and tolerance," the Constitution's vision of how to achieve this end does in fact involve some "singl[ing] out" of religious speech by the government. This is consistent with "the lesson of history that was and is the inspiration for the Establishment Clause, the lesson that in the hands of government what might begin as a tolerant expression of religious views may end in a policy to indoctrinate and coerce." Lee, 505 U.S., at 591–592.

Second, the Court contends that the lower courts erred by introducing a false tension between the Free Exercise and Establishment Clauses. The Court, however, has long recognized that these two Clauses, while "express[ing] complementary values," "often exert conflicting pressures." Cutter, 544 U.S., at 719. See also Locke v. Davey, 540 U.S. 712, 718 (2004) (describing the Clauses as "frequently in tension"). . . .

... The proper response is to identify the tension and balance the interests based on a careful analysis of "whether [the] particular acts in question are intended to

establish or interfere with religious beliefs and practices or have the effect of doing so."
Walz, 397 U.S., at 669. [T]hat inquiry leads to the conclusion that permitting Kennedy's
desired religious practice at the time and place of his choosing, without regard to the
legitimate needs of his employer, violates the Establishment Clause in the particular
context . . . here.

. . . The Court now says for the first time that endorsement simply does not matter,
and completely repudiates the test established in *Lemon* . . . . Both of these moves are
erroneous . . . and novel.

. . .

Given . . . concern for the political community, it is unsurprising that the Court has
long prioritized endorsement concerns in the context of public education. See, e.g., *Santa
Fe*, 530 U.S., at 305; *Wallace*, 472 U.S., at 60–61; *Edwards*, 482 U.S., at 578, 593; see
also *Lee*, 505 U.S., at 618–619 (Souter, J., concurring) (explaining that many of the
Court's Establishment Clause holdings in the school context are concerned not with
whether the policy in question "coerced students to participate in prayer" but with
whether it " 'convey[ed] a message of state approval of prayer activities in the public
schools' " . . . .[4] No subsequent decisions in other contexts, including the cases about
monuments and legislative meetings on which the Court relies, have so much as
questioned the application of this core Establishment Clause concern in the context of
public schools. In fact, Town of Greece v. Galloway, 572 U.S. 565, which held a prayer
during a town meeting permissible, specifically distinguished *Lee* because *Lee*
considered the Establishment Clause in the context of schools. 572 U.S., at 590 (plurality
opinion).

. . . [T]he endorsement inquiry dictated by precedent is a measured, practical, and
administrable one, designed to account for the competing interests present within any
given community.

. . .

The Court now . . . overrul[es] *Lemon* entirely and in all contexts. It is wrong to do
so. . . .

[T]he purposes and effects of a government action matter in evaluating whether
that action violates the Establishment Clause, as numerous precedents beyond *Lemon*
instruct in the particular context of public schools. Neither the critiques of *Lemon* as
setting out a dispositive test for all seasons nor the fact that the Court has not referred
to *Lemon* in all situations support this Court's decision to dismiss that precedent
entirely, particularly in the school context.

Upon overruling one "grand unified theory," the Court introduces another: It holds
that courts must interpret whether an Establishment Clause violation has occurred
mainly "by 'reference to historical practices and understandings.' " . . . [W]hile the Court
has long referred to historical practice as one element of the analysis in specific
Establishment Clause cases, the Court has never announced this as a general test or
exclusive focus.

The Court reserves any meaningful explanation of its history-and-tradition test for
another day . . . . It should not escape notice, however, that the effects of the majority's
new rule could be profound. . . .

---

[4] The Court attempts to recast *Lee* and *Santa Fe* as solely concerning coercion, but both cases
emphasized that it was important to avoid appearances of " 'state endorsement of prayer in public
schools.' " *Santa Fe*, 530 U.S., at 308; see *Lee*, 505 U.S., at 590 (finding that the "degree of school
involvement" indicated that the "prayers bore the imprint of the State").

For now, it suffices to say that the Court's history-and-tradition test offers essentially no guidance for school administrators. . . . [T]he Court simply sets the stage for future legal changes that will inevitably follow the Court's choice today to upset longstanding rules.

Finally, the Court['s] . . . analysis of coercion misconstrues both the record and this Court's precedents.

. . . The Court's suggestion that coercion must be "direc[t]" to be cognizable under the Establishment Clause is contrary to long-established precedent. The Court repeatedly has recognized that indirect coercion may raise serious establishment concerns, and that "there are heightened concerns with protecting freedom of conscience from subtle coercive pressure in the elementary and secondary public schools." *Lee*, 505 U.S., at 592 (opinion of the Court) . . . .

. . .

. . . [Kennedy's] prayers did not need to be broadcast. His actions spoke louder than his words. His prayers were intentionally, visually demonstrative to an audience aware of their history and no less captive than the audience in *Santa Fe*, with spectators watching and some players perhaps engaged in a song, but all waiting to rejoin their coach for a postgame talk. Moreover, Kennedy's prayers had a greater coercive potential because they were delivered not by a student, but by their coach, who was still on active duty for postgame events.

. . . [N]owhere does the Court engage with the unique coercive power of a coach's actions on his adolescent players.

. . . [T]he Court . . . draw[s] a bright line between Kennedy's years-long practice of leading student prayers, which the Court does not defend, and Kennedy's final three prayers, which BHS students did not join, but student peers from the other teams did. . . . The question . . . is not whether a coach taking a knee to pray on the field would constitute an Establishment Clause violation in any and all circumstances. It is whether permitting Kennedy to continue a demonstrative prayer practice at the center of the football field after years of inappropriately leading students in prayer in the same spot, at that same time, and in the same manner, which led students to feel compelled to join him, violates the Establishment Clause. It does.

. . . Even on the Court's myopic framing of the facts, at two of the three games on which the Court focuses, players witnessed student peers from the other team and other authority figures surrounding Kennedy and joining him in prayer. The coercive pressures inherent in such a situation are obvious. . . .

. . . Importantly, nothing in the Court's opinion should be read as calling into question that Kennedy's conduct may have raised other concerns regarding disruption of school events or misuse of school facilities that would have separately justified employment action against Kennedy.

. . .

Today, the Court . . . elevates one individual's interest in personal religious exercise, in the exact time and place of that individual's choosing, over society's interest in protecting the separation between church and state, eroding the protections for religious liberty for all. Today's decision is particularly misguided because it elevates the religious rights of a school official, who voluntarily accepted public employment and the limits that public employment entails, over those of his students, who are required to attend school and who this Court has long recognized are particularly vulnerable and deserving of protection. In doing so, the Court sets us further down a perilous path in forcing States to entangle themselves with religion, with all of our rights hanging in the balance. As much as the Court protests otherwise, today's decision is no victory for religious liberty. I respectfully dissent.

2. THE FREE EXERCISE OF RELIGION

Page 1874. Replace Roman Catholic Diocese of Brooklyn v. Cuomo with the following:

Tandon v. Newsom

593 U.S. ___, 141 S.Ct. 1294 (2021).

To combat the spread of COVID-19 during the global coronavirus pandemic, California restricted at-home gatherings to no more than three households, at least for a period of time. Plaintiffs sought a preliminary injunction against application of this restriction to at-home religious exercises in larger groups. The district court denied their motion, and the Ninth Circuit denied their application for emergency injunctive relief pending appeal. The Supreme Court granted the latter request, however, in a 5–4 per curiam ruling. The majority opinion said in relevant part:

"The Ninth Circuit's failure to grant an injunction pending appeal was erroneous. This Court's decisions have made the following points clear.

"First, government regulations are not neutral and generally applicable, and therefore trigger strict scrutiny under the Free Exercise Clause, whenever they treat *any* comparable secular activity more favorably than religious exercise. Roman Catholic Diocese of Brooklyn v. Cuomo, 592 U.S. ___, ___–___ (2020) (per curiam) .... It is no answer that a State treats some comparable secular businesses or other activities as poorly as or even less favorably than the religious exercise at issue....[a]

"Second, whether two activities are comparable for purposes of the Free Exercise Clause must be judged against the asserted government interest that justifies the regulation at issue. Id., at ___ ... (describing secular activities treated more favorably than religious worship that either 'have contributed to the spread of COVID-19' or 'could' have presented similar risks). Comparability is concerned with the risks various activities pose, not the reasons why people gather....

"Third, the government has the burden to establish that the challenged law satisfies strict scrutiny. To do so in this context, ... narrow tailoring requires the government to show that measures less restrictive of the First Amendment activity

---

[a] The *Roman Catholic Diocese* case involved capacity restrictions in *public* spaces, including churches and businesses. With the same 5–4 division among the Justices, the per curiam majority there also had granted emergency injunctive relief pending appeal, the majority concluding that the "regulations cannot be viewed as neutral because they single out houses of worship for especially harsh treatment" compared to lesser capacity restrictions on "essential" and "even nonessential" businesses. Chief Justice Roberts would have avoided granting injunctive relief, because the Governor had "revised the designations of the affected areas" and "it is a significant matter to override determinations made by public health officials concerning what is necessary for public safety in the midst of a deadly pandemic"— even though he thought the numerical capacity limits "do seem unduly restrictive" and "may well ... violate the Free Exercise Clause." A dissent by Justice Breyer, joined by Justices Sotomayor and Kagan, agreed that there was "no need now to issue [the] injunction[,]" but also thought the merits of the free exercise claim were "far from clear[.]" And Justice Sotomayor's separate dissent, joined by Justice Kagan, thought the regulations treated "religious institutions equally or more favorably than comparable secular institutions" like concerts, movie showings, lectures and sporting events, which were subject to more restrictive capacity limits. Businesses were dissimilar in her view, because religious services involved "large groups of people gathering, speaking, and singing in close proximity indoors for extended periods of time."

could not address its interest in reducing the spread of COVID. Where the government permits other activities to proceed with precautions, it must show that the religious exercise at issue is more dangerous than those activities even when the same precautions are applied. Otherwise, precautions that suffice for other activities suffice for religious exercise too. . . .

"Fourth, even if the government withdraws or modifies a COVID restriction in the course of litigation, that does not necessarily moot the case. And so long as a case is not moot, litigants otherwise entitled to emergency injunctive relief remain entitled to such relief where the applicants 'remain under a constant threat' that government officials will use their power to reinstate the challenged restrictions. . . .

"These principles dictated the outcome in this case . . . . First, California treats some comparable secular activities more favorably than at-home religious exercise, permitting hair salons, retail stores, personal care services, movie theaters, private suites at sporting events and concerts, and indoor restaurants to bring together more than three households at a time. . . . Second, the Ninth Circuit did not conclude that those activities pose a lesser risk of transmission than applicants' proposed religious exercise at home. The Ninth Circuit erroneously rejected these comparators simply because this Court's previous decisions involved public buildings as opposed to private buildings. . . . Third, instead of requiring the State to explain why it could not safely permit at-home worshipers to gather in larger numbers while using precautions used in secular activities, the Ninth Circuit erroneously declared that such measures might not 'translate readily' to the home. . . . The State cannot 'assume the worst when people go to worship but assume the best when people go to work.' Roberts v. Neace, 958 F.3d 409, 414 (CA6 2020) (per curiam). And fourth, although California officials changed the challenged policy shortly after this application was filed, the previous restrictions remain in place until April 15th, and officials with a track record of 'moving the goalposts' retain authority to reinstate those heightened restrictions at any time. . . .

"Applicants are likely to succeed on the merits of their free exercise claim; they are irreparably harmed by the loss of free exercise rights 'for even minimal periods of time'; and the State has not shown that 'public health would be imperiled' by employing less restrictive measures. *Roman Catholic Diocese*, ... Accordingly, applicants are entitled to an injunction pending appeal.

"This is the fifth time the Court has summarily rejected the Ninth Circuit's analysis of California's COVID restrictions on religious exercise. . . . It is unsurprising that such litigants are entitled to relief. California's Blueprint System contains myriad exceptions and accommodations for comparable activities, thus requiring the application of strict scrutiny. . . ."

Chief Justice Roberts did not file an opinion but would have denied the application. Justice Kagan, joined by Justices Breyer and Sotomayor, dissented, writing in part:

". . . California limits religious gatherings in homes to three households. If the State also limits all secular gatherings in homes to three households, it has complied with the First Amendment. And the State does exactly that: It has adopted a blanket restriction on at-home gatherings of all kinds, religious and secular alike. California need not, as the per curiam insists, treat at-home religious gatherings the same as hardware stores and hair salons—and thus unlike at-home secular gatherings, the obvious comparator here. . . . [T]he law does not require that the State equally treat apples and watermelons.

"And even supposing a court should cast so expansive a comparative net, the per curiam's analysis . . . defies the factual record. . . . [As the Ninth Circuit majority explained,] those [public] activities do pose lesser risks for at least three reasons. First, 'when people gather in social settings, their interactions are likely to be longer than they would be in a commercial setting,' with participants 'more likely to be involved in prolonged conversations.' . . . Second, 'private houses are typically smaller and less ventilated than commercial establishments.' . . . And third, 'social distancing and mask-wearing are less likely in private settings and enforcement is more difficult.' . . . These are not the mere musings of two appellate judges: The district court found each of these facts based on the uncontested testimony of California's public-health experts. . . ."

Page 1886. Add after Masterpiece Cakeshop, Ltd. v. Colorado Civil Rights Commission:

Fulton v. City of Philadelphia
593 U.S. ___, 141 S.Ct. 1868, 210 L.Ed.2d 137 (2021).

■ CHIEF JUSTICE ROBERTS delivered the opinion of the Court.

[The City's Department of Human Services assumes custody of children who cannot remain in their homes and pursues foster care placements for them through standard annual contracts with state-licensed private foster agencies like Catholic Social Services (CSS). Under Pennsylvania law, foster agencies must conduct a home study review of prospective foster parents and decide whether to "approve, disapprove or provisionally approve the foster family." When the Department seeks a referral, the agencies "report whether any of their certified families are available, and the Department places the child with what it regards as the most suitable family."]

. . . Because [CSS] understands the certification of prospective foster families to be an endorsement of their relationships, it will not certify unmarried couples—regardless of their sexual orientation—or same-sex married couples. CSS does not object to certifying gay or lesbian individuals as single foster parents or to placing gay and lesbian children. No same-sex couple has ever sought certification from CSS. If one did, CSS would direct the couple to one of the more than 20 other agencies in the City, all of which currently certify same-sex couples. For over 50 years, CSS successfully contracted with the City to provide foster care services while holding to these beliefs.

But . . . in 2018[, after a newspaper report] in which a spokesman for the Archdiocese of Philadelphia stated that CSS would not be able to consider prospective foster parents in same-sex marriages[, the] City Council called for an investigation, . . . [t]he Philadelphia Commission on Human Relations launched an inquiry[, a]nd the Commissioner of the Department [met] with the leadership of CSS. . . . Immediately after the meeting, the Department informed CSS that it would no longer refer children to the agency. The City later explained that the refusal of CSS to certify same-sex couples violated a non-discrimination provision in its contract with the City as well as the non-discrimination requirements of the citywide Fair Practices Ordinance. The City stated that it would not enter a full foster care contract with CSS in the future unless the agency agreed to certify same-sex couples.

CSS . . . [sued] the City, the Department, and the Commission[,] . . . alleg[ing] that the referral freeze violated the Free Exercise and Free Speech Clauses of the First Amendment. . . .

The District Court denied preliminary relief. It concluded that the contractual non-discrimination requirement and the Fair Practices Ordinance were neutral and generally applicable under Employment Division, Department of Human Resources of Oregon v. Smith, 494 U.S. 872 (1990), and that the free exercise claim was therefore unlikely to succeed.

The . . . Third Circuit affirmed. . . .

CSS . . . challenged the Third Circuit's determination that the City's actions were permissible under *Smith* and also asked this Court to reconsider that precedent.

. . .

II

A

. . . [I]t is plain that the City's actions have burdened CSS's religious exercise by putting it to the choice of curtailing its mission or approving relationships inconsistent with its beliefs. The City disagrees. In its view, certification reflects only that foster parents satisfy the statutory criteria, not that the agency endorses their relationships. But CSS believes that certification is tantamount to endorsement. And "religious beliefs need not be acceptable, logical, consistent, or comprehensible to others in order to merit First Amendment protection." Thomas v. Review Bd. of Ind. Employment Security Div., 450 U.S. 707, 714 (1981). . . .

Smith held that laws incidentally burdening religion are ordinarily not subject to strict scrutiny under the Free Exercise Clause so long as they are neutral and generally applicable. . . . CSS urges us to overrule *Smith*, and the concurrences in the judgment argue in favor of doing so. . . . But we need not revisit that decision here. This case falls outside *Smith* because the City has burdened the religious exercise of CSS through policies that do not meet the requirement of being neutral and generally applicable. . . .

Government fails to act neutrally when it proceeds in a manner intolerant of religious beliefs or restricts practices because of their religious nature. See Masterpiece Cakeshop, Ltd. v. Colorado Civil Rights Comm'n, . . .); *Lukumi*, ... CSS points to evidence in the record that it believes demonstrates that the City has transgressed this neutrality standard, but we find it more straightforward to resolve this case under the rubric of general applicability.

A law is not generally applicable if it "invite[s]" the government to consider the particular reasons for a person's conduct by providing " 'a mechanism for individualized exemptions.' " *Smith*, ...[;] Sherbert v. Verner, 374 U.S. 398 (1963)[. . . .]

. . . *Smith* [held] that "where the State has in place a system of individual exemptions, it may not refuse to extend that system to cases of 'religious hardship' without compelling reason." . . .

A law also lacks general applicability if it prohibits religious conduct while permitting secular conduct that undermines the government's asserted interests in a similar way. . . . Church of Lukumi Babalu Aye, Inc. v. Hialeah . . . .

B

. . . [S]ection 3.21 of [the City's] standard foster care contract . . . is not generally applicable as required by *Smith*. . . . [It] specifies in pertinent part:

> "**Rejection of Referral**. Provider shall not reject a child or family including, but not limited to, . . . prospective foster or adoptive parents, for Services based upon . . . their . . . sexual orientation . . . unless an exception is granted by the Commissioner or the Commissioner's designee, in his/her sole discretion."

. . .

Like the good cause provision in *Sherbert*, section 3.21 incorporates a system of individual exemptions, made available in this case at the "sole discretion" of the

Commissioner. The City has made clear that the Commissioner "has no intention of granting an exception" to CSS. . . . But the City "may not refuse to extend that [exemption] system to cases of 'religious hardship' without compelling reason." *Smith*, 494 U.S., at 884 . . . .

The City . . . argue[s] that governments should enjoy greater leeway under the Free Exercise Clause when setting rules for contractors than when regulating the general public. . . .

. . . We have never suggested that the government may discriminate against religion when acting in its managerial role. And *Smith* itself drew support for the neutral and generally applicable standard from cases involving internal government affairs. See 494 U.S., at 883–885, and n. 2 (citing Lyng v. Northwest Indian Cemetery Protective Assn., 485 U.S. 439 (1988) . . . . The City . . . accordingly ask[s] only that courts apply a more deferential approach in determining whether a policy is neutral and generally applicable in the contracting context. We find no need to resolve that narrow issue in this case. No matter the level of deference we extend to the City, the inclusion of a formal system of entirely discretionary exceptions in section 3.21 renders the contractual nondiscrimination requirement not generally applicable.

. . .

The City . . . add[s] that, notwithstanding the system of exceptions in section 3.21, a separate provision in the contract independently prohibits discrimination in the certification of foster parents. That provision, section 15.1, bars discrimination on the basis of sexual orientation, and it does not on its face allow for exceptions. . . . But state law makes clear that . . . an exception from section 3.21 also must govern the prohibition in section 15.1, lest the City's reservation of the authority to grant such an exception be a nullity. As a result, the contract as a whole contains no generally applicable non-discrimination requirement.

Finally, the City . . . contend[s] that the availability of exceptions under section 3.21 is irrelevant because the Commissioner has never granted one. That misapprehends the issue. The creation of a formal mechanism for granting exceptions renders a policy not generally applicable, regardless whether any exceptions have been given, because it "invite[s]" the government to decide which reasons for not complying with the policy are worthy of solicitude, *Smith*, 494 U.S., at 884—here, at the Commissioner's "sole discretion."

. . .

C

. . . [T]he City [also] argues that CSS's refusal to certify same-sex couples constitutes an "Unlawful Public Accommodations Practice[ ]" in violation of the Fair Practices Ordinance. That ordinance forbids "deny[ing] or interfer[ing] with the public accommodations opportunities of an individual or otherwise discriminat[ing] based on his or her race, ethnicity, color, sex, sexual orientation, . . . disability, marital status, familial status," or several other protected categories. Phila. Code § 9–1106(1) (2016). The City contends that foster care agencies are public accommodations and therefore forbidden from discriminating on the basis of sexual orientation when certifying foster parents.

. . . We conclude that . . . foster care agencies do not act as public accommodations in performing certifications.

The ordinance defines a public accommodation in relevant part as "[a]ny place, provider or public conveyance, whether licensed or not, which solicits or accepts the patronage or trade of the public or whose goods, services, facilities, privileges, advantages or accommodations are extended, offered, sold, or otherwise made available to the public." § 9–1102(1)(w). Certification is not "made available to the public" in the usual sense of the words.... A Pennsylvania antidiscrimination statute similarly defines a public accommodation as an accommodation that is "open to, accepts or solicits the patronage of the general public." ... The "common theme" is that a public accommodation must "provide a benefit to the general public allowing individual members of the general public to avail themselves of that benefit if they so desire." Blizzard v. Floyd, 149 Pa. Commw. 503, 506, 613 A. 2d 619, 621 (1992).

Certification as a foster parent, by contrast, is not readily accessible to the public. It involves a customized and selective assessment that bears little resemblance to staying in a hotel, eating at a restaurant, or riding a bus. The process takes three to six months. Applicants must pass background checks and a medical exam. Foster agencies are required to conduct an intensive home study during which they evaluate, among other things, applicants' "mental and emotional adjustment," "community ties with family, friends, and neighbors," and "[e]xisting family relationships, attitudes and expectations regarding the applicant's own children and parent/child relationships." 55 Pa. Code § 3700.64. Such inquiries would raise eyebrows at the local bus station.... [T]he one-size-fits-all public accommodations model is a poor match for the foster care system.

[Justice Gorsuch's] concurrence adopts the City's argument, seeing no incongruity in deeming a private religious foster agency a public accommodation. We respectfully disagree .... The District Court did not take into account the uniquely selective nature of the certification process, which must inform the applicability of the ordinance. We agree with CSS's position ... that its "foster services do not constitute a 'public accommodation' under the City's Fair Practices Ordinance, and therefore it is not bound by that ordinance." ... We therefore have no need to assess whether the ordinance is generally applicable.

III

The contractual non-discrimination requirement imposes a burden on CSS's religious exercise and does not qualify as generally applicable.... Because the City's actions are therefore examined under the strictest scrutiny regardless of *Smith*, we have no occasion to reconsider that decision here.

... [S]o long as the government can achieve its interests in a manner that does not burden religion, it must do so.

The City asserts that its non-discrimination policies serve three compelling interests: maximizing the number of foster parents, protecting the City from liability, and ensuring equal treatment of prospective foster parents and foster children.... The question ... is not whether the City has a compelling interest in enforcing its non-discrimination policies generally, but whether it has such an interest in denying an exception to CSS.

Once properly narrowed, the City's asserted interests are insufficient. Maximizing the number of foster families and minimizing liability are important goals, but the City fails to show that granting CSS an exception will put those goals at risk. If anything, including CSS in the program seems likely to increase, not reduce, the number of available foster parents. As for liability, the City offers only speculation that it might be sued over CSS's certification practices. Such speculation is insufficient to satisfy strict scrutiny, ... particularly because the authority to certify foster families is delegated to agencies by the State, not the City ....

That leaves the interest of the City in the equal treatment of prospective foster parents and foster children. We do not doubt that this interest is a weighty one, for "[o]ur society has come to the recognition that gay persons and gay couples cannot be treated as social outcasts or as inferior in dignity and worth." *Masterpiece Cakeshop*, ... On the facts of this case, however, this interest cannot justify denying CSS an exception for its religious exercise. The creation of a system of exceptions under the contract undermines the City's contention that its nondiscrimination policies can brook no departures. See *Lukumi*, 508 U.S., at 546–547. The City offers no compelling reason why it has a particular interest in denying an exception to CSS while making them available to others.

* * *

. . . CSS seeks only an accommodation that will allow it to continue serving the children of Philadelphia in a manner consistent with its religious beliefs; it does not seek to impose those beliefs on anyone else. The refusal of Philadelphia to contract with CSS for the provision of foster care services unless it agrees to certify same-sex couples as foster parents cannot survive strict scrutiny . . . .

In view of our conclusion that the actions of the City violate the Free Exercise Clause, we need not consider whether they also violate the Free Speech Clause.

The judgment . . . is reversed, and the case is remanded . . . .

■ JUSTICE BARRETT, with whom JUSTICE KAVANAUGH joins, and with whom JUSTICE BREYER joins as to all but the first paragraph, concurring.

. . . Petitioners, their *amici*, scholars, and Justices of this Court have made serious arguments that *Smith* ought to be overruled. While history looms large in this debate, I find the historical record more silent than supportive on the question whether the founding generation understood the First Amendment to require religious exemptions from generally applicable laws in at least some circumstances. In my view, the textual and structural arguments against *Smith* are more compelling. As a matter of text and structure, it is difficult to see why the Free Exercise Clause—lone among the First Amendment freedoms—offers nothing more than protection from discrimination.

Yet what should replace *Smith*? The prevailing assumption seems to be that strict scrutiny would apply whenever a neutral and generally applicable law burdens religious exercise. But I am skeptical about swapping *Smith*'s categorical antidiscrimination approach for an equally categorical strict scrutiny regime, particularly when this Court's resolution of conflicts between generally applicable laws and other First Amendment rights—like speech and assembly—has been much more nuanced. There would be a number of issues to work through if *Smith* were overruled. To name a few: Should entities like Catholic Social Services—which is an arm of the Catholic Church—be treated differently than individuals? Cf. Hosanna-Tabor Evangelical Lutheran Church and School v. EEOC, 565 U.S. 171 (2012). Should there be a distinction between indirect and direct burdens on religious exercise? Cf. Braunfeld v. Brown, 366 U.S. 599, 606–607 (1961) (plurality opinion). What forms of scrutiny should apply? Compare Sherbert v. Verner, 374 U.S. 398, 403 (1963) (assessing whether government's interest is " 'compelling' "), with Gillette v. United States, 401 U.S. 437, 462 (1971) (assessing whether government's interest is "substantial"). And if the answer is strict scrutiny, would pre-*Smith* cases rejecting free exercise challenges to garden-variety laws come out the same way? See *Smith*, 494 U.S., at 888–889.

We need not wrestle with these questions in this case, though, because the same standard applies regardless whether *Smith* stays or goes. A longstanding tenet of our free exercise jurisprudence—one that both pre-dates and survives *Smith*—is that a law burdening religious exercise must satisfy strict scrutiny if it gives government officials discretion to grant individualized exemptions. . . . And all nine Justices agree that the City cannot satisfy strict scrutiny. I therefore see no reason to decide in this case whether *Smith* should be overruled, much less what should replace it. I join the Court's opinion in full.

■ JUSTICE ALITO, with whom JUSTICE THOMAS and JUSTICE GORSUCH join, concurring in the judgment.

. . .

Regrettably, the Court declines to [confront whether *Smith* should be reconsidered.] Instead, it reverses based on what appears to be a superfluous (and likely to be short-lived) feature of the City's standard annual contract with foster care agencies. *Smith*'s holding about categorical rules does not apply if a rule permits individualized exemptions, 494 U.S., at 884, and the majority seizes on the presence in the City's standard contract of language giving a City official the power to grant exemptions. The City tells us that it has never granted such an exemption and has no intention of handing one to CSS, . . . but the majority reverses . . . because the contract supposedly confers that never-used power.

This decision might as well be written on the dissolving paper sold in magic shops. The City has been adamant about pressuring CSS to give in, and if the City wants to get around today's decision, it can simply eliminate the never-used exemption power. If it does that, then, voilà, today's decision will vanish—and the parties will be back where they started. The City will claim that it is protected by *Smith*; CSS will argue that *Smith* should be overruled; the lower courts, bound by *Smith*, will reject that argument; and CSS will file a new petition in this Court challenging *Smith*. What is the point of going around in this circle?

. . .

We should reconsider *Smith* without further delay. The correct interpretation of the Free Exercise Clause is a question of great importance, and *Smith*'s interpretation is hard to defend. It can't be squared with the ordinary meaning of the text of the Free Exercise Clause or with the prevalent understanding of the scope of the free-exercise right at the time of the First Amendment's adoption. It swept aside decades of established precedent, and it has not aged well. Its interpretation has been undermined by subsequent scholarship on the original meaning of the Free Exercise Clause. Contrary to what many initially expected, *Smith* has not provided a clear-cut rule that is easy to apply, and experience has disproved the *Smith* majority's fear that retention of the Court's prior free-exercise jurisprudence would lead to "anarchy." 494 U.S., at 888.

II

A

. . .

The test distilled from *Sherbert*—that a law that imposes a substantial burden on the exercise of religion must be narrowly tailored to serve a compelling interest—was the governing rule for the next 37 years. Applying that test, the Court sometimes vindicated free-exercise claims. . . .

. . .

Other cases applied *Sherbert* but found no violation. . . .

B

This is where our case law stood when *Smith* reached the Court. . . .

. . .

. . . [W]ithout briefing or argument on whether *Sherbert* should be cast aside, the Court adopted what it seems to have thought was a clear-cut test that would be easy to apply: A "generally applicable and otherwise valid" rule does not violate the Free Exercise Clause "if prohibiting the exercise of religion . . . is not [its] object . . . but merely the incidental effect of" its operation. 494 U.S., at 878. Other than cases involving rules that target religious conduct, the *Sherbert* test was held to apply to only two narrow categories of cases: (1) those involving the award of unemployment benefits or other schemes allowing individualized exemptions and (2) so-called "hybrid rights" cases. See 494 U.S., at 881–884.

To clear the way for this new regime, the majority was willing to take liberties. Paying little attention to the terms of the Free Exercise Clause, it was satisfied that its interpretation represented a "permissible" reading of the text, *Smith*, 494 U.S., at 878, and it did not even stop to explain why that was so. The majority made no effort to ascertain the original understanding of the free-exercise right, and it limited past precedents on grounds never previously suggested. *Sherbert*, *Thomas*, and *Hobbie* were placed in a special category because they concerned the award of unemployment compensation, *Smith*, 494 U.S., at 883, and *Yoder* was distinguished on the ground that it involved both a free-exercise claim and a parental-rights claim, *Smith*, 494 U.S., at 881. Not only did these distinctions lack support in prior case law, the issue in *Smith* itself could easily be viewed as falling into both of these special categories. After all, it involved claims for unemployment benefits, and members of the Native American Church who ingest peyote as part of a religious ceremony are surely engaging in expressive conduct that falls within the scope of the Free Speech Clause. See, e.g., Texas v. Johnson, 491 U.S. 397, 404 (1989).

None of these obstacles stopped the *Smith* majority from adopting its new rule and displacing decades of precedent. . . .

. . .

Smith's impact was quickly felt, and Congress . . . attempted to restore the *Sherbert* test. . . . [T]he Religious Freedom Restoration Act (RFRA), passed in the House without dissent, was approved in the Senate by a vote of 97 to 3, and was enthusiastically signed into law by President Clinton. . . . And when this Court later held in *City of Boerne*, 521 U.S. 507, that Congress lacked the power under the 14th Amendment to impose these rules on the States, Congress responded by enacting the Religious Land Use and Institutionalized Persons Act (RLUIPA) under its spending power and its power to regulate interstate commerce. . . . RLUIPA imposed the same rules as RFRA on land use and prison regulations. . . . RLUIPA passed both Houses of Congress without a single negative vote and, like RFRA, was signed by President Clinton. . . .

RFRA and RLUIPA have restored part of the protection that *Smith* withdrew, but they are both limited in scope and can be weakened or repealed by Congress at any time. They are no substitute for a proper interpretation of the Free Exercise Clause.

III

A

That project must begin with the constitutional text. . . .

. . .

B

. . . [W]e can . . . focus on . . . the term "prohibiting" and the phrase "the free exercise of religion."

. . . [T]he ordinary meaning of "prohibiting the free exercise of religion" was (and still is) forbidding or hindering unrestrained religious practices or worship. That straightforward understanding is a far cry from the interpretation adopted in *Smith*. It certainly does not suggest a distinction between laws that are generally applicable and laws that are targeted.

As interpreted in *Smith*, the Clause is essentially an antidiscrimination provision: It means that the Federal Government and the States cannot restrict conduct that constitutes a religious practice for some people unless it imposes the same restriction on everyone else who engages in the same conduct. *Smith* made no real attempt to square that equal-treatment interpretation with the ordinary meaning of the Free Exercise Clause's language, and it is hard to see how that could be done. The key point for present purposes is that the text of the Free Exercise Clause gives a specific group of people (those who wish to engage in the "exercise of religion") the right to do so without hindrance. The language of the Clause does not tie this right to the treatment of persons not in this group.

. . .

C

. . .

[To the possible argument that e]ven if a law prohibits conduct that constitutes an essential religious practice, it cannot be said to "prohibit" the free exercise of religion unless that was the lawmakers' specific object[, Justice Alito responded as follows:]

This is a hair-splitting interpretation. It certainly does not represent the "normal and ordinary" meaning of the Free Exercise Clause's terms. . . . Consider how it would play out if applied to some . . . hypothetical laws . . . . A law categorically banning all wine would not "prohibit" the celebration of a Catholic Mass? A law categorically forbidding the slaughter of a conscious animal would not "prohibit" kosher and halal slaughterhouses? A rule categorically banning any head covering in a courtroom would not "prohibit" appearances by orthodox Jewish men, Sikh men, and Muslim women who wear hijabs? It is no wonder that *Smith*'s many defenders have almost uniformly foregone this argument.

D

Not only is it difficult to square Smith's interpretation with the terms of the Free Exercise Clause, the absence of any language referring to equal treatment is striking. . . .

. . . Other constitutional provisions contain non-discrimination language. For example, Art. I, § 9, cl. 6, provides that "[n]o Preference shall be given by any Regulation of Commerce or Revenue to the Ports of one State over those of another." Under Art. IV, § 2, cl. 1, "[t]he Citizens of each State shall be entitled to all Privileges and Immunities of Citizens in the several States." Article V provides that "no State, without its Consent, shall be deprived of its equal Suffrage in the Senate." Language mandating equal treatment of one sort or another also appeared in the religious liberty provisions of colonial charters and state constitutions. But Congress eschewed those models. The contrast between these readily available anti-discrimination models and the language that appears in the First Amendment speaks volumes.

IV

A

While we presume that the words of the Constitution carry their ordinary and normal meaning, we cannot disregard the possibility that some of the terms in the Free Exercise Clause had a special meaning that was well understood at the time. . . .

. . . [W]e must ask whether the Free Exercise Clause protects a right that was known at the time of adoption to have defined dimensions. But in doing so, we must keep in mind that there is a presumption that the words of the Constitution are to be interpreted in accordance with their "normal and ordinary" sense. . . .

B

1

What was the free-exercise right understood to mean when the Bill of Rights was ratified? And in particular, was it clearly understood that the right simply required equal treatment for religious and secular conduct? When *Smith* was decided, scholars had not devoted much attention to the original meaning of the Free Exercise Clause, and the parties' briefs ignored this issue, as did the opinion of the Court. Since then, however, the historical record has been plumbed in detail, and we are now in a good position to examine how the free-exercise right was understood when the First Amendment was adopted.

By that date, the right to religious liberty already had a long, rich, and complex history in this country. . . . [B]y 1789, every State except Connecticut had a constitutional provision protecting religious liberty. . . . In all of those State Constitutions, freedom of religion enjoyed broad protection, and the right "was universally said to be an unalienable right." . . .

2

. . .

When we look at these provisions, we see one predominant model. This model extends broad protection for religious liberty but expressly provides that the right does not protect conduct that would endanger "the public peace" or "safety."

. . .

3

The model favored by Congress and the state legislatures—providing broad protection for the free exercise of religion except where public "peace" or "safety" would be endangered—is antithetical to *Smith*. If, as *Smith* held, the free-exercise right does not require any religious exemptions from generally applicable laws, it is not easy to imagine situations in which a public-peace-or-safety carveout would be necessary. Legislatures enact generally applicable laws to protect public peace and safety. If those laws are thought to be sufficient to address a particular type of conduct when engaged in for a secular purpose, why wouldn't they also be sufficient to address the same type of conduct when carried out for a religious reason?

Smith's defenders have no good answer. . . .

. . .

. . . [T]he ordinary meaning of offenses that threaten public peace or safety must be stretched beyond the breaking point to encompass all violations of any law.

C

That the free-exercise right included the right to certain religious exemptions is strongly supported by the practice of the Colonies and States. When there were important clashes between generally applicable laws and the religious practices of particular groups, colonial and state legislatures were willing to grant exemptions— even when the generally applicable laws served critical state interests.

[Justice Alito cited as examples oath exemptions for religious objectors, exemptions from military conscription, colonial exemptions from special taxes for supporting ministers of established churches, and other exemptions.]

In an effort to dismiss the significance of these legislative exemptions, it has been argued that they show only what the Constitution permits, not what it requires. *City of Boerne*, 521 U.S., at 541 (opinion of Scalia, J.). But legislatures provided those accommodations before the concept of judicial review took hold, and their actions are therefore strong evidence of the founding era's understanding of the free-exercise right. . . .

D

Defenders of *Smith* have advanced historical arguments of their own, but they are unconvincing, and in any event, plainly insufficient to overcome the ordinary meaning of the constitutional text.

. . .

. . . Indeed, the case against *Smith* is very convincing.

V

. . .

In assessing whether to overrule a past decision that appears to be incorrect, we have considered a variety of factors, and four of those weigh strongly against *Smith*: its reasoning; its consistency with other decisions; the workability of the rule that it established; and developments since the decision was handed down. . . . No relevant factor, including reliance, weighs in *Smith*'s favor.

A

Smith's reasoning. As explained in detail above, *Smith* is a methodological outlier. . . .

. . .

[Among other deficiencies,] there is the problem that the hybrid-rights exception would largely swallow up *Smith*'s general rule. A great many claims for religious exemptions can easily be understood as hybrid free-exercise/free-speech claims. Take the claim in *Smith* itself. To members of the Native American Church, the ingestion of peyote during a religious ceremony is a sacrament. When Smith and Black participated in this sacrament, weren't they engaging in a form of expressive conduct? Their ingestion of peyote "communicate[d], in a rather dramatic way, [their] faith in the tenets of the Native American Church," and the State's prohibition of that practice "interfered with their ability to communicate this message" in violation of the Free Speech Clause. McConnell, Free Exercise Revisionism 1122. And, "if a hybrid claim is one in which a litigant would actually obtain an exemption from a formally neutral, generally applicable law under another constitutional provision, then there would have been no reason for the Court in [the so-called] hybrid cases to have mentioned the Free Exercise Clause at all." *Lukumi*, 508 U.S., at 566–567 (opinion of Souter, J.) . . . . It is telling that this Court has never once accepted a "hybrid rights" claim in the more than three decades since *Smith*.

In addition to all these maneuvers—creating special categories for unemployment compensation cases, cases involving individualized exemptions, and hybrid-rights cases—*Smith* ignored the multiple occasions when the Court had directly repudiated the very rule that Smith adopted.

Smith's rough treatment of prior decisions diminishes its own status as a precedent.

B

Consistency with other precedents. . . . *Smith* did not overrule *Sherbert* or any of the other cases that built on *Sherbert* from 1963 to 1990, and . . . *Smith* is tough to harmonize with those precedents.

The same is true about more recent decisions [like] Hosanna-Tabor Evangelical Lutheran Church and School v. EEOC, 565 U.S. 171 (2012), [and] Our Lady of Guadalupe School v. Morrissey-Berru, 591 U.S. ___, ___–___ (2020) . . . .

There is also tension between *Smith* and our opinion in Masterpiece Cakeshop, Ltd. v. Colorado Civil Rights Comm'n, ... In that case, we observed that "[w]hen it comes to weddings, it can be assumed that a member of the clergy who objects to gay marriage on moral and religious grounds could not be compelled to perform the ceremony without denial of his or her right to the free exercise of religion." . . . The clear import of this observation is that such a member of the clergy would be entitled to a religious exemption from a state law restricting the authority to perform a state-recognized marriage to individuals who are willing to officiate both opposite-sex and same-sex weddings.

. . .

C

Workability. One of *Smith*'s supposed virtues was ease of application, but . . . at least four serious problems have arisen and continue to plague courts when called upon to apply *Smith*.

1

. . . The "hybrid rights" exception, which was essential to distinguish *Yoder*, has baffled the lower courts. . . .

. . .

It is rare to encounter a holding of this Court that has so thoroughly stymied or elicited such open derision from the Courts of Appeals.

2

Rules that "target" religion. Post-*Smith* cases have also struggled with the task of determining whether a purportedly neutral rule "targets" religious exercise or has the restriction of religious exercise as its "object." . . .

. . .

Decisions of the lower courts on the issue of targeting remain in disarray. . . .

3

The nature and scope of exemptions. There is confusion about the meaning of *Smith*'s holding on exemptions from generally applicable laws. Some decisions apply this special rule if multiple secular exemptions are granted. . . . Others conclude that even one secular exemption is enough. . . . And still others have applied the rule where the law, although allowing no exemptions on its face, was widely unenforced in cases involving secular conduct. . . .

4

Identifying appropriate comparators. To determine whether a law provides equal treatment for secular and religious conduct, two steps are required. First, a court must identify the secular conduct with which the religious conduct is to be compared. Second, the court must determine whether the State's reasons for regulating the religious conduct apply with equal force to the secular conduct with which it is compared. See *Lukumi*, 508 U.S., at 543. In *Smith*, this inquiry undoubtedly seemed straightforward: The secular conduct and the religious conduct prohibited by the Oregon criminal statute were identical. But things are not always that simple.

Cases involving rules designed to slow the spread of COVID-19 have driven that point home. State and local rules adopted for this purpose have typically imposed different restrictions for different categories of activities. Sometimes religious services have been placed in a category with certain secular activities, and sometimes religious services have been given a separate category of their own. To determine whether COVID-19 rules provided neutral treatment for religious and secular conduct, it has been necessary to compare the restrictions on religious services with the restrictions on secular activities that present a comparable risk of spreading the virus, and identifying the secular activities that should be used for comparison has been hotly contested.

. . .

Smith seemed to offer a relatively simple and clear-cut rule that would be easy to apply. Experience has shown otherwise.

D

Subsequent developments. . . . The *Smith* majority thought that adherence to *Sherbert* would invite "anarchy," but experience has shown that this fear was not well founded. Both RFRA and RLUIPA impose essentially the same requirements as *Sherbert*, and we have observed that the courts are well "up to the task" of applying that test. Gonzales v. O Centro Espírita Beneficente União do Vegetal, 546 U.S. 418, 436 (2006). . . .

Another significant development is the subsequent profusion of studies on the original meaning of the Free Exercise Clause. When *Smith* was decided, the available scholarship was thin, and the Court received no briefing on the subject. Since then, scholars have explored the subject in great depth.

. . .

E

. . . Reliance is often the strongest factor favoring the retention of a challenged precedent, but no strong reliance interests are cited in any of the numerous briefs urging us to preserve *Smith*. . . .

. . .

Smith was wrongly decided. As long as it remains on the books, it threatens a fundamental freedom. And while precedent should not lightly be cast aside, the Court's error in *Smith* should now be corrected.

VI

A

If *Smith* is overruled, what legal standard should be applied in this case? . . . A law that imposes a substantial burden on religious exercise can be sustained only if it is narrowly tailored to serve a compelling government interest.

Whether this test should be rephrased or supplemented with specific rules is a question that need not be resolved here because Philadelphia's ouster of CSS from foster care work simply does not further any interest that can properly be protected in this case. . . . CSS's policy has not hindered any same-sex couples from becoming foster parents, and there is no threat that it will do so in the future.

CSS's policy has only one effect: It expresses the idea that same-sex couples should not be foster parents because only a man and a woman should marry. Many people today find this idea not only objectionable but hurtful. Nevertheless, protecting against this form of harm is not an interest that can justify the abridgment of First Amendment rights.

We have covered this ground repeatedly in free speech cases. In an open, pluralistic, self-governing society, the expression of an idea cannot be suppressed simply because some find it offensive, insulting, or even wounding. . . .

The same fundamental principle applies to religious practices that give offense. The preservation of religious freedom depends on that principle. Many core religious beliefs are perceived as hateful by members of other religions or nonbelievers. . . .

Suppressing speech—or religious practice—simply because it expresses an idea that some find hurtful is a zero-sum game. While CSS's ideas about marriage are likely to be objectionable to same-sex couples, lumping those who hold traditional beliefs about marriage together with racial bigots is insulting to those who retain such beliefs. . . .

. . .

After receiving more than 2,500 pages of briefing and after more than a half-year of post-argument cogitation, the Court has emitted a wisp of a decision that leaves religious liberty in a confused and vulnerable state. Those who count on this Court to stand up for the First Amendment have every right to be disappointed—as am I.

■ JUSTICE GORSUCH, with whom JUSTICE THOMAS and JUSTICE ALITO join, concurring in the judgment.

[Justice Gorsuch's opinion is sharply critical of the majority's interpretation of the City's contract provisions, the City's Fair Practices Ordinance, and state law, as embodying policies that are not "generally applicable," thereby avoiding the need to confront directly whether *Smith* should be overruled.]

. . . One way or another, the majority seems determined to declare there is no "need" or "reason" to revisit *Smith* today.

But tell that to CSS. Its litigation has already lasted years—and today's (ir)resolution promises more of the same. Had we followed the path Justice Alito outlines—holding that the City's rules cannot avoid strict scrutiny even if they qualify as neutral and generally applicable—this case would end today. Instead, the majority's course guarantees that this litigation is only getting started. As the final arbiter of state law, the Pennsylvania Supreme Court can effectively overrule the majority's reading of the Commonwealth's public accommodations law. The City can revise its FPO to make even plainer still that its law does encompass foster services. Or with a flick of a pen, municipal lawyers may rewrite the City's contract to close the § 3.21 loophole.

Once any of that happens, CSS will find itself back where it started. The City has made clear that it will never tolerate CSS carrying out its foster-care mission in accordance with its sincerely held religious beliefs. . . . The City has expressed its determination to put CSS to a choice: Give up your sincerely held religious beliefs or give up serving foster children and families. . . .

. . .

We hardly need to "wrestle" today with every conceivable question that might follow from recognizing *Smith* was wrong. See (Barrett, J., concurring). To be sure, any time this Court turns from misguided precedent back toward the Constitution's original public meaning, challenging questions may arise across a large field of cases and controversies. But that's no excuse for refusing to apply the original public meaning in the dispute actually before us. Rather than adhere to *Smith* until we settle on some "grand unified theory" of the Free Exercise Clause for all future cases until the end of time, the Court should overrule it now, set us back on the correct course, and address each case as it comes.

. . .

Page 1900. Add after Espinoza v. Montana Department of Revenue:

Kennedy v. Bremerton School District
597 U.S. ___, 142 S.Ct. 2407 (2022).

[The report of this case appears *supra*, at p. 137.]

Carson v. Makin
596 U.S. ___, 142 S.Ct. 1987 (2022).

Maine provided tuition assistance for families to send their children to accredited or approved private secondary schools in areas of the State that lacked public secondary schools, but only if the private school the family chose to have the children attend was not a religious school. The Court, in a 6–3 majority opinion by Chief Justice Roberts, relied on Trinity Lutheran Church of Columbia, Inc. v. Comer and Espinoza v. Montana Department of Revenue, *supra*, and held that the eligibility exclusion of sectarian schools violated the Free Exercise Clause.

As "the most rural State in the Union," Maine confronts "realities of remote geography and low population density" that make it difficult for the State's responsible school administrative units (SAUs)—more than half of which do not operate a public secondary school—to comply with state law requiring "that every school-age child in Maine 'shall be provided an opportunity to receive the benefits of a free public education[.]' " Maine's tuition assistance program is designed to address that challenge by providing that "if an SAU neither operates its own public secondary school nor contracts with a particular public or private school for the education of its school-age children, the SAU must 'pay the tuition . . . at the public school or the approved private school of the parent's choice at which the student is accepted.' Me. Rev. Stat. Ann., Tit. 20–A, § 5204(4) (Cum. Supp. 2021)." The tuition assistance obligation applies to private schools only if they are accredited or approved and only up to a specified maximum rate. Before 1981, "parents could [and did sometimes] direct the tuition assistance payments to religious schools." At that point, "however, Maine imposed a new requirement that any school receiving tuition assistance payments must be 'a nonsectarian school in accordance with the First Amendment of the United States Constitution.' Me. Rev. Stat. Ann., Tit. 20–A, § 2951(2)." Chief Justice Roberts then noted that the Court "subsequently held, however, that a benefit program under which private citizens 'direct government aid to religious schools wholly as a result of their own genuine and independent private choice' does not offend the Establishment Clause. Zelman v. Simmons-Harris, 536 U.S. 639, 652 (2002)." Nonetheless, Maine decided to retain its "nonsectarian" requirement.

Responding to this suit by two sets of parents who challenged that requirement, Chief Justice Roberts wrote that "we have repeatedly held that a State violates the Free Exercise Clause when it excludes religious observers from otherwise available public benefits." Just as in *Trinity Lutheran Church* and *Espinoza*, Maine's requirement could not satisfy strict scrutiny:

". . . [A] neutral benefit program in which public funds flow to religious organizations through the independent choices of private benefit recipients does not offend the Establishment Clause. See *Zelman*, 536 U.S., at 652–653. Maine's decision to continue excluding religious schools from its tuition assistance program after *Zelman* thus promotes stricter separation of church and state than the Federal Constitution requires. . . .

"But as we explained in both *Trinity Lutheran* and *Espinoza*, such an 'interest in separating church and state "more fiercely" than the Federal Constitution . . . "cannot qualify as compelling" in the face of the infringement of free exercise.' . . . Justice Breyer stresses the importance of 'government neutrality' when it comes to religious matters, but there is nothing neutral about Maine's program. The State pays tuition for certain students at private schools—so long as the schools are not religious. That is discrimination against religion. A State's antiestablishment interest does not justify enactments that exclude some members of the community from an otherwise generally available public benefit because of their religious exercise."

Chief Justice Roberts then addressed two attempts by the First Circuit panel and Maine to distinguish this case from *Trinity Lutheran* and *Espinoza*:

". . . First, the panel defined the benefit at issue as the 'rough equivalent of [a Maine] public school education,' an education that cannot include sectarian instruction. . . . Second, the panel defined the nature of the exclusion as one based not on a school's religious 'status,' as in *Trinity Lutheran* and *Espinoza*, but on religious 'uses' of public funds. . . . Neither of these formal distinctions suffices . . . ."

As for the first, it was not true that the public benefit Maine is offering is a free public education. The statute does not say that, and the "benefit is *tuition* at a public *or* private school, selected by the parent, with no suggestion that the 'private school' must somehow provide a 'public' education." Differences in operation between private schools eligible for tuition assistance and Maine public schools "are numerous and important." They include the fact that private schools "do not have to accept all students"; that tuition at many private schools is "several times the maximum benefit that Maine is willing to provide"; that "the curriculum taught at participating private schools need not even resemble that taught in the Maine public schools"; that "[p]articipating schools need not hire state-certified teachers"; and that the private schools "can be single-sex." Hence, "it is simply not the case that these schools, to be eligible for state funds, must offer an education that is equivalent—roughly or otherwise—to that available in the Maine public schools." Moreover, "were we to accept Maine's argument, our decision in *Espinoza* would be rendered essentially meaningless. By Maine's logic, Montana could have obtained the same result that we held violated the First Amendment simply by redefining its tax credit for sponsors of generally available scholarships as limited to 'tuition payments for the rough equivalent of a Montana public education'—meaning a secular education." The Chief Justice concluded this part of the analysis this way:

"The dissents are wrong to say that under our decision today Maine 'must' fund religious education. Maine chose to allow some parents to direct state tuition payments to private schools; that decision was not 'forced upon' it. The State retains a number of options: it could expand the reach of its public school system, increase the availability of transportation, provide some combination of tutoring, remote learning, and partial attendance, or even operate boarding schools of its own. As we held in *Espinoza*, a 'State need not subsidize private education. But once a State decides to do so, it cannot disqualify some private schools solely because they are religious.' "

As for the second, the Chief Justice said this:

". . . In *Trinity Lutheran* and *Espinoza*, we held that the Free Exercise Clause forbids discrimination on the basis of religious status. But those decisions never suggested that use-based discrimination is any less offensive to the Free Exercise Clause. This case illustrates why. '[E]ducating young people in their faith, inculcating its teachings, and training them to live their faith are responsibilities that lie at the very core of the mission of a private religious school.' Our Lady of Guadalupe School v. Morrissey-Berru, ...

"Any attempt to give effect to such a distinction by scrutinizing whether and how a religious school pursues its educational mission would also raise serious concerns about state entanglement with religion and denominational favoritism. . . . Indeed, Maine concedes that the Department barely engages in any such scrutiny when enforcing the 'nonsectarian' requirement. . . . That suggests that any status-use distinction lacks a meaningful application not only in theory, but in practice as well. In short, the prohibition on status-based discrimination under the Free Exercise Clause is not a permission to engage in use-based discrimination."

Justice Breyer's dissent, joined by Justice Kagan and mostly by Justice Sotomayor, faulted the majority for paying "almost no attention" to the Establishment Clause and "almost exclusive attention" to the Free Exercise Clause, thus "fail[ing] to recognize the ' "play in the joints" ' between the two Clauses." To him, "[t]hat 'play' . . . sometimes allows a State to further antiestablishment interests by withholding aid from religious institutions without violating the Constitution's protections for the free exercise of religion. In my view, Maine's nonsectarian requirement falls squarely within the scope of that constitutional leeway." He elaborated in part as follows:

"On the one hand, the Free Exercise Clause ' "protect[s] religious observers against unequal treatment." ' *Trinity Lutheran*, ...

"On the other hand, the Establishment Clause 'commands a separation of church and state.' . . .

". . . Together they attempt to chart a 'course of constitutional neutrality' with respect to government and religion. . . . They were written to help create an American Nation free of the religious conflict that had long plagued European nations with 'governmentally established religion[s].' . . .

"The Religion Clauses thus created a compromise in the form of religious freedom. They aspired to create a 'benevolent neutrality'—one which would 'permit religious exercise to exist without sponsorship and without interference.' . . . We have historically interpreted the Religion Clauses with these basic principles in mind. . . .

"And in applying these Clauses, we have often said that 'there is room for play in the joints' between them. . . . This doctrine reflects the fact that it may be difficult to determine in any particular case whether the Free Exercise Clause *requires* a State to fund the activities of a religious institution, or whether the Establishment Clause *prohibits* the State from doing so. . . . [W]e have made clear that States enjoy a degree of freedom to navigate the Clauses' competing prohibitions. . . . This includes choosing not to fund certain religious activity where States have strong, establishment-related reasons for not doing so. See, e.g., *Locke*, 540 U.S., at 719–722. And, States have freedom to make this choice even when the Establishment Clause does not itself prohibit the State from funding that activity. *Id.*, at 719 ('[T]here are some state actions permitted by the Establishment Clause but not required by the Free Exercise Clause'). The Court today nowhere mentions, and I fear effectively abandons, this longstanding doctrine."

In the portion of his opinion that Justice Sotomayor did not join, Justice Breyer expressed his belief that the "Religion Clauses . . . should be interpreted to advance their goal of avoiding religious strife" and noted "the increased risk of religiously based social conflict when government promotes religion in its public school system." A "Nation with well over 100 different religious groups" presents a "greater risk of religiously based strife, conflict, and social division." As "[n]ot all state-funded programs that have religious restrictions carry the same risk of creating social division and conflict[,] . . . [r]ecognition that States enjoy a degree of constitutional leeway allows States to enact laws sensitive to local circumstances while also allowing this Court to consider those circumstances in light of the basic values underlying the Religion Clauses."

Zelman "concluded that a State *may*, consistent with the Establishment Clause, provide funding to religious schools through a general public funding program if the 'government aid . . . reach[es] religious institutions only by way of the deliberate choices of . . . individual [aid] recipients.' . . .

"But . . . [w]e have never previously held what the Court holds today, namely, that a State *must* (not *may*) use state funds to pay for religious education as part of a tuition program designed to ensure the provision of free statewide public school education.

"What happens once 'may' becomes 'must'? Does that transformation mean that a school district that pays for public schools must pay equivalent funds to parents who wish to send their children to religious schools? Does it mean that school districts that give vouchers for use at charter schools must pay equivalent funds to parents who wish to give their children a religious education? What other social benefits are there the State's provision of which means—under the majority's interpretation of the Free Exercise Clause—that the State must pay parents for the religious equivalent of the secular benefit provided? The concept of 'play in the joints' means that courts need not, and should not, answer with 'must' these questions that can more appropriately be answered with 'may.' "

Trinity Lutheran and *Espinoza* were not controlling, as "Maine denies tuition money to schools not because of their religious affiliation, but because they will use state funds to promote religious views." "State funding of religious activity risks the very social conflict based upon religion that the Religion Clauses were designed to prevent. And, unlike the circumstances present in *Trinity Lutheran* and *Espinoza*, it is religious activity, not religious labels, that lies at the heart of this case." Both religious schools at issue in this case could not satisfy Maine's "nonsectarian" requirement because of the pervasive nature of their religious education:

"A school fails to meet that requirement (and is deemed 'sectarian') only if it is *both* (1) ' "associated with a particular faith or belief system" ' *and also* (2) ' "promotes the faith or belief system with which it is associated and/or presents the [academic] material taught through the lens of this faith." ' 979 F. 3d, at 38 (quoting Maine's then-education commissioner). To determine whether a school is sectarian, the ' "focus is on what the school teaches through its curriculum and related activities, and how the material is presented." ' . . . ' " [A]ffiliation or association with a church or religious institution . . . is not dispositive" ' of sectarian status. . . ."

The "Maine legislators who endorsed the State's nonsectarian requirement . . . did not want Maine taxpayers to finance, through a tuition program designed to ensure the provision of free public education, schools that would use state money for teaching religious practices." They "thought that government payment for this kind of religious education would be antithetical to the religiously neutral education that the Establishment Clause requires in public schools." Further,

"Nothing in our Free Exercise Clause cases *compels* Maine to give tuition aid to private schools that will use the funds to provide a religious education. . . . [W]e have never said that the Free Exercise Clause prohibits States from withholding funds because of the religious *use* to which the money will be put. . . . Maine does not refuse to pay tuition at private schools because of religious status or affiliation. The State only denies funding to schools that will use the money to promote religious beliefs through a religiously integrated education—an education that, in Maine's view, is not a replacement for a civic-focused public education. . . . This makes Maine's decision to withhold public funds more akin to the state decision that we upheld in *Locke*, and unlike the withholdings that we invalidated in *Trinity Lutheran* and *Espinoza*.

". . . Maine endeavors to provide children the religiously neutral education required in public school systems. And that, in significant part, reflects the State's antiestablishment interests in avoiding spending public money to support what is essentially religious activity. The Religion Clauses give Maine the ability, and flexibility, to make this choice."

Justice Breyer offered one further argument:

"In my view, Maine's nonsectarian requirement is also constitutional because it supports, rather than undermines, the Religion Clauses' goal of avoiding religious strife. Forcing Maine to fund schools that provide the sort of religiously integrated education offered by Bangor Christian and Temple Academy creates a similar potential for religious strife as that raised by promoting religion in public schools. It may appear to some that the State favors a particular religion over others, or favors religion over nonreligion. Members of minority religions, with too few adherents to establish schools, may see injustice in the fact that only those belonging to more popular religions can use state money for religious education. Taxpayers may be upset at having to finance the propagation of religious beliefs that they do not share and with which they disagree. And parents in school districts that have a public secondary school may feel indignant that only *some* families in the State—those families in the more rural districts without public schools—have the opportunity to give their children a Maine-funded religious education.

"Maine legislators who endorsed the State's nonsectarian requirement understood this potential for social conflict. . . . Legislators also recognized that these private schools make religiously based enrollment and hiring decisions. Bangor Christian and Temple Academy, for example, have admissions policies that allow them to deny enrollment to students based on gender, gender-identity, sexual orientation, and religion, and both schools require their teachers to be Born Again Christians. . . . Legislators did not want Maine taxpayers to pay for these religiously based practices— practices not universally endorsed by all citizens of the State—for fear that doing so would cause a significant number of Maine citizens discomfort or displeasure. . . . The nonsectarian requirement helped avoid this conflict—the precise kind of social conflict that the Religion Clauses themselves sought to avoid.

"Maine's nonsectarian requirement also serves to avoid religious strife between the State and the religious schools. . . .

"This . . . situation . . . forces Maine into the position of evaluating the adequacy or appropriateness of the schools' religiously inspired curriculum. Maine does not want this role. . . .

"Nor do the schools want Maine in this role. . . . The nonsectarian requirement ensures that Maine is not pitted against private religious schools in these battles over curriculum or operations, thereby avoiding the social strife resulting from this state-versus-religion confrontation. By invalidating the nonsectarian requirement, the majority today subjects the State, the schools, and the people of Maine to social conflict of a kind that they, and the Religion Clauses, sought to prevent.

"I emphasize the problems that may arise out of today's decision because they reinforce my belief that the Religion Clauses do not require Maine to pay for a religious education simply because, in some rural areas, the State will help parents pay for a secular education. After all, the Establishment Clause forbids a State from paying for the practice of religion itself. And state neutrality in respect to the *teaching* of the practice of religion lies at the heart of this Clause. . . . There is no meaningful difference between a State's payment of the salary of a religious minister and the salary of someone who will teach the practice of religion to a person's children. . . ."

Justice Sotomayor also filed a dissent "to add three points." First, the "Court should not have started down this path five years ago" in *Trinity Lutheran*. That decision "revolutionized Free Exercise doctrine by equating a State's decision not to fund a religious organization with presumptively unconstitutional discrimination on the basis of religious status." And the Court, despite having drawn the distinction in *Trinity Lutheran* and *Espinoza*, "now holds for the first time that 'any status-use distinction' is immaterial in both 'theory' and 'practice.'. . . As a result, in just a few years, the Court has upended constitutional doctrine, shifting from a rule that permits States to decline to fund religious organizations to one that requires States in many circumstances to subsidize religious indoctrination with taxpayer dollars."

Second, "[f]rom a doctrinal perspective, the Court's failure to apply the play-in-the-joints principle here . . . leaves one to wonder what, if anything, is left of it[,]" and "[f]rom a practical perspective, today's decision directs the State of Maine (and, by extension, its taxpaying citizens) to subsidize institutions that undisputedly engage in religious instruction." As a result, "Maine must choose between giving subsidies to its residents or refraining from financing religious teaching and practices."

Finally, "the Court's decision is especially perverse because the benefit at issue is the public education to which all of Maine's children are entitled under the State Constitution. As this Court has long recognized, the Establishment Clause requires that public education be secular and neutral as to religion."

Justice Sotomayor concluded her opinion with this:

". . . Today, the Court leads us to a place where separation of church and state becomes a constitutional violation. If a State cannot offer subsidies to its citizens without being required to fund religious exercise, any State that values its historic antiestablishment interests more than this Court does will have to curtail the support it offers to its citizens. With growing concern for where this Court will lead us next, I respectfully dissent."